POPULAR AUTOCRACY
IN GREECE
1936–41

POPULAR AUTOCRACY IN GREECE
1936–41

A Political Biography of
General Ioannis Metaxas

P. J. Vatikiotis

Emeritus Professor of Near East Politics, University of London

FRANK CASS
LONDON • PORTLAND, OR

First Published in 1998 in Great Britain by
FRANK CASS PUBLISHERS.
Newbury House, 900 Eastern Avenue
London, IG2 7HH

and in the United States of America by
FRANK CASS PUBLISHERS
c/o ISBS, 5804 N.E. Hassalo Street
Portland, Oregon, 97213-3644

Website http://www.frankcass.com

British Library Cataloguing in Publication Data:

Vatikiotis, P.J. (Panayiotis Jerasimof), 1928–
Popular autocracy in Greece,1936–41: a political
biography of General Ioannis Metaxas
1. Metaxas, Ioannis 2. Statesmen–Greece–Biography
3. Greece–Politics and government–1935–67
I. Title
949.5'074'092

ISBN 0-7146-4869-8 (cloth)
ISBN 0-7146-4445-5 (paper)

Library of Congress Cataloging-in-Publication Data:

Vatikiotis, P.J. (Panayiotis Jerasimof), 1928–
Popular autocracy in Greece, 1936–41: a political biography of
General Ioannis Metaxas / P.J. Vatikiotis.
p. cm.
Includes index.
ISBN 0-7146-4869-8 (cloth) ISBN 0-7146-4445-5 (paper)
1. Metaxas, Ioannis, 1871–1941. 2. Dictators–Greece–Biography.
3. Generals–Greece–Biography. 4. Greece–History–1917–1944.
5. Greece–Politics and government–1935–1967. I. Title.
DF849.58.M48V37   1998
949.507–dc21   97-39080
                                                         CIP

Typeset by
Vitaset, Paddock Wood, Kent
Printed in Great Britain by
Creative Print and Design (Wales), Ebbw Vale

Contents

PART III
Prelude to Power: The Momentum of Leadership

PART IV
Radical Reformer and Wartime Leader,
Architect of Military Victory

List of Illustrations

Preface and Acknowledgements

I embarked on this work after I retired from university teaching. The generosity of the British Academy and the Leverhulme Trust helped me embark on this study. My friend John Campbell, Emeritus Fellow of St Antony's College, Oxford, a social and cultural anthropologist and leading scholar of modern Greece, was a steady reference on things Greek and modern Greek society. The work of a younger generation of Greek scholars, many of them incidentally, trained, supervised and nurtured by John Campbell himself over the last three decades in Oxford, was enlightening and helpful. The fact that on the two or three occasions I had ventured to comment in print on limited aspects of modern Greek politics and had engaged the lively attention of some Greeks in Greece, including critics in the media and a number of university colleagues, I found encouraging.

Thanos Veremis, Professor of Modern European Political History at the University of Athens, and Director of ELIAMEP (Helenic Foundation For European and Foreign Policy) was always helpful with references and suggestions; Ioanna Pepelasi-Minoglou, Nicos Mouzelis, Dimitris Livanios, Yannis Nicolaou, Mina Kalogridou, Yannis Koliopoulos, and many others helped by discussing with me their own research. Petros Gavallas, a semi-retired Athenian journalist, was a veritable 'Who's Who' about Athenian politicians and Athenian society of the interwar period; he clarified for me the links between them, the web of alliances and alignments proving to me finally that what Petros Gavallas did not know about the Athens of the last sixty years is not worth knowing.

Most valuable was the time I spent in Athens working closely with the late Professor Yannis Georgakis, when he was Karamanlis's Special Ambassador to the Arab countries in the Middle East. I helped him with the expertise of the specialist, and slaved valiantly, albeit without much success, to introduce the Greeks on an institutional level and in a more systematic fashion to the world of Islam and the Middle East. A man of vision, intelligence and fertile imagination – and incidentally a great admirer of Venizelos – a veteran of the wartime Axis occupation during which he was director of the Regent's (Archbishop Damaskinos) cabinet, Georgakis offered great service to the Greek and Allied underground Resistance in Greece. Widely and popularly known also as 'the professor', Georgakis was one of the gifted German-trained young Greek jurists of the interwar period – he taught Criminal Law at the Panteios School in Athens. Though a highly controversial figure, he was still counted among the Great and the Good, and served successively as Prefect of the Ionian Islands and Governor of the Dodecanese after the War. A close friend and confidant of the legendary shipping tycoon Aristotle Onassis, Georgakis also made his mark in the aviation industry as Chairman of the Olympic Airways Board, and in the 1980s as president of the Onassis Foundation, after which he persuaded his political friends, Mitsotakis and Karamanlis, to launch the Foundation for Hellenic Culture – a kind of 'Greek British Council' – in June 1992, with himself as its first President. Georgakis introduced me to the nitty gritty of mundane – raw – Greek politics, with all its charms and evils. I also experienced at close range the generosity, splendour, power – and corruption – of a political patron's salon (of an oriental potentate's *diwan* or *seraglio*), the petty personalized fractiousness of Greek – perhaps all Mediterranean – politics. Although repelled, I was at the same time fascinated, and I was determined that I would learn more about the political conduct of this last remaining Ottoman society of my compatriots.

St Antony's College, Oxford, kindly offered me its hospitality as one of its Senior Associate Members, where I could take advantage of the facilities of the Middle East Centre and the European Studies Programme, for which I am grateful.

I am grateful to my old friend and editor Alastair Everitt for helping me to contain the text within manageable length and proportions, and to Professor George Krimbas of Athens University for the large number of illustrations he supplied me with from his father's, Elias Krimbas's, photographic archive, many of which are reproduced in this book. I also wish to thank two other sources of illustrations produced here: the Greek Literary and Historical Archive (ELIA) in Athens, and Mrs Nana Metaxas-Foka, the surviving younger daughter of Ioannis Metaxas.

I acknowledge with gratitude the assistance of the above-mentioned individuals and institutions. Last but not least I am deeply indebted to my wife, who suffered quietly through all of this, and dextrously kept me alive, the foremost requisite for undertaking and completing this project, and to the professional advice, treatment and care of the Cardiology Clinic at the John Radcliffe Hospital, Oxford, headed by Dr Gribbin. For what is presented here, however, I am solely responsible.

P.J. VATIKIOTIS
Oxford, Autumn 1997

Introduction

This is not intended to be a full biography of Ioannis Metaxas, only a political biography, in fact, a political profile of the man, a prosopography. Needless to say both are difficult undertakings, especially as so many of his associates as well as his opponents, and generally the people associated with his career or involved in his 4th August Regime [1936–1941] have long been dead. What I present here is a political portrait of Ioannis Metaxas, drawn mainly, if not exclusively, from Greek sources. I emphasize more the early years of his life; his background, his conduct and style in entering the world of Greek politics during the decade 1910–20, and his road to state power from 1920 to 1936.[1] There is less emphasis on his own 4th August Regime, no elaborate historical narrative of it and its policies, beyond its relevance for an assessment of the man and his political performance. To this extent it follows very closely – even explicitly – his *Diary*,[2] his own record of his own life, his correspondence, and the written evidence – diaries, reminiscences, memoirs, memoranda – of his close associates and his critics.[3] Less attention is paid to the detail of the policies of his regime, except in general terms, that is, the broad aims and spirit of these policies.[4] At the same time I tried to avoid the temptation of essaying a historical narrative of his regime. Making the task even more difficult was the inhibiting knowledge that Metaxas is generally a controversial and unpopular figure in the political consciousness and experience of the average contemporary Greek. He is in fact a prominent feature of the contemporary Greek's political demonology, for he elicits hostility and opprobrium. This may explain, in part, the glaring lack, until very recently, of serious studies by Greeks about Metaxas and his notorious regime, especially when he represents such a virulent figure of political 'evil' in their view

– but also reminds them perhaps uncomfortably of so many personal and political traits that they, as a nation, share with him,[5] such as authoritarianism and autocracy which they have yet to overcome; only now in the mid-1990s do they sustain them with the protection of membership in, and the fig leaf of, the European Union!

A recent fifty-year Anniversary Supplement of the newspaper *TO VIMA*, Athens 6 August 1986, still considered the Metaxas regime a national nightmare. Several contributors put together a rather thin, confused and therefore misleading text, one of them claiming that 'the Metaxas regime was the first in modern Greek history of a systematic attempt at a permanent distortion of the political values, liberal perceptions and national orientation of the Greek people'. Needless to say such a statement is an exaggeration for it ignores the documentation available for research and other evidence. Marios Ploritis, an editor of the paper, discusses the permanence of the regime, with its promised 'Third Greek Civilization' as a chimera and a typical claim of such other European totalitarian regimes as the 'One Thousand Year Third German Reich' of the Nazis, and the new Roman Empire of Fascist Italy. Nicos Mouzelis makes the unoriginal proposition that the ideology of the Metaxas regime of 4th August 1936 was neither a fascist nor simply an anti-democratic episode in the long-term parliamentary history of the country. Rather he adjudges it to have been a mixed autocratic regime. He thought that while it exhibited certain totalitarian features such as the predomination of society and the Nation over the individual, or the state over the citizen, it also affected a link with classical Greece.

It is important in this connection to distinguish between what others said about Metaxas when he was in power and much later, say, in the mid-1980s. His detractors while he was in power did not make their comments in the context of the Right vs. Left antithesis, but rather of the Liberal or Republican vs. the Conservative or Monarchist autocracy; and basically because both sides were autocratic or authoritarian when in power, they shared what one might call for the sake of convenience the post-1909 political ethos and idiom.

What one can say with some certainty based on the documentary evidence is that Metaxas was a protégé of the Royal Court; he was opposed to what he considered mindless adventure in Asia Minor, the quixotic gestures of partisan politicians with their disorganized and inordinate partisan intrigues. In fact, Metaxas disapproved of and disliked certain traits, and especially weaknesses in his contemporary modern fellow Greek. He wished for the higher standards based on a disciplined, measured ideal, self-controlled and balanced. He craved orderly endeavour among the Greeks; in short, all the attributes to be found in his perception of the efficient German, and his idealization of the latter because he followed a classical Greek ideal! The question – in fact the conundrum – for Metaxas was how to fashion a new Greek on this ideal model. The task he set himself was not only unrealistic, but in the final analysis an unpleasantly arrogant and pompous one too; and in any case he failed in carrying it out. The average Greek was impulsive, spontaneous and disorderly, whereas Metaxas was compulsive and calculating about order and discipline – a German-style RSM in an Army of Greeks!

A question that is often asked about Metaxas is, did his dictatorship break the cycle of royalist vs. republican military coups? It has been difficult to give a categorical answer because of the Second World War and the Civil War. The Left, of course, claims that the Metaxas regime consecrated the right into long-term power in Greece. The evidence, however, only suggests that the Metaxas regime of 4th August 1936 destroyed, or displaced, the Traditional Right, so that a New Right emerged from the crucible of the Occupation and the subsequent Civil War.[6] Although General Tsalakoglou who collaborated with the Nazi occupiers was anti-Venizelist, he was not a typical pro-Metaxas officer; he was simply an anti-Venizelist one. Nor was Brigadier Thrasyvoulos Tsakalotos one either. He was anti-Venizelist and commanded the Rimini Brigade, the first unit of the regular Greek Army to engage the forces of the Left in combat in Athens in 1944. What is also certain is that Metaxas weakened and ridiculed the traditional political and social elite of Athenian and other urban salon-fähigkeit gemütlich urban bourgeoisie. But the War itself, the Occupation and the Civil War further eroded the authority and position of this elite. I have tried to show that Metaxas personally was ambivalent about this elite, or better still, intended to found his own for he detested it while at the same time was desperate at some point to join it. Politically though Metaxas wished to be the leader of the people: he tended to be a populist who aimed at the establishment of a popular autocracy, using the monarch as a figurehead and symbol of national unity while he wielded actual power. He often came across as a social leveller, the castigator of class in favour of social cohesion and national solidarity. At the same time, he was didactically conscious of his educational role in constructing a new society, a 'new Greek'.[7]

The *TO VIMA* Supplement also describes the Metaxas regime as a Police State; this has been a popular perception among several scholars of that period in Greek political history. Again this must be approached with caution as a relative term and depiction: a Police State in relation to what and to whom? To be sure the Metaxas dictatorship or autocracy lacked a party base or any substitute for it, unless one considers the unlikely case of his National Youth Organization, *Ethniki Organosis Neoleas (EON)*, or its forerunners at different stages of the political career of Metaxas, such as the small Party of *Eleftherophrones*, the Group of Reformers (*Metarythmistes*), the Associations or Clubs of *Epistratoi* (Conscripts), and the Popular Political Clubs of 1920–21 in Cephalonia. The Metaxas regime in fact rested on the support of the King and an anti-Venizelist faction that dominated the security forces, Army and Police. Metaxas was indispensable to the King: thus on 5 March 1936 he became his Minister of Army Affairs in order to deal with disloyal and seditious army officers. As Prime Minister a month later Metaxas suspended certain basic articles of the Constitution (what in effect constituted the nearest thing to a Bill of Rights), dissolved Parliament and proclaimed Martial Law (in effect, he abolished partisan politics). All of his immediate objectives were music to the King's ears: Metaxas promised to keep the army officers out of politics; keep Venizelists out of the Army; neutralize the politicians; and promote closer ties with Britain. That is why in addition to the premiership, Metaxas combined the portfolios of Foreign Affairs and Defence, and after the 4th August he added those of Education and, for all practical purposes, Interior too. He was overworked because it was difficult to find suitable ministers. Moreover, his objectives were rather idiosyncratic. He was suspicious, overbearing and could be vindictive to boot. Able cabinet ministers like C. Zavitsianos, Andreas Hatzikyriakos, G. Logothetis and Alex. Koryzis tended to resign within two to three years. C. Kotzias and C. Maniadakis were closest to Metaxas among his cabinet ministers and constituted his inner circle or kitchen cabinet – *Camarilla* – along with Theologos Nicoloudis (Minister of Press and Tourism), I. Diakos (a minister without portfolio, but a successful power broker, journalist-publicist and political fixer). Yet none of these people had the ability, idealism and intellectual cultivation of Metaxas; they were conveniently lesser types.

One can only conclude that Metaxas did not want professional traditional party politicians in his government. He was trying to break with the old Greek political world and its mould, to create a new state without politicians, one based on corporatist representation. The fact remains that there were in the regime many ex-army officers from the 1923 Leonardopoulos–Gargalides abortive coup against the Liberal–

Republican–Venizelist–Plastiras post-Asia Minor movement. This abortive coup and the subsequent purge of the army officers accused of being associated with it, constituted a bond between them and Metaxas, reputedly the inspiration and prime mover of the coup. Others in his administration came from the world of banking, especially the National Bank of Greece, and some major local industries like the Bodosakis armaments and weapons manufacturer.

Metaxas depoliticized the army officer corps. He used the expanded police force developed by Venizelos twenty years earlier in order to control the opposition and suppress unrest in the country. He increased the perks of the Gendarmerie (the *Chorofylaki*), and generally strengthened General Security Agencies which since 1929 at least (under the *Idionym Law*) chased up the Communists, and deported political dissidents and seditious elements to the islands and remote countryside. General Security also supplied the Service for the Defence of the State and against the threat of war in the form of counter-espionage: a highly efficient Aliens department was created under the direction of the General Security Undersecretary C. Maniadakis. In fact and in actual practice, the Metaxas regime in this area built on existing institutions and practices. By expanding the training and educational facilities for the Police, it made them a far more efficient agency of state control·– a counterweight to the Army perhaps? – eliciting as a result a wider public perception of the regime as a Police State.[8] Yet another source of public resentment of the regime was its high taxation policies and its plainly coercive and intimidating fund-raising for national purposes. Metaxas though enjoyed better relations with the armed forces among whom he commanded wide respect for his brilliant past record as a Staff Officer in the Balkan Wars, and later for setting out the overall strategy of resistance to the Italian invasion in October 1940. Navy Chief Admiral Sakellariou however disliked Metaxas, and at some point the latter dismissed his deputy Economou. Although these were anti-Venizelist, they were primarily monarchist officers. Thus the initial reaction of the army to the Metaxas Palace coup on 4th August was one of acquiescence; many of them happened to be Kondylist – Populist officers. But there was rising discontent in the next two years, especially as they came to resent the new institution favoured by Metaxas, the paramilitary *EON* or National Youth Organization. There were weak unsuccessful coup attempts by the odd officers and minor politicians, some of them allegedly inspired by the Palace.[9] Some blatantly pro-German officers at inopportune times were sacked as for example, General Platys, especially when Metaxas and the King were trying to balance a foreign policy of neutrality with a pro-British bias so as not to provoke an Italian attack.

Certain concrete achievements of the Metaxas regime remain, lasting developments that are popularly associated with it: the Demotic Grammar of Triandafylides commissioned by Metaxas, a committed demoticist himself; the IKA system of Social Security – National Insurance, and Old Age Pension – a scheme considered earlier by the previous Venizelos regime, but for one reason or another sidetracked; the further development of the Piraeus–Kifissia Electric Railway; the Albania National Epic. Many agree that his personality and strong will kept wartime Greek morale up; there was a total collapse after his death in January 1941. It is interesting that Metaxas never really liked, or at least never respected, General Alexander Papagos; he considered him militarily incompetent or at least inadequate. A joke making the rounds of Greek GHQ at the Grande Bretagne Hotel in 1940, probably inspired and obviously propagated by Metaxas himself went like this: 'Imagine what would happen if the Italians found out that Aleko is our Chief of Staff …'.

II

The fact is that Metaxas was a dominant figure in the Greek political consciousness and discourse for at least three decades, if not longer – roughly the first half of this century. Originally he was a central figure in the passionate national schism in Greece from 1916 to 1936 and beyond; and later was often invoked by his supporters and enemies alike in the discussion of the tragic post-Second World War developments in Greece. Simply on this basis, Metaxas deserves the attention of historians, and especially so over half a century after his death. But he merits attention too as a major Greek national figure who, at the moment of deadly threat to the territorial integrity and sovereign independence of the country, not only rose to the occasion of leading its defence against a powerful, though cowardly, aggressor in October 1940, but, as it transpired, also had the prescience, the foresight, and vision during the preceding four years in power to organize and equip the Greek armed forces and bring them up to a strength of over 750,000 men under arms, and achieve a modicum of national rehabilitation – even unity, albeit under an autocratic regime – to be able to cope with such a critical challenge. Even his most severe detractors among his

Greek critics grant him this much.[10] The novelist Giorgos Theotokas believed that:

> The worth of Metaxas is that at the fateful moment (which was also the supreme moment in his life) he felt clearly without hesitation the demands of the deeper instincts of Greece … I greatly appreciate two things about Metaxas. One the fact that from the first moment and without hesitation he placed the national interest above any other – the regime, political or social interest – and in this he towered over Mussolini and the leaders of the French Right. The other, his political sensitivity to the fact that not only all of Greece would be for war till the end or to the last, but what direction it would take. Thus Metaxas became the agent of the deeper passions of the nation. Good general, good intellectual.[11]

On pages 205–6 of his *Diary* Theotokas quotes the impression of Metaxas by Demetra Vakka (Mrs Kenneth Brown):

> While Colonel Metaxas is widely considered the most capable of King Constantine's entourage, he did not make as strong an impression on me: he is a small fat man, an ordinary dark-complexioned type. While a student in Germany's *Berlinkriegsakademie* they called him 'Little Moltke'. It is reported one day the Kaiser put his hand on Metaxas's shoulder and told [his brother-in-law] King Constantine, 'If I had five like him, I'd conquer the world.' Despite his German training and education, Colonel Metaxas did not consider Germany invincible and was not for neutrality at all. Proof of this is all the work he did to prepare a military plan for the capture of Constantinople. His plan was submitted to the Entente, but Britain rejected it.

And Queen Sophia of Greece told her brother, the Kaiser, 'Wir haben unser man in Atene, das ist Yannaki.' Philip Dragoumis in one of the volumes of his memoirs, *Dichasmos 1916–1919* (Athens, 1995), in the entry for 28 July 1919 [p.447] reports, 'The Queen is the only one who continues to rely on the worth of Metaxas.' Furthermore Theotokas in the entry of 31 January 1941 in his *Diary* [p.238] reveals more in his description of the state funeral of Metaxas when he reports,

> It is clear people were sad about his death, especially in view of OXI and repulsing the Italian invasion. The past is erased; what is left is the glorious moment in Metaxas's life, the one that guarantees his fame. But there

wasn't the same kind of anguish as there was over Venizelos's death. The
relationship of Metaxas to the people was never one of love; he was rather
cold, logical and calculating. It was like grieving or mourning over the
loss of a valuable partner. But also one of undoubted respect: Metaxas,
who was so maligned in the political arena in the past and who till age
sixty-five was considered a failure, managed in the end to command
respect. He achieved what he wanted, that is, to govern Greece, and
entered history as leader and saviour of the country. He made us follow
his funeral with grief over his loss, and respect for his strength, judgment,
exceptional perseverance and courage.

And in the entry of 16 February 1941 [pp.337–8] Theotokas describes
the Metaxas *Diary* as one in which the dictator wore his 'Sunday best',
constituting a significant historical document of the last thirty years
(1910–40), and wholly convincing of Metaxas's patriotism. 'I have no
difficulty accepting this', Theotokas concludes, 'because I never believed
in the conscious treachery of Metaxas, his ministers or generals. But I
deplore the Metaxas regime for its niggardly spirit (*mikropsychia*), narrow
mindedness and strategic incompetence, and the reigning dynasty
(which can be deplored) for its hereditary, traditional, incurable stupidity,
and humble devotion to its material interests and personal safety.'

Beyond that, Metaxas himself gave an extensive explanation of his
actions and policy in a major statement to the Greek Press, the owners,
editors and publishers of the national dailies (the Athens Press) at the
Grande Bretagne Hotel on 2 November 1940.[12]

III

It was only after I had completed the research for this book that I ventured
to visit the Metaxas home, a modest Italianate villa at No. 10 Danglis
Road in Kifissia, a suburb of Athens, where I met his surviving younger
daughter Mrs Nana Foka, a sprightly welcoming lady in her early
eighties. She showed me around the house and all the mementos connected with her father and his regime; regaled me with stories and
episodes about his closest associates; insisted that I occupy the lounge
chair in which the Italian Ambassador Emmanuelle Grazzi sat when
he delivered Il Duce's infamous ultimatum to Metaxas at 3 a.m. on
28 October 1940. A plaque on the left-hand side of the front wall of the
villa commemorates that momentous occasion.

A gifted linguist, Mrs Foka also described vividly too me her mother's arrest by ELAS during the Communist Insurgency or Civil War. Her main complaint was about the absence of any reference to her father on any of the national occasions the Greeks celebrate or commemorate in connection with the Second World War. She finds this deliberate lack of recognition, tantamount to a denial of her father's contribution to Greek national survival and his other services to the Greek nation, spitefully petty and undeserved. When I asked what she remembered best about her father when she was growing up, she replied, 'He always admonished us not to trust anybody.' Typical of a suspicious autocrat, dictator? When I asked her who her father's close friends were, she snapped, 'he had no friends'; in Greek, 'Itan aphilos'.[13]

IV

Why sketch a political portrait or profile of someone like Metaxas who after all was the authoritarian Prime Minister of a small Balkan country on the eve of the Second World War? His impact on his own country was overwhelming so long as he lived, but not permanent; and he hardly had any than a passing impact on a wider society beyond the boundaries of Greece, including the sizeable Greek communities of the diaspora in Egypt, North America, and Africa. There must be though a natural fascination with an individual of extraordinary talent, achievement or power, and who radiates some kind of glamour. The Chief of the Greeks – 'Great Governor' (O Megalos Kyvernites) of Greece – radiated a glamour of sorts if only because he insisted and succeeded, albeit temporarily, in imposing his will and vision on his country and its people unopposed for at least four years. One is therefore curious about any special abilities Metaxas had that compelled him to act in the public domain and his hopes and vision which many other Greeks may have shared but could not pursue or implement themselves.

Needless to say no biographer or prosopographer, including this one, is free of bias. Both social context and emotional elements constitute conditioning factors. Even the much vaunted documentation which is invoked and purveyed as evidence is not always wholly dependable or trustworthy. Finally, why Metaxas and not someone else? Perhaps to the extent that in his general perception of politics in modern Greece and overall vision of Greece as the expression of Hellenism, Metaxas may have left behind him a broad legacy that lingers on in certain corners of the Traditional Political Right, reflected in the Military Establishment and remnants of the Monarchist Establishment. His legacy may even encompass the remnants of the underlying anti-Western cultural streak in contemporary Greek nationalism. Yet this particular tendency has always been present in Greek literary/cultural writing and discussion since 1880 at least.[14] Is Greece, in the Eastern Mediterranean, more Hellenistic than Hellenic? Is it more Byzantine Oriental (Near Eastern as per D.G. Hogarth, 1902, and Vatikiotis, 1974)[15] than classical Greek or Western Hellenic? But that is another vast and never ending argument.

V

Interesting too is the fact that there are no serious biographies of the two rivals, Venizelos and Metaxas, whose publicly aired political differences dominated the Greek political scene and divided the Greek nation, both in mainland Greece and in the Diaspora for nearly thirty years.

The contrast in the personality of the two men is relevant here. Venizelos was mercurial, charismatic, clannish, tribal, imperious and autocratic. Possessing an enormous ego, he was seen by the mythopoeic Greeks as a hero and a saviour of the nation.[16] A party political animal, he was a master of political intrigue. A perusal of his voluminous correspondence suggests a contradictory personality, a slippery customer difficult to grasp or pin down. Neither man was a mainland Greek; both were islanders. Metaxas was from Cephalonia that was free of Ottoman influence, and rather more Italianate by virtue of the Venetian occupation of over two centuries followed by a brief French occupation with its fall-out of the ideas of the Renaissance, the Enlightenment and the French Revolution. He was conscious of his family's Byzantine origins and its subsequent ennoblement by the Venetian rulers in the seventeenth century. He was proud of the fact that in the past members of his family had served as governors of the island of Ithaca for several generations, while others had been prominent soldiers, men of letters, doctors and lawyers. In contrast, Venizelos from Ottoman-ruled Crete, was from a rougher, less genteel, background and of a rebellious disposition.

Venizelos was a lawyer and professional politician, whereas Metaxas was a professional soldier turned politician. Impulsive, empathic, impressionable and ponderous, Venizelos came to power in 1910 on the back of an army coup d'état. In contrast, Metaxas, detached, or even semi-detached, and openly more snobbish, haughty, coolly analytical, calculating and deliberate, was a highly and widely respected Army staff officer who clawed his way on to the national political scene after having been a notorious courtier, a client of the Greek royal family. In yet sharper contrast, Venizelos was an 'Ottoman' Greek, whose romantic political liberalism and republicanism of convenience were largely the result of French Enlightenment influence. Metaxas was rather Teutonic, impressed by the 19th-century German love of classical Greek 'kultur', Prussian military prowess and efficiency. But he could not match the charm and charisma of Venizelos which verged on demagogy and hero worship.[17] Whereas Venizelos was adulated, actually worshipped by the masses even when he governed them in a 'popular autocracy', nobody worshipped Metaxas. Erudite and a romantic about classical Greek civilization, loyalty and duty were his social-political priorities, civic values and the supreme virtues, not rebellion or pandering to the fickle masses. An elitist and a monarchist pitted against the Greek bourgeois political establishment, Metaxas was determined to impose a new order and discipline on the Greek state and society, and to counter the sentimentality of national dreams woven by Venizelos.

Whereas Metaxas was cautious and premonitional in his political judgment, Venizelos was impulsive and flamboyant. Paradoxically perhaps Metaxas was more radical in his domestic national perceptions and consistently anti-bourgeois, whereas Venizelos was the uncrowned king of the Greek bourgoisie, the darling of the liberal political salons of the Greek 'chattering classes' (to borrow a late 20th-century British metaphor) at home and abroad.[18] He attracted and enjoyed tremendous affection from his followers, whereas Metaxas elicited fear and resentment from his critics and enemies, respect and obedience from his political allies, supporters and collaborators.

VI

Like a period in the history of the ancient Greeks, the Trojan War, the public career of Ioannis Metaxas as a prominent soldier and politician began with a quarrel which led to the Schism (*Ethnikos Dichasmos*), in the country and which lasted for thirty years, at least, from 1915 to 1945, and which was both epochal and significant in the life and political destiny of Greece. There are at least four main reasons why the reconstruction of the public life and political career of Metaxas is difficult; some will aver impossible. One is the man's complex personality and his own extraordinary description and dissection of it in a *Diary*[19] unique among the personal records left by public men in Greece; there is also a mass of state and private papers, *selectively* collected and preserved in the Greek State Archives, including an intimate correspondence with his wife during the first twenty years of their marriage. Another is the nature of his authoritarian regime under which he governed Greece as an autocrat, a classical dictator from 4 August 1936 to 29 January 1941. The third is that his rule coincided with the greatest epic of the modern Greeks, their heroic and successful resistance against the Italian invaders in Albania in 1940–41. The fourth reason is Metaxas's own unclear and undefined relation to Mediterranean and European fascism, the shift in his political career from a parliamentary politician to being an anti-parliamentarian autocrat. His quarrel with Venizelos dominated the Greek political scene in the interwar period and fuelled the passionate division of Greek politics which emphasizes personal preference and promotes violent factionalism.

The more empathic among us Greeks also find Metaxas an unattractive personality, dry, over-logical, and lacking charisma. Teutonically erudite, pedantic? There are several things we hold against him. The comfortable bourgeois middle class among us which arose under the Tricoupis regimes of the 1880s and 1890s and its successors, and dominated Greek politics from the late 19th century to 1936, find Metaxas a tedious lower middle class (petty bourgeois) clever upstart despite his own claim that he was the descendant of declassé nobility of Frankish counts with Byzantine ancestors. What the 'chattering classes' among us cannot forgive too is his having abolished our favourite sport, namely party politics, or the politics of factionalism – he denied us our clubland world of political gossip and intrigue. Many also cannot forgive him for having been more successful as the champion of greater social justice for the people, the lower toiling classes of farmers and workers. Perhaps most insulting of all to us was the fact that Metaxas managed to govern the country for four and a half years under a practically *personal* regime of enlightened despotism, unsupported by any national political party, and one strictly based on an understanding – not free incidentally of mutual suspicion – with the King, the personal loyalty of a few old collaborators and political cronies, a thoroughly purged army officer corps which respected him as a one-time brilliant staff officer and retired general, and a brilliantly efficient state security service, *Asfaleia*, as well as his own impressive moral authority.

Initially my interest in Metaxas did not derive from any passing acquaintance with recent Greek political history, but from my wider interest in 'strong man rule' in the Mediterranean in the interwar period, and my more specialized study about a parallel phenomenon in the modern Middle East, illustrated in my study, *Nasser and his Generation* (London and New York, 1978), and 'Authoritarianism and Autocracy in the Middle East', *Arab and Regional Politics in the Middle East* (London and New York, 1984, French Gallimard).[20] After going through his state and private papers, examining his personal library which he bequeathed to *EON* and which his family gifted to the nation and housed in the Benaki Museum-Library, I was intrigued enough to hazard what I offer here. But it must be understood that whatever portrait I have managed to construct of the man is strictly drawn from records and documents, that is from the available historical record, and to this extent it did not have the benefit of live interlocutors who may have known my subject. If however I have managed to illustrate the personal factor in modern Greek politics, to illuminate the intensity of factionalism to the point of tragedy and its role in the Greek epic of 1940 which to some degree assuaged the lingering humiliation and frustration over the national catastrophe in Asia Minor in 1914–22, I will have also depicted Greek *hubris* in its contemporary guise and inadvertently strengthened those Greeks and foreigners who still believe that the Greek 'character' – if there is such a national trait – has not really changed significantly from what it was during the ancient period.

VII

In trying to draw a portrait of Metaxas here I do basically five things: (1) inquire into Metaxas's beginnings, his family background, his military education and early career; (2) look into his earliest political activities as a staff officer, his political choices in the spectrum of Greek political factionalism, his relationship to that great national figure Venizelos, the quarrel between them and its consequences for the country; (3) consider his early retirement from active military service with the rank of major general – and his involvement in national politics as leader of a small and minor political party, member of Parliament, political writer and polemicist, cabinet minister, political intriguer, and leading royalist engaged in a deadly contest for national power with the republican factions; (4) examine him as prime minister and head of the 4th August

Regime, 1936–41, founder of the 'new Greek state' based on a minimal, oversimplified political ideology vaguely akin to that of European (Mediterranean) fascism, social and economic reformer, and national war leader; and (5) consider Metaxas as a mirror of Greek politics and society from 1900 to 1940, especially as reflected in his *Diary* and other private writings.

NOTES

1. Much of the excitement in reconstructing the political career of Metaxas was in his struggle for power. Once he attained absolute power, one feels he considered his 4th August Regime was an anti-climax, taken up mainly with keeping the state solvent, the desperate search for the procurement of arms to defend the country in an imminent world war, and the suppression of any opposition. Even on the eve of his own apotheosis as the architect of the Greek victory over Italian aggression, the Greek Albanian Epic, October 1940–March 1941, Metaxas was a very sick man, and already as of April 1940 literally dying.
2. Ioannis Metaxas, *To Prosopiko tou Imerologio, 1897–1941* (I. Metaxas, His Personal Diary) in four volumes. The first two volumes, edited with an Introduction, Prologue and Notes by Christos Christidis, Athens, Estia, 1951; volume iv (1933–41) edited by Phaidon Vranas, Preface by Lela and Loukia Metaxas, Athens, Ikaros, 1960; and volume iii (1921–32) edited by Pan. M. Sifnaios, Athens, Ikaros, 1964. All translations from the *Diary* and from all other Greek sources are mine.
3. Many of these are in the Private Papers of I. Metaxas deposited in the State Archives in Athens, and many of them are reproduced in the Appendices to the volumes of the *Diary*.
4. I take the view and approach the Metaxas episode not as a violent departure or radical break with a presumed long political tradition of liberal democracy in modern Greek history, but on the contrary as the culmination and logical conclusion of a long political tradition and culture of authoritarianism and autocracy. I shall argue that the ideological dimension of the Metaxas regime was a limited and opportunistic one, not as elaborate as some of the younger contemporary students of Greece seem to think or believe; that in fact, the Metaxas regime was a highly personal one, loath to emulate or be part of the wider European Fascist or totalitarian political trend of the inter-war period, but keen to develop its own authoritarianism and self-sufficiency on largely Hellenic, i.e., native indigenous historical roots, antecedents and experiences. If one must have a parallel to anything comparable in southern Europe, then I suggest Salazar of Portugal with his *Estado Novo*, or New State as of July 1932. On Salazar, see among others, A. Ferro, *Salazar: Portugal and her Leader*, English translation by H. de Barros Gomez and J. Gibbons, 1939, *Salazar, Doctrine and Action* (Speeches, 1928–50), translated by R.E. Broughton, 1951, F.C.C. Egerton, *Salazar, Rebuilder of Portugal*, 1943, and Michael Derrick, *The Portugal of Salazar*, 1938. The journalist who conducted the interview with Metaxas for the *Echo de Paris* on 16 September 1936, drew a parallel if not similar conclusion about an autocrat at the head of an authoritarian state. See *Diary*, iv, pp.654–5.
5. But see Nicolas Karras, *O Ioannis Metaxas*, Athens, 1994, I. Kolliopoulos, *Restoration,*

Dictatorship, War, Athens, 1985, and I. Koliopoulos, H Diktatoria tou Metaxa kai o polemos tou Saranta '40, Thessaloniki, 1994.

6. But cf. Constantine Sarandis, 'The Ideology and Character of the Metaxas Regime', *Aspects of Greece 1936–40, The Metaxas Dictatorship*, edited by Robin Higham and Thanos Veremis, Athens, 1993, pp.147–77, based on an earlier (1979) Oxford D.Phil. Thesis, *The Emergence of the Right in Greece*, 1920–40.

7. This role may be extrapolated and defined from I. Metaxas, *Logoi* (Speeches), 1936–40, 2 vols, Athens, The National Society, 1939 and Athens, 1941, some of which are reproduced in relevant sections of his *Diary*.

8. See D.H. Close, 'The Police in the 4th August Regime', *Journal of the Hellenic Diaspora*, vol.13, pp.91–105, and 'The Power Base of the Metaxas Dictatorship', *Aspects of Greece 1936–40, The Metaxas Dictatorship*, edited by Robin Higham and Thanos Veremis, Athens, 1993, pp.15–40. See also, D.H. Close, *The Character of the Metaxas Dictatorship: An International Perspective*, New York, 1990.

9. As for instance the conspiracy 'Fighters for Popular Liberties' headed by Generals Tsangarides and Matalas. It was uncovered in March 1938 to the alarm of Metaxas, and led to an extensive purge of the officer corps, especially in the Athens Garrison. Another weak conspiracy led by the minor politicians A. Livieratos and G. Kartalis, never really got off the ground. See G. Dafnis, *I Ellas Metaxy Dio Polemon, 1923–40* (Greece Between Two Wars), Athens, Ikaros, 1974, esp. pp.11, 433–67. In fact Metaxas records his own version of the above-mentioned abortive army coup in the entry to his *Diary* for 12 March 1938, the day he set out for Ankara and the reception of his stopover in Thessaloniki. The conspiracy was initiated by George Papandreou who together with some anti-Venizelist politicians sought to mount a coup d'état led by the CO of the 12th Division, Major-General I. Tsangaridis and the Inspector of Artillery Major General J. Matalas, both Venizelist officers who disapproved of the 1935 coup but who looked to Andreas Michalakopoulos to succeed Metaxas in government.

10. As an illustration of this effort, see the voluminous correspondence with H. Simopoulos, the Greek Ambassador in London, and the top secret submission by the Chief of the General Staff about staffing and personnel needed in the Armed Forces, as well as equipment in the event of a general mobilization, dated May 1939. In the Private Papers of I. Metaxas.

11. Giorgos Theotokas, *Tetradhia Imerologiou* (Notebooks of a Diary), *1929–53*, Athens, Estia, 1987, p.198.

12. Document in typescript in Metaxas Private Papers; reproduced in the documents appendices of the *Diary*.

13. My earlier study of Nasser of Egypt, *Nasser and his Generation*, London, 1978, found that 'that autocrat or despot on the Nile' had no close friends either. Is friendlessness the fate of dictators and autocrats; and is that a reflection of their not being able to trust anyone?

14. By the turn of the century a fairly identifiable school of letters with, among others, Pericles Yannopoulos, K.S. Sokolis and especially Ion Dragoumis occupying prominent positions.

15. D.G. Hogarth, *The Nearer East*, 1902, and P.J. Vatikiotis, *Greece: A Political Essay*, London, The Washington Papers, No.22, Sage Publications, 1974.

16. See Penelope Delta's hagiographic volume of excerpts from her *Diary, Memoirs and Correspondence* – her private archive – about E. Venizelos, edited by P.A. Zannas, Athens, 1983.

17. Ibid.

18. Cf. the Ioannis Metaxas *Diary*, 4 vols, and Penelope Delta on Venizelos, *op. cit.*, as

well as G. Ventiris, *The Greece of 1910–1920*, 2 vols, Athens, 1970 (first edition, Athens, Pyrsos, 1931).

19. *Op. cit.*
20. Pp.135–51, and the expanded French version of it, 'Autoritarisme et Autocratie au Proche-Orient', *Islam et Politique au proche-Orient Aujourd'hui*, Paris, Le Debat, Gallimard, 1991, pp.177–209.

PART I

Formative Years: School, Military Training,
Cultural and Political Influences

1

Origins and Formative Years

The putative Byzantine origins of the family of Ioannis Metaxas go back to one Mark Anthony (Marcantonio) Metaxas, a soldier of the last Byzantine Emperor Constantine Paleologos. After the fall of Constantinople in 1453, he fled to Cephalonia, settling down in the town of Franzata, later re-named Metaxata. Other members of the Metaxas family were prominent in the Venetian–Turkish wars, some of them having led Cephalonian mercenaries in these wars against the Turks in Crete and other parts. Thus Angelo and Anastasios Metaxas were reputedly prominent in the Morozini-led campaign against the Turks on the Greek mainland. It was presumably for such mercenary services to the Venetians – the Franks – that some of the Metaxas family were created counts in c.1690.

The fortunes of the extended Metaxas family are reflected in the variety of offices and activities its members were engaged in from the 16th to the 19th century. Several of them – such as General Constantine and his brother Andreas – became prominent in the War of Greek Independence (1821–30). Before that they had been governors of nearby Ithaca (1558–1795), physicians to Ali Pasha of Yannina,[1] as well as clergymen. Others among them were academics and scientists teaching in Italian universities. Members of the Metaxas family (e.g., Stavros Metaxas) were among the leaders of the revolt against English rule in Cephalonia in 1848. Others chose to play a role in world commerce: thus Count Baptiste Metaxas founded in 1841 a commercial 'House of Metaxas' in England. In short the Metaxas was an established prominent and leading family in Cephalonia; its rival was the other prominent family of Anninos on the island.

Ioannis Metaxas, who belonged to the Angelo branch (the Anjulati) of the Metaxas clan, as distinguished from the Anastasios branch, was born in Vathy on Ithaca, where Panagis, his father, was a local government officer, probably a provincial district officer. By all accounts not too bright, Panagis had inherited a smallholding in Argostoli on Cephalonia. In social terms he could best be described as being from a declassé aristocratic background. Politically he was a client of Alexander Koumoundouros (1817–83), a politician from Mani, who served as minister of Finance and Prime Minister. In 1868 Koumoundouros founded his own newspaper, *Ethnikon Pneuma* (National Spirit) and short-lived party. He was reputedly leaning towards France and England among the European Powers, but feared Russia. Although he had played a leading role in the new dynasty and the introduction of the new Constitution in 1863–64, he subsequently disagreed with King George I over Greek policy during the Eastern Question and the Congress of Berlin in 1876–78.[2] He exercised his patronage by securing for Panagis the post of district officer in Ithaca.

The mother of Ioannis Metaxas, Eleni Trigoni, was the daughter of a landowner from Agrinion on the mainland, with Macedonian antecedents, and connections. Just before that the Metaxas family had been living in Cephalonia off the meagre income from the inherited small landholding at Kontogourata. Panagis was by all accounts not too extrovert, rather conservative, and very conscious of his aristocratic or noble antecedents, as well as of his declassé status. Unfortunate circumstances forced him to sell his land and seek public employment through the influence of his patron Alexander Koumoundouros, in the local administration – the gendarmerie, county office or treasury. And so Ioannis Metaxas was born in the District Office building in Vathy, Ithaca, on 15 August 1871, where his father, Panagis, was district officer. Panagis reported a troublesome birth due to a congenital complication – whatever that may have been – for its nature was never alluded to or reported in any of the sources. Later in life Ioannis Metaxas suffered periodically occasional internal-intestinal bleeding of unknown or undisclosed etiology, as well as bouts of pharyngitis, as recorded in his *Diary*.[3] Panagis had reported that the midwife allowed the infant to bleed profusely, but in spite of that the infant survived. It must have been difficult for her and the physician to abandon the newborn infant to its fate in order to look after the mother and save her life.

Panagis had married Eleni Trigoni, Ioannis's mother, in March 1870. Ioannis Metaxas was born seventeen months later in August 1871. The modest real estate legacy which Panagis had inherited from his father in Kontogourata he sold in 1871, soon after Ioannis was born, for the sum of 6,000 drachmas; and by 1880 when Ioannis was nine years old Panagis owned no landed property of any kind. Rather he now faced financial difficulties, having become a minor public employee in the local-provincial administration for the rest of his life, moving from one posting to another. Thus in 1873 Panagis became the district officer in Ithaca, a position he held for six years, during which period the boy Ioannis attended primary school there. His school report for the year 1878–79 recorded that Ioannis had excelled in mathematics and Greek. This was also the year his father Panagis was fired from his position in local government. The family returned to Argostoli, where Ioannis attended secondary school. Having sold the inherited property at Kontogourata, Panagis and his family suffered a drop in living standards to the level of the lower middle class (the *mikroastikoi*). Ioannis was once again reported as being top in maths in school, and described widely as bookish, serious, circumspect and conservative, helped along by his ambitious mother, who was reportedly brighter than her husband Panagis. Ioannis acquired the reputation of an introspective lad who loved solitary walks in the countryside. His solitude and concentration were complemented by a highly developed sense of dignity and self-respect (*axioprepeia*). Unlike many of his contemporaries Ioannis did not believe in fate (*moira*), but rather in ability, competence and presentiment.[4]

NOTES

1. 'The Lion of Yanina', 1741–1822.
2. (Greek) *Encyclopaedia Biographical Dictionary*, vol.8.
3. See the four volumes of the Metaxas *Diary* for episodes of haemorrhaging, stomach complaints and other ailments.
4. See D. Kallona, *O Ioannis Metaxas, Mathitis, Stratiotis, Agonistis, Kyvernitis* (Ioannis Metaxas: Student, Soldier, Politician, Fighter, Governor-Ruler), Athens, 1938. See also the relatively recent monograph, *O Ioannis Metaxas Autopsychoanalyetai* (I Metaxas Psychoanalyses Himself), Athens, 1988, by Andreas Kapoyannopoulos. I have not ascertained whether Kapoyannopoulos is a professional, qualified psychoanalyst, or a medically qualified psychiatrist; but his monograph is rather original in its approach to the construction of a profile of I. Metaxas.

2

Early Military Career

Ioannis Metaxas entered Military College, *Scholé Evelpidhon*, in 1885 from which he graduated as a second lieutenant in 1890. Not much is known about his early military postings beyond the fact that between 1890 and 1892 – the first two years after graduation and commission – Ioannis lived in Corfu, but served in different posts or assignments. In August 1892, Ioannis entered the School for Military Engineers, *To Mechaniko*, as it was known, which led to the first interesting assignment of his military career. In 1894 we find Lieutenant Ioannis Metaxas as the Chief Engineer of the Nafplion garrison, where a year later in 1895 he supervised the construction of the seafront promenade (*Corniche*) to Arvanitia on the waterfront.[1]

His father, Panagis, was now Chief Executive of the local authority. For the next three years till the outbreak of the 1897 Thessaly Greco–Turkish War, Metaxas led an uneventful life, very much tied to the garrison and family routine. He did though become a member of the National Society, where he took an active part in the discussions of young officers about certain burning national issues of the day, such as the liberation of Crete from Turkish rule and its union with mainland Greece, as well as the national struggle in Macedonia.[2]

During this early period in his military career, Metaxas established wider contacts and close relations with other officers, including his superiors or commanding officers who were to influence his future career. One such dominating influence was his CO, Captain Victor Dousmanis,[3] Mechanical Corps, Senior GHQ Staff Officer, mentor and patron but also, according to Metaxas, his 'exploiter', who between 1899 and 1908 helped Crown Prince Constantine to reorganize the Army. Twenty-three years later, in 1920, Metaxas finally rebelled and broke off this particular close relationship.[4]

Another transient relationship with a negative impact on Ioannis

Metaxas was that with Lt Col. Constantine Sapoundzakis, an officer of the 'old school', very close to the royal court and Chief of Staff during the ill-fated 1897 Thessaly War. Metaxas considered Sapoundzakis an incompetent officer.[5] Thanks to the influence of his relative Nicolaki Metaxas, a government minister – Minister of Army Affairs in 1885 and 1897 – Metaxas secured after the Thessaly War the posting of staff officer of the First Mechanized Division in Larissa.

The 1897 Thessaly War itself was a traumatic experience for the young officer Metaxas as well as for many others. Precipitated by the mindless zeal of ultra nationalism and patriotic chauvinism, it pushed an inadequately trained and ill-equipped army into a senseless, fruitless war with Turkey, and led to the loss, instead of the intended gain, of territory, as well as the further unwelcome involvement of foreign powers in the affairs of the newly independent Greek state. Just before that the insurrection in Crete elicited the expression of the earliest anti-European, anti-foreign – anti-Western – sentiments by Metaxas:

> The English tried to obstruct the landing of Greek troops in Crete, and the European press is unfriendly. Since Europe wishes to prevent our national integration, we should foment a general revolt in Turkey, and involve all nations in a worse conflict and if we are destroyed we will have dragged the whole of Europe to disaster … We all demand a European world war, since they [foreigners] are seeking to bury us … The spirit that pervades Greece is that if they prevent us from occupying Crete, we must invade Macedonia and bring about a European War … The position of the Great Powers is undoubtedly to sacrifice Crete and Greece for their own interests … Europe at the end of the 19th century appears in a dreadful state which does not augur well for its future. [*Diary*, I, pp.140–3]

During the Crete insurrection which called for union with mainland Greece, Metaxas was of the view that the resolution of that crisis depended very much on the stand of England. He records in his *Diary*, I, 135 ff. on 24 January 1897, that the insurrection in Crete calling for union with Greece had already begun, and that (our) National Society supports and encourages it. He also records the next day news of massacres in Chania in Crete of Christians by Turks. There was partial mobilization, an army regiment was sent up to the frontier in Thessaly, and the destroyer navy fleet under Prince George sailed with orders to prevent the landing of a Turkish army on Crete. There was a full-blown crisis by the end of January 1897: Europe was in a way inattentive and

England was concerned mainly with its policy of reform of the Turkish state. In February the Powers' fleets shelled rebel concentrations in Halepa (home town of E. Venizelos); there were widespread clashes in Crete; the King rejected European power pressure and resolved to deal with the Crete crisis himself; there was widespread enthusiasm for war: 'My only wish is war, war to the end, a holocaust that will burn the whole of corrupt European society' [*Diary*, I, p.145]. By mid-February 1897, Metaxas complains, 'the whole of official Europe is fighting us; only members of the European public support us', and then stops suddenly any further comment on events beyond repeating, 'Greek hatred of all Europeans is at its height' [*Diary*, I, p.147]. But, he goes on, 'I am not writing history, only my impressions, and sentiments.'

At this point Metaxas goes into a rather incoherent harangue about his feeling of injustice, regret over his mindless patriotism, depression about the poor standard of the army and its officer corps. He describes how his particular duties during the War with access to the top secret papers of the minister – 'my position is confidential: I am in charge of the minister's correspondence' – gave him real insight into the dreadful internal condition of the army leading him to a state of disappointment and depression. The morale of the army officers was low: idleness, lack of training, petty rivalries within the corps caused their corruption. Metaxas does not resume the entries in his *Diary* until two weeks later from Larissa, where Major Pallis was Chief of Staff, and where he also found Dousmanis who promised to find Metaxas an assignment with HQ Staff. He further reports about the state of the army, consisting of poorly trained troops, suffering many shortages and led by officers of low morale, and poor leadership. But he also hoped that his fellow officer Xenofon (Fondas) Strategos (later with Metaxas in Berlin) would help him get assigned to the staff of the Crown Prince. In actual fact though Metaxas ended up working with Dousmanis on the staff of the First Division, commanded by seventy year old Major General Makris, a nice man but of limited military education and training [*Diary*, I, pp.152–3]. Metaxas has much praise for Dousmanis, his immediate superior: 'broad intellect, practical thought; hardworking, dynamic, brilliant ... but sadly undermined by his GHQ superiors'. On the whole, in his thumbnail profiles of the officers at HQ, Metaxas tends to belittle their military abilities, as well as criticising their character [*Diary*, I, pp.153–5].

The entries in the *Diary* for this period, especially on the eve of the 1897 War are long, reflective and of a personal nature. He writes about the formation of his character at a time when war was inevitable:

What is certain is that despite all of my struggles, my character has yet to be formed. I hope, however, that experience and my will to improve will lead to that character formation. Despite the clerical nature of my assignment at HQ – *officier d'administration* – like everybody else, I did not wish to leave because, remaining at the centre, I could observe all the movements of the army, and because I assumed that hearing about me at GHQ people would think me someone – an officer – above the average ... And God keeps me. [*Diary*, I, pp.154–6]

It was during this early part of 1897 that Metaxas acquired a rather high opinion of himself as a staff officer, and more generally of his military abilities. At HQ he was involved in the drafting of operational orders in the office of Dousmanis and Chief of Staff General Sapoundzakis, a time when he became convinced that other officers around were seeking to undermine his privileged position because they were envious and resented his recognized competence. The complaint about the envy of others so common in this very early period of his military career was to become a permanent feature throughout the rest of his stratopolitical career.

NOTES

1. Funding for this major public work was supplied by the Archbishop of Argos Nikandros Delouka. Cited in *Diary*, I, p.51, quoting the local Nafplion newspaper *Anexartisia*, number 548 of 8 May 1895.
2. On the founding, membership, objectives, activities and finances of the National Society, see *Istoria tou Ellinikou Ethnous* (History of the Greek Nation, vol.4, 1881–1913), Athens, 1977, pp.93–100.
3. Dousmanis was the descendant of a noble Corfu family of Albanian origins, whose ancestors, like those of Metaxas, fought alongside the Venetians against the Turks. He was born in 1861 – ten years before Metaxas – the grandson of Anthony Dousmanis, a politician who published in Italian the record of the Gladstone Mission to Corfu. After Military Academy he joined the Corps of Engineers (Michaniko), served as an instructor in the Military Academy, as Chief of Staff, in the Ministry of Army Affairs (Stratiotikon), 1899–1909. He was promoted Colonel after the Balkan Wars, and became Aide to King Constantine and Venizelos. After the deposition of Constantine Dousmanis went into exile in 1917. He was tried and convicted along with other officers of GHQ, given a life sentence, but freed after the November 1920 elections. He was re-arrested by the Plastiras Revolution regime in 1922, but after interrogation was released. He published *The History of Thessaly* (1927), and *An Inside View of the Asia Minor Campaign* (1928). P. Dragoumis, *Dichasmpos, 1916–1919* (Diary), Athens, 1995, describes Dousmanis as the most dangerous opponent of Venizelos, p.433, and reports that the Queen insisted on proclaiming the value and worth of Metaxas, p.447.

4.   General A. Mazarakis–Ainian reports in his *Apomnemoneumata* (Memoirs), Athens,
      1948, p.414, the reply of Dousmanis to the comments by Metaxas on his book
      about the military catastrophe in Asia Minor, where he said: 'Metaxas always
      intrigued and conspired against me, and tried to undermine me with Venizelos in
      order to replace me as Chief of Staff. In a meeting in my office, where he (Metaxas)
      came to see me about his posting to Drama, and where I did not receive him
      warmly, I told him drily that his new assignment was fitting after his continuous
      hostile stand against me, and added, I recognize you are an excellent staff officer,
      but you have a lousy character. If I were convinced that even now you would improve
      I would keep you here at HQ. Crying, he embraced me. I was moved by his
      sentimentalism, believed him and kept him at HQ. But he went on undermining
      me. He is Greece's man of destiny.'
5.   See *Diary*, I, (entry for Easter at Farsala), pp.180–200, reporting on the 1897 War
      and many of his fellow staff officers at GHQ, for his contradictory statements about
      the Chief of Staff Sapoundzakis. Within a matter of days after lauding him as one
      of the best educated officers in the Army, Metaxas condemned him as incompetent
      and had to be replaced. Mrs Sapoundzakis, incidentally, was Lady-in-Waiting to
      the Queen.

3

The 1897 Greek–Turkish Thessaly War

I

When the Thessaly War broke out in March 1897 the 26-year-old Metaxas served as a junior officer in the headquarters of the Commander in Chief, Crown Prince Constantine. This posting was to prove crucial for his military career, early politicization and future political career. Metaxas was diligent and very observant from that rather privileged posting and left us in his *Diary* one of the best descriptive narratives of that war [*Diary*, I, pp.157–330]. He was however shocked by the incompetence of senior officers, and at the same time realized the folly of nationalist zeal in fighting a war when the country was in utter political and military disarray. The experience convinced him – as it did most young officers in the Army – of the need and importance of the reform and reorganization of the Army and society wider afield. In short, he foresaw the ensuing condition of stasis which led to the Goudi Army coup in 1909 against the political establishment (the *ancien régime* of 1864–1900), the old political parties with their traditional bourgeois politicians surrounding the monarchy, and the conservative leadership of a pre-modern army.

Another and perhaps most decisive influence on Metaxas at this early stage of his career was Crown Prince Constantine, to whom he became blindly loyal and totally devoted. He was needless to say close to one or two of the other royal princes, especially Nikolaos and Andreas, who were fellow serving officers in the Army. He soon owed his chance to further his military studies at the *Berlinkriegsakademie* to the patronage of the Crown Prince – the major influence in his life and career. At the end of the Thessaly War in September 1897, Metaxas, along with other staff officers, prepared the Crown Prince's Report on that disastrous war. He also wrote his own technical study which he submitted to an army competition conducted by the Chief Inspector of the Engineer Corps, and for which he won the first prize. The study was subsequently published by the Ministry of the Army with the title, 'The Role of the Engineer Corps in Military Expeditions'. It is the only technical military study by Metaxas ever published.

Interesting – and possibly upon reflection rather significant – is the fact that during and just before the War Metaxas managed to do some paid private surveyor and construction jobs in his spare time: his *Diary* entries in November and December 1896 are introspective and revealing: pondering the situation in the country Metaxas confided 'by noon I was overwhelmed with despair over the blackness of my future. The truth is that I am nothing' [*Diary*, I, p.120]. He was possessed by self doubt.[1] The affairs of the National Society were not going well. Equally Athens was riddled with political scandals. 'Athens with the mindlessness of all those who inhabit it; the doings of the political parties in Parliament … God help us' [*Diary*, I, p.119]. He reports a number of resignations from the Officers Club, transfers and problems with promotions. The King demanded of the prime minister certain reforms in the army, a suspected deal between King and Prime Minister Deliyannis in order to forestall any explosion in the Army. At the same time the policy of Greece was changing vis-à-vis the other Balkan countries, especially Romania and Serbia [*Diary*, I, p.121]. At this time Metaxas took long walks, often with his sister Marianthe but mainly with fellow officers or played cards with the latter late into the night and pondered further on his and the country's situation. On Tuesday, 3 December:

> I left early for Argos to carry on with the costing of the construction of the army camp there. After lunch I met Logothetis, who was having difficulty in walking due to his rheumatism and excessive drinking. He offered me coffee and regaled me with stories of his family, wishing that his son would become somebody in the future. I was saddened watching a man destroyed by drink and other abuses but still clinging on to his aristocratic past. I sympathized with his rueful remarks and his dreams for the future of his son, because despite the democratic veneer surrounding me, there remained always in the depths of my soul aristocratic ideas – values. [*Diary*, I, p.122]

Then back to mundane concerns of financial interest: 'I am swamped: the work for the army camp in Argos, and a private contract – the copying of plans for which I received 25 drachmas. I am relieved' [*Diary*, I, p.123].

During that early period in his career Metaxas assisted his family financially, so that any extra income was welcome. But as he put it, he was going through rough, stormy days of melancholy and depression. The politics of the National Society – viz., elections preoccupied him. He did not win the Presidency of the Society because he records in his *Diary*, 'they (the other officer members) resent me because they feel I am ahead of them (my excellence)' [*Diary*, I, p.124]. Also at that early stage, Metaxas believed like most other Greeks then and today that the Ecumenical Patriarchate was a source of Greek strength in the Balkans. 'The Serbs and the Bulgars may be stronger militarily, but this is not enough. I believe that because this nation (the Greek) is endowed with so many charismatic qualities it is the only cultural element in the East, and God will not abandon it' [*Diary*, I, p.125]. He worried desperately about the state of the nation, its fragmented government, fractious army and politicians: 'May God preserve Greece and guard the Race (to genos).' Metaxas concludes his *Diary* at the end of 1896, 'A critical year for me' expressing an early tenet of his, 'I want everyone to be in his place', celebrates the fact that his health has improved, that his belief in God, the immortality of the soul, morality and progress has been restored – a kind of general euphoria and self-congratulation [*Diary*, I, p.128].

That part of his *Diary* which comprises a record of his experiences in the 1897 Thessaly War is critical for an understanding of the changes in the views of Metaxas about the army officer corps, the dynasty, and the politicians. His idealism and patriotic enthusiasm reflected in his membership of the National Society and the views he held while at Nafplion about the resolution of national issues had been eroded and undermined by the experience of that war. He reports the war campaign in detail: his entries in April 1897 deplore the incompetence of the staff and line officers, the weakness of the infantry, the disarray of the troops at the front, the rout and general retreat in Thessaly after hardly any combat, with a minimum of casualties, so that before the retreat to Farsala the army of Thessaly was non-existent. He witnessed the rottenness of Greek political and military organization, the ignorance and ill-disposition of army officers [*Diary*, I, p.184]. Undisciplined troops tended to pillage and plunder during their retreat; sanitation and health services were poor despite good quality medical officers: they lacked transport, were deprived of supplies, and most personnel were not devoted to duty. Metaxas's brief profile of HQ officers is equally bitter and disappointed: thus a certain Goulimis was a bad influence on HQ; so was the new

Chief of Staff Major Pallis: 'old professor of mine whom I respect and expected much from him; but I begin to doubt his worth. We shall see' [*Diary*, I, p.190]. After painting a grim picture of the overall condition of the army, he refers to the need for a ceasefire, but also alludes to the political anarchy in the country. The War, he came to think, was partly the result of domestic politics, especially the clash between the government of Deliyannis and the opposition led by Rallis and the press. Much of the blame for the Greek military collapse in the War was put by the Opposition and the press on the monarch and the royal princes. The Crown Prince and the princes with army command were to be made scapegoats of the failure in the war. In his *Diary* for that period Metaxas also emphasizes inadequate military preparation, poor equipment, the debilitating rivalries among senior and staff officers, and the clash between some of the latter and the Crown Prince who was Commander in Chief. In describing the progress of the Crown Prince and his HQ Staff in the Larissa area, Metaxas records the Crown Prince's efforts to regroup and galvanize the troops on the line which elicited their cheers; Metaxas comments, 'The Greeks shout a great deal, but seldom act' [*Diary*, I, p.166]; in other words, they are all noise with no action. The general retreat that turned into a rout of the Greek forces, south of Lamia, prompted the Athens government on 19 May to beg the representatives of the Great Powers to intervene, and the Tsar pressed the Sultan. Hostilities in Thessaly virtually ceased on 19 May, and on the 20th a ceasefire was agreed. A Peace Treaty was concluded and signed in Istanbul on 20 November, 1897.

Actually as early as May 1897, if one is to stay with his *Diary*, Metaxas is already a disillusioned 'patriot'. Thus he records that fellow officer Yannakis Petmezas, arriving from Crete, regaled him and Papavasileiou at HQ about the bravery and tenacity of the Cretans, and his belief that they will persevere against European and all other opposition till victory, and comments, 'he seems to me over-enthusiastic and exaggerates. I would have been the same before the War; but now I am different' [*Diary*, I, p.267]. In disgust, he reports simply, 'In general, the troops or army units, with the exception of artillery and engineer units, moved in great disarray; their officers showed no interest in their well-being' [*Diary*, I, p.268]. In fact, already, on the eve of the War in March 1897, Metaxas was concerned and unimpressed: 'Our army, on the whole, has excellent morale, but also great needs and shortages: it is short of horses, good organization and proper logistics and most important leaders. Nearly all the unit commanders are unsuitable, uneducated. May God help us'

[*Diary*, I, p.152]. One of his complaints as a staff officer was not simply the rivalry between officers at HQ, but the fact that the intrigues prevented any systematic work on strategy and tactics or operations: 'Not a single study, no preparation about future hostilities. Orders are issued without proper study and are constantly modified or changed. No officer is ever sent out on reconnaissance missions or to reconnoitre the area of operations or battle' [*Diary*, I, p.272]. But Metaxas also seems to vacillate in his approval and disapproval of the two Chiefs of Staff, Pallis and Sapoundzakis. Thus towards the end of the war, he concludes on 21 May, 'the more I think of the matter, I recognize that under Sapoundzakis we always acted correctly, but with Pallis I confess that the activity of HQ Staff was and remains negligible (really naught, *midameni*)'. He also records his ridicule of another officer, Drosopoulos, who was praising events in Crete by saying, 'he speaks of the events of war mindlessly; he does not really know what war is like: he thinks it is like the odd skirmishes in Crete'. It was an exchange with one of his relatives, the officer George Metaxas, which set him wondering whether the Staff HQ was up to the task and which led him to express his revised view of the two Chiefs of Staff [*Diary*, I, pp.272–5].

Back in Athens in the autumn of 1897, Metaxas reverted to the routine existence of an officer, marked by time spent in the fashionable and popular Zacharatos Café. During that time, Metaxas also developed a closer relationship with his younger schizophrenic and ill-fated brother Costaki, who was a medical student. 'Costakis', Metaxas recorded in his *Diary* at one point, 'is constantly pursued by imaginary enemies; there is no person who is not continuously concerned with how to harm him' [*Diary*, I, p.410], clearly a paranoid persecution complex. Having completed his tour of duty at Army GHQ where he was assigned to the Crown Prince's Staff engaged in preparing the official Army Report on the 1897 Thessaly War, Metaxas set out to visit his family who were still in Nafplion. Just before setting out on this journey, he stopped to bid the Crown Prince, his commander in chief, farewell. During that encounter the Crown Prince 'asked me if I wanted to go to Europe. My answer is easy to surmise. He told me he planned to send me, Papavasileiou and Strategos, to Germany; now that his relations with the Emperor [Kaiser] were good we would be accepted into the Academy in Berlin. He hoped that the government will send us, and told me we should learn German' [*Diary*, I, p.343]. Leaving Athens this time Metaxas was very happy over his prospects, and even happier to see his family again, especially his mother and sister Marianthe. 'What a transformation', he remarks, 'I do not recognize myself; the War has transformed me from a youth to a man, relieving me of my neurotic oversensitivity, and removing the veil from my eyes which hid from me the reality of things … And so ended here the turbulent period of my life' [*Diary*, I, p.345].

He had just been through a harrowing and depressing period, marked by a series of family crises which were to shake up Metaxas and undermine his confidence and feeling of security about his future military career. 'What a thunderbolt! May God have mercy.' His sister became ill with depression, but eventually recovered to marry and have children (she died in 1928). It was his brother, Costaki, as we shall see, whose bouts of severe mental illness became a source of great unhappiness for Metaxas. Although Costaki qualified in medicine he never practised. These incidents of ill health in the family were compounded by the difficulties engendered when Metaxas's father was dismissed from his job in the provincial administration by his boss for party political reasons, accusing him of service anomalies, that is, venality. Metaxas records traditional feelings of honour and shame: his father's public disgrace is a disgrace for the whole family. 'I cannot remain in the army. I shall leave Greece to look for a job elsewhere in order to support my family', he records angrily in his *Diary* [I, p.337]. His father was transferred to Arta on the mainland, and after that back to the island of Zakynthos (Zante). Meanwhile, on his return journey by rail to Athens, Metaxas read *Faust* to relieve his melancholy and depression. 'I too have my religion to console me in these terrible moments: *Faust*, Goethe's magnificent poem, is my Gospel' [*Diary*, I, p.339]. All the same, for good measure he resorted to the accepted recourse of nepotism in an effort to help his father, using the intercession of his superior officer Lt Col. Sapoundzakis who gave him a letter of introduction to the relevant government minister Korpas. 'But surely they cannot treat him (his father) unjustly; the sycophancy of the Provincial Prefect is apparent, and they fear us. Costakis attributes much value to my strength – my proximity to the Crown Prince. While I doubt this, my optimism has been restored' [*Diary*, I, p.342].

From November to the end of 1897, Metaxas was preoccupied with his sister's and brother's mental illnesses, hysteria and schizophrenia respectively, as well as with his father's employment difficulties. In fact, he withdrew from his social circle of friends in order to devote all his attention and spare time to his family and their difficulties. His father had been transferred in the meantime and Metaxas became responsible for the domestic well-being of the family including the shopping. Thus the very long entry of 2 November 1897 in his *Diary* is a painful and detailed catalogue of these trials and tribulations. At one point Metaxas wonders if Marianthe's illness was hereditary, and wondered about his own health: 'I became nervous, irritable and disturbed ... I was drained of all stamina ...' (these were the first indications of hypochondria in Metaxas). 'And so amidst the tears and agony and misfortune, this year (1897) that was so productive for me came to a close' [*Diary*, I, p.354].

The prospect of further military study and training at the *Berlin-kriegsakademie* (The Berlin War Academy) came at a crucial stage in the career of Metaxas, offering him a relief from the succession of family disasters, and allowing him to experience life in Western Europe.

II

Between the end of 1897 and February 1899, that is, on the eve of his departure to Germany, Metaxas did not keep up his *Diary* entries on a daily or regular basis. He was too distracted by family matters and difficulties. Thus he tried to describe the year 1898 in two–three lengthy entries, such as the one covering the period from July to mid-October, and from mid-October to the end of the year. He did nevertheless consider 1898 on the whole as a happier year even though he had remained in Nafplion on his own for some time after his family had left town. He used this period of time to write his paper, referred to earlier, for the Ministry of Army Affairs competition and for which he received the first prize, but which to his deep and bitter disappointment did not lead to his promotion. During this period of the year Metaxas faced a severe moral-psychological personal crisis, before he was posted back to Athens on the threshold of wider horizons and opportunities, and at the start of his concern with and involvement in more public matters and issues, now that family trials and tribulations were at least temporarily behind him.

At this time, suffering from a bout of influenza, Metaxas refers to his chronic pharyngitis.[2] He also mentions briefly his correspondence with Captain Dousmanis who from Athens kept Metaxas informed about the attacks on the King, the Crown Prince and his GHQ Staff, but he claims that during his illness he rarely read the newspapers. He did though read a great deal of fiction, as well as materials for the preparation of his paper, 'The Role of the Engineer Corps in Military Expeditions'. At some point in 1898 Metaxas was assigned by the Ministry to translate pieces from

the 'Ecole des Mines', and he continued to read *Faust* in his spare time.
He was now in Nafplion on his own, his family having returned to
Zakynthos. Leisure amusement was provided by the Kotopouli Theatre
in Nafplion which he frequented. Yet he was deeply hurt when he was
passed over for promotion, and saw officers his junior promoted ahead
of him. He became resentful and imagined all kinds of revenge against
the Army and an ungrateful society which refused to recognize his worth.
'I decided to leave the Army at the first opportunity', he threatened
[*Diary*, I, p.362]. 'In addition to overwork, a severe winter and a protracted bout of influenza were added to my natural impulses and passions
(ormai) … Suddenly now, once I overcame the family difficulties, these
natural passions exploded and remained unabated …'. He was, moreover, disappointed and could not withstand the frustration any longer:

> My toils, struggles and morality were not rewarded. Why should I suffer
> any longer; why should not I enjoy life as it was offered to me; what
> meaning was there to decency, dignity, honour and morality? They were
> all futile; enjoyment is all. I was like a madman; only the will, the deter-
> mination to finish the paper for the competition kept me at work. Often
> I felt like tearing up all my notes and giving myself wholly over to hedonism
> and pleasure … but something – a spark of latent ambition – held me
> back. And I carried on working while the ignorant and incompetent
> around me got promoted … Bitterness and disappointment dominated
> my soul. [*Diary*, I, p.363]

Approaching Spring made matters worse. Metaxas followed super-
ficially the events of the Spanish–American War; he ignored domestic
or national politics. Yet 'amidst the moral and national ruin which fed
my soul, one figure remained intact, untainted: the King and his dynasty.
My devotion to them grew. There was a moment – only a moment –
when I hated my country, but not my kind. I needed a prop – an anchor
and support – and I found it in this sentiment for my King' [*Diary*, I,
p.365].

Metaxas spent Easter and attended the Royal tour in Nafplion. He
had applied for home leave to Zakynthos where he planned to complete
the work on his paper for the competition. But in the meantime he was
unexpectedly transferred to a posting with his regiment in Athens. It was
an unwelcome assignment (Metaxas planned to spend the summer in
Nafplion) which revived his neurasthenia, so that for a while he was
overwhelmed by total despair: 'I considered my life a failure; I had no

future … I could see no hope of any improvement, and the only solution was for me to abandon my military career and seek to make a living in business. Depression, despair and disappointment possessed me.' He confided many of his feelings to his mother. Nevertheless he enjoyed his home leave in Zakynthos between reading the papers at the Club and walking in the countryside. But this did not relieve or dispel his depression. After a short stop at Nafplion to pick up his kit Metaxas resumed his regimental duties in Athens which occupied him till noon of each day. 'I was still wholly pessimistic about my future', he hastens to add, 'but was more inclined to rationalize the situation. I frequented the theatre and the Zacharatos Bar, almost an unemployed – well, at least underemployed – Athenian' [*Diary*, I, pp.369–70]. At the same time Metaxas settled into a flat in Kolonos, established a liaison with a girl supplied by a Mrs Eleni, and otherwise flirted with the girls in the neighbourhood.

Having discovered that his paper received first prize in the Army Competition, Metaxas concluded: 'It indicated I had a road before me other than the road of hedonism and pleasure; that of honour and glory' [*Diary*, I, p.373]. The politics of the military were a bore: Smolenski against Zorba,[3] and Zorba against the King. Yet the strength of the monarchy to which I was devoted as the only hope for the country, was about to be restored, and all its Café detractors thwarted [*Diary*, I, p.374]. And ever since Metaxas returned to Athens he never stopped seeing Dousmanis in his office in the palace of the Crown Prince. 'He was the first person I went to see in Athens, and I often stopped in his office. I thought they could take me back in this office, although I did not request or demand this, nor did I have the right to do so' [*Diary*, I, p.374]. But he soon joined in the regular discussions of Dousmanis and his circle of officers at Zacharatos. 'We talked about culture, Art and Philosophy: our ideas, views, beliefs and hopes were similar over many things. What is certain is that this man (i.e., Dousmanis) had a great influence over me, the formation of my character, or at least in my development' [*Diary*, I, p.374]. The close relationship between them showed Metaxas that 'work saves' until 'the choice before me was clear: Either honour and grandeur, or hedonism and corruption' [*Diary*, I, p.375].

Although unhappy about his progress in learning German, Metaxas and Papavasileiou persevered with their lessons. He was also distracted by his violent, insatiable passion for women, which was satisfied temporarily by a 24-year-old textile worker in the neighbourhood with whom he carried on an affair for several weeks. He alluded again briefly to the old complaint of his being passed over for promotion to Prince George who had just been appointed High Commissioner in Crete, thereby adding to the popularity of the royal family: 'Everyone now appreciates the role of the dynasty of King George in Greece; the hostility and mistrust between it and the nation were dispelled; except for the parliamentarians – the bourgeoisie, as Costakis called them, of the political parties who plot and intrigue constantly in pursuit of a bit of power' [*Diary*, I, p.380]. The Crown Prince's Report on the 1897 War, on which Metaxas worked too, was published after all, so that despite the difficulties, Metaxas viewed the future with hope; his doubts and reservations overcome.

Eighteen ninety-nine was an important year in the life of Metaxas. It was the critical year in his military education and training when he entered the Berlin War Academy to follow an advanced course. It compensated in part for the dreadful and dramatic family crisis over his father's waning career, his brother's and sister's mental illness – all of these unpleasant, unhappy episodes that seriously influenced the views of Metaxas of Greek society and Greek political life, as well as the formation of his own character. He records in his *Diary* for January–February 1899 that the 1897 War Report by the Crown Prince he helped prepare was released by Dousmanis to the press: *Estia* published a summary of it, and there were comments about it in other papers. The overall public reaction to the Report was excellent, and despite the opposition of the paper *Embros*, the Report retained its credibility. The press gave it wide coverage and notice for three weeks, and the Crown Prince was praised as a brave Greek, until in the end he was 'deified'. Yet there was always something for the neurotic Metaxas to fret about. Thus he claims that his impending mission, together with that of Papavasileiou and Strategos to the Berlin War Academy, was in jeopardy when he learned from Colonel Paraskevopoulos that legislation was being prepared for the selection of officers to go to Europe for further training by examination. Metaxas felt that this threatened his position and prospects and sought, through his oldest patrons Dousmanis and the Crown Prince, to protect it, since getting to Berlin also required the appropriate legislation and specific government decrees.

Amidst all this commotion and anxiety Metaxas carried on a torrid affair with a Miss R. who was at the same time herself entangled with another man – an army sergeant. Metaxas was working again in the office of the Crown Prince, where Col. Pallis had requested him as an aide because he was about to draft the Reorganization of the Army Plan in the name of the Crown Prince for submission to the Minister. Interestingly – and characteristically – Metaxas complains about the superficiality of Pallis which the Crown Prince had not yet spotted. But it was also a time of general elections which the incumbent Deliyannis lost to Theotokis. Metaxas mentions in passing requests from his family to use his connection with the Crown Prince to help his father and brother. 'Unfortunately, they (the family) misunderstand and misinterpret my position with the Crown Prince; they assume I can extract important favours' [*Diary*, I, p.386], and he makes it clear he is reluctant to resort to that level of nepotism, as it could displease his major patron, the Crown Prince. Nevertheless, he sought it via his immediate Army superior officers, Col. Pallis, Capt. Dousmanis and Lt Col. Sapoundzakis. What is most interesting about this period in his life, as reflected in his *Diary* entries, is the fear of Metaxas that Palace conspiracies as well as GHQ intrigues would undermine his position and future. Thus he suffered constant and acute anxiety that something would go wrong – the first sign of paranoia? [*Diary*, I, 11 Feb. 1899, p.387]. Interesting too – even if in a minor way – is the fact that Metaxas began at this time to adopt a new style of life as an officer and a different social routine, such as lunching at the Officers Club and frequenting popular or well known society bistros. Yet his comments occasioned by the funeral of the famous philanthropist Syngros, recorded in his *Diary* on Sunday, 14 February 1899 [*Diary*, I, pp.388–9] are equally relevant for his perception of the Greeks in general and Athenian society in particular. He refers again to the nepotism he had to resort to with the Crown Prince via his superior officers Pallis, Mazarakis and others [*Diary*, I, p.389].

By early March however Metaxas is despondent once again: his failed love affair – sexual liaison really; his indisposition caused him disquiet and left him without any zest for work. 'I feel bitter that I cannot amuse myself at all, and disgust for my monstrous life … Since morning', he notes on Thursday, 2 March 1899, 'I have been enveloped by black thoughts. My future is bleak … My mind cannot sustain any work …'. On the following day though his nervous condition improved, and he was able to do some studying. 'Costakis believed it was due to mental fatigue. I too suspect that I suffer from a neurasthenia', he confided in an aside in his *Diary* [I, p.395]. By Wednesday, 24 March Metaxas was referring to a new routine set on a course of work for the new Army Reorganization Plan under Pallis and Dousmanis, and his German lessons with a new tutor, Dietrich [*Diary*, I, p.395]. The political crisis arising out of the Deliyannis–Theotokis rivalry allowed Zaimis to form a new government in April 1899. The press sang the praises of Zaimis and attacked the Crown Prince for his attempts to suppress constitutional institutions. The old game of a parliamentary regime, as far as Metaxas was concerned, was resumed. 'I was discouraged. The Crown Prince's lack of boldness brought us back to the awful parliamentarianism' [*Diary*, I, p.398]. Metaxas insists on commenting on political changes and crises from the perspective of their effect on his personal fortunes, and how he had lost out in love too. It forced him to abandon his *Diary* for a while, and in May 1899 he was complaining, 'My age is that of ambition, and I have yet to experience true love' [*Diary*, I, p.401]. During that month Metaxas took part in extensive army manoeuvres.

NOTES

1. Metaxas had been reading *Studies in the History of Mankind* by the Belgian historian Francis Laurent which seemed to influence his thinking at that time.
2. See Ch.16, below, about causes of death.
3. Col. Smolenski distinguished himself as a line officer in the 1897 Thessaly War; he was subsequently posted to the Royal Household. Colonel Nicholas Zorba, an artillery officer, commanded the 3rd Artillery Regiment in the 1897 War, pursued advanced military training in France, served as an Adjutant in the Ministry of Army Affairs, and Commandant of the Military Academy *(Scholé Evelpidhon)*. Accusations of alleged disobedience of orders in the 1897 Thessaly War led to a difficult stage in his military career, without further promotion. His hostility to the royal family served to land him the leadership of the 1909 Goudi Army coup, as leader of the Military or Army League *(Stratiotikos Syndesmos)*.

4

The European Experience: The *Berlinkriegsakademie*, 1899–1903

Metaxas bid his family farewell and left Zakynthos on 24 August 1899 apprehensive and tormented by doubts of insecurity, the search among his patrons for protection and support, and his questioning of the existence of God. In order to calm his disturbed psyche, he wondered, 'Is there a God – does God exist?' [*Diary*, I, p.458]. Accompanied on the journey by his two fellow officers, Strategos and Papavasileiou, and after stops in Trieste and Vienna, Metaxas arrived in Berlin on 13 September 1899.

> We arrived in Trieste at noon on Friday. My initial impression of the first big European city from the steamship, was unsatisfactory, because most of the City was hidden from view in a valley. After 1½ hours we disembarked at the quay where Gougalis, the cousin of Strategos, welcomed us and was most helpful throughout our stop in Trieste … Most impressive, as we were arranging for our baggage to be sent on to the railway station, was the cleanliness of the streets, the green of the many trees. On the premises of the famous Post and Telegraph Office I admired the order, trust and security in which people received their letters inside the small boxes … We promenaded at Miramar, a marvellous experience, especially for us who were not used to the art by which Europeans transform nature. And yet we missed our sky and sea … The women are good looking, graceful and pleasant, and must enjoy sex. They are nothing like the wild – primitive – Athenians …. [*Diary*, I, pp.463–4]

Metaxas goes on to describe the train journey from Trieste to Vienna, where they arrived the following morning of a wet and misty day, checking into the Metropol Hotel.

The sight of the city and its streets stunned us; we went around with gaping mouths. But I felt ill, took quinine, and could not enjoy the *Venedig in Wien*. The following day, despite my indisposition, we toured many of the sights – mainly Gothic churches – in town. The women are totally free. We attended Rigoletto at the Opera and visited the *Kunsthistorichen museum*. [*Diary*, I, pp.464–5]

On the eve of their departure from Vienna though, Metaxas became possessed once again by anxiety and worry about his family back home. A week after they left Greece, they were on the train taking them from Vienna to Berlin. On the Austrian–German border customs officers desisted from examining their baggage as soon as they discovered they were army officers. 'Ja' was the only word uttered by the customs man. We were soldiers and therefore for him highly respected – demigods. 'This was my first impression of Germany' [*Diary*, I, p.467]. Order and notices about smoking on the train: 'On the whole I felt intermingled, always delicately, the firm directing hand of the State.'

Interesting is his attempted contrast between himself and his two travelling companions, Papavasileiou and Strategos – a contrast he will keep returning to throughout their stay in Germany. Metaxas remarks about their extroversion: 'On the train coach they engaged Germans in conversation; they find relations easy, they are Mediterraneans (from the Mezzogiorno). I don't like this; perhaps my unhappy childhood and the trials of my earlier life have made me reserved and melancholy. Those two however were happy like children' [*Diary*, I, p.468]. He found moreover that they did not share his sense of time (a very unGreek trait). Instead they wasted much of it gazing at shopwindows. According to the Greek Ambassador in Berlin, Rangavis, 'Our entry into the War Academy was the first indication of the transformation of Greek relations with Germany. The German Emperor recognized this change in his toast at an officers' dinner in honour of his sister Princess Sophia, wife of the Crown Prince of Greece.

In his *Diary* entry for 19 September in Berlin covering most of the first year one gleans the views of Metaxas about his experience but also the way he related to his two Greek colleagues, and his intention to render the Berlin experience meaningful not only for his personal educational and cultural development (see for example his personal library), but for his future military–political career as well.

The *Diary* entries of this early period in Berlin when, with his two companions, he was househunting and arranging for private German language lessons with Dr Kampe, Metaxas risks detailed descriptions of the character and behaviour of his two companions, especially Papavasileiou. He found the latter a spoilt indecisive Athenian. He concedes however his own meanness and inordinate concern with money [*Diary*, I, pp.475–8], but insists he had to lecture his colleagues about the ills of expensive ostentation, the importance of being prudent and provident; he also sang the praises of genuine true nobility as against the corrupt bourgeoisie (*'prostychoi astoi'*). Interesting too is his comparison of his two fellow students, Strategos and Papavasileiou. The former he found honest, straight, steady, logical and practical; his main failing being his bad manners. The latter he found to be lacking in integrity, devious, secretive, sly, underhanded and petty [*Diary*, I, p.480]. All three were attached to the 2nd Infantry Regiment of the Imperial Guard, to which the Greek Crown Prince, the Kaiser's brother-in-law, also belonged.

At one point Metaxas thought of having calling cards (*billieta* as he called them) printed with his own coat of arms. 'I want to carry my title, of which I am proud', he records, 'but I don't wish to do it precipitately, so as not to arouse the envy of my colleagues.' On 22 October, Metaxas records, 'At last we have started a normal life', having reported to the Regiment and the CO of the Guards [*Diary*, I, p.484]. While Papavasileiou complained about their treatment by the German officers, Metaxas on the contrary found the Mess most welcoming and pleasant. But he is still careful with money and frets over his finances: 'Yesterday and today I bought several textbooks for the course in the Academy. In addition, I was forced to pay 9 Marks to satisfy a sexual need, which I very much regret, especially since due to my inexperience I did not enjoy it' [*Diary*, I, p.487].

The *Diary* entry for 8 October 1899 is interesting and significant:

One of the greatest deprivations of my generally deprived youth has been love. Poor, timid and modest due to my poverty and misfortune, and lacking an attractive appearance, I have kept away from women ... One of my dreams therefore here in Germany is to forge an easy liaison–relationship, not with a public woman (prostitute) ... but an innocent young girl who makes no demands. There is a 'but' however in all of this: such a relationship would constitute a tie which I may find difficult to break. In the meantime it would consume my time away from my studies and my duty; it would entail the expenditure of money – the money of my country intended for my training and education as an officer, and which I should use otherwise to assist my unfortunate needy family

anyway. Above all I had undertaken before God the obligation that my
life would be one of priestly – hieratical – devotion to my duty … which
is to work hard and continuously for my King and Country. My duty is
also to save money to help my brother Costaki, and with the needs of my
family.

Metaxas chose duty and hastened to add ruefully:

> But such victories have a high price: My youth is past; I am 29 and I
> embark upon the age of full manhood with the bitterness of past
> deprivations, but with the determination to fulfil my duty towards God,
> people, the King and the country, and my beloved family. [*Diary*, I, p.489]

Metaxas and his two fellow officers had audiences with the King of
Greece who was visiting the Kaiser that autumn. They also spoke with
his son, Prince Nikolaos, brother of the Crown Prince. The Greek royal
visit to Berlin reflected the rapprochement between the two countries,
as well as improved relations with Turkey [*Diary*, I, p.492]. Metaxas,
though, never ceased to worry over the condition of his brother Costakis
back home. He was at the same time exercised by the attitude of his
companions, especially Papavasileiou, over work in the Academy, and
their resentment of his aristocratic noble background. Yet he avers, 'I
expect to become something by relentless hard work. Should I sacrifice
this too?' [*Diary*, I, pp.493–4]. 'Suffering from the lack of women – sex
– and not satisfied with the whores I resorted to, I tried to forge a
relationship with a sweet young woman from Vienna' [*Diary*, I, p.495].
For a while, then, Metaxas neglected his studies. The affair with Elsie
ended and he returned to his work. After several disagreements and
rows with Strategos and Papavasileiou, Metaxas stopped any further
close relations with them, as he felt he could no longer trust them. But
it is also clear Metaxas himself was not an easy colleague to get on with.
Mistrust seems to have been part of his nature. Equally, sensitivity
about his dignity, status and self-respect were prominent traits of his
personality.

By December 1899 there was an improvement in the fortunes of his
family back in Cephalonia, but Metaxas continued to assist them financially with his occasional remittances. One of his recorded comments at
the close of the year referred to the renewed conflict between the Crown
Prince and Parliament over the Reorganization of the Army Bill, and
concludes, 'Well, I'll do something too to suck some parliamentary blood;

the occasion will present itself' [*Diary*, I, p.500], referring to the political rot in parliament, and the need for the King to deal with it boldly and firmly. Indication of the intense hatred Metaxas had for the party politicians? On 23 December, Metaxas tried to fill the gaps in his *Diary* which he had neglected for a couple of months, during which time he nearly contracted cystitis, was tortured by the lack of sex, but frequented the theatre. He cannot resist complaining about his colleague Papavasileiou: 'He judges the Germans through a neo-Hellenic lens; he is mistaken. He expected them to receive him with open arms, and he was unhappy with their reserved but always polite manner' [*Diary*, I, p.502]. On 10 January in recording his night spent with a woman for 10 marks, Metaxas opines, 'The advice of prudence and good sense is one thing; the impulsive acts of youth quite another' [*Diary*, I, p.503]. His closing remarks at the end of the year relate to his anxiety over his father's threatened position, his brother's illness, confessing that he is entrusting his hopes in God: 'I am a sinner' [*Diary*, I, p.505].

Worthy of note about his second year at the Academy is that Metaxas did not keep up his regular *Diary* entries on a daily basis. In May–June he successfully sat examinations in Tactics, Fortifications and Military History. He was simultaneously tortured by the desire for women. Relations with his two colleagues worsened, marked by frequent rows. The difficulties of his family continued, especially his brother's illness, (Costakis experienced renewed fears of persecution) and Metaxas continued to assist them financially.[1] 'I decided not to go with women, to attend the theatre less frequently in order to save money' [*Diary*, I, p.516]. More significant was the development of his political views, especially his pro-monarchism and the more intense consciousness of his noble and Byzantine antecedents. Parts of his resolution to lead a more sedate life was a result of his reading of the short stories by Guy de Maupassant. A bout of influenza and a spell in bed drove him to more extensive reading. He even re-read his *Diary* and noted that the early part, from 1896 to the events in Crete, was written by a thoroughly moral person: 'I was that then', suggesting he had been corrupted since [*Diary*, I, p.519]. He even remembers to comment on the Boer War: 'The tide has turned in favour of the English' [*Diary*, I, p.520]. He continued to attend the Opera, especially Wagner. He was nonetheless plagued by bad news from home. By early March 1900 his brother's illness had worsened. 'I begin to despair completely over Costaki … might I also be responsible for his illness?' [*Diary*, I, p.522]. He also feared about the family's endurance and difficulties over his brother's advancing illness.

Costakis had been admitted into the Dromokaiteion asylum. Metaxas's deep depression was partly alleviated by his participation in a programme of war games. But the guilt feeling over his brother remained causing him to suffer stomach upsets and other psychosomatic symptoms of illness. A suspected hypochondriac Metaxas took to his bed to rise from it only to attend a ball on Saturday, 17 March 1900. Later that month he saw a performance of Tannhäuser, and met more German and American ladies. During this period of doubt and illness Metaxas heard Beethoven for the first time in his life. Until mid-June Metaxas occupied himself with political developments in Greece, and recorded extensive comments about them in his *Diary*.

The passage of the Reorganization of the Army Bill reflected the Crown Prince's abandonment of his earlier Court policy of ready compromise with the political parties in Parliament, and the initiation of a bolder royal policy:

> Since Parliamentary institutions have failed, the Crown Prince ... appears with great courage to lay the defeat of 1897 at the door of Parliamentary direction of the Army, and undertakes to redress the balance ... In the matter of principles there is no via media, middle road: If it is shown that the Monarchy replacing Parliament in the affairs of the Army has succeeded, nothing can stop the nation from veering towards it. The struggle in Greece between Monarchism and Parliamentarism will be joined. There is no monarchist party in Parliament; it lies outside parliament; it is the Crown Prince who depends on and is supported by those who by virtue of their origin or character and preference are devoted to the idea of the monarchy – and these are few – and on those who suffer in the long or short term at the hands of intemperate Parliamentarism, and seek refuge in the Monarchy – and these constitute the majority of the Nation.

Metaxas then goes on to proclaim his own stand in this major political division over the preferred type of rule in Greece:

> I have set my course a long time ago: I am a soldier and a nobleman, and I place my sword in the service of the king; I dedicate my life and soul to him. It is immaterial to me if the King is good or bad, harmful or useful, for I don't examine whether his actions are good or bad for the Nation. I follow him blindly; his will for me is law ... I have no other ambition than to fulfil my duty towards the King and the Crown Prince. I consider

the King the representative of the Nation, of the past, present and future of the Nation. All opposition to him from whatever quarter I reject and find repulsive. [*Diary*, I, p.527]

Of course, Metaxas hastens to add,

there has been a transformation in me in the last four years. Thus the War put me in my place (i.e., sobered him up). I became aware of what I owed as a soldier and above all as a nobleman and a Metaxas: I belong to that aristocracy which fought for the King and the State long before the birth of the modern Greek nation state. This Greece was born from its struggles and sacrifices. For me therefore the motherland is not the Greece of 1821, because as a Metaxas I belong to a species and generation that antedated, existed before this one, and that belonged to another larger mother country which now only the King can represent, because it gave rise to the Monarchy we have now. Monarchy was not born in Greece after a treaty; it was the deepest, innermost desire of the Nation, which during its enslavement – the Turkish occupation – always awaited the moment at which the Monarchy whose sway was interrupted in 1453 (with the fall of Constantinople to the Ottoman Turks) would resume its life ... The Monarchy in Greece is a continuation of the one my ancestors served. It is therefore my duty to serve it too. [*Diary*, I, pp.527–8]

Thus Metaxas states clearly his belief in the link between the monarchy and modern Greece and the Byzantine state half a century earlier.

Metaxas deplores and mocks the use by the Greeks of pompous though by now meaningless phrases like 'freedom' and the 'War against Tyranny' [*Diary*, I, p.529]. Much of this is a foretaste of his dubious attitude towards his fellow Greeks and foreshadows his own approach to the governing of the country when in absolute power in 1936–41. He himself asserts, 'In a way, by winter of 1898 my character had acquired its final form which it kept till the end' [*Diary*, I, p.528]. At the same time, it is significant after he heard Bach's *Passionmusik*, to admit he was moved by the great personality of Jesus; 'I felt I too am a Christian' [*Diary*, I, p.528]. Metaxas thought he would spend the Easter vacation studying but the good Spring weather, nature, the countryside and the *libido carnis* upset his plans and pushed aside his good intentions. Nevertheless he managed to pass his examinations in May–June, returned more regularly to his *Diary*, and took part in military exercises including training in bridge construction that took him to Cologne and other parts of Germany. He also sent money to his family, and continued to worry about his *Diary* which he was trying to update and keep in order. 'Could I be suffering neurologically as always?' [*Diary*, I, p.534].

The military exercises near Paderborn in September 1900 lasted for a fortnight. Metaxas also travelled along the Rhine as far as Mainz and Wiesbaden. Then after five days in Brussels, he visited Waterloo before returning to Berlin. Characteristic during this period is Metaxas's complaint against his two fellow student officers, claiming that his better results in the examinations generated some resentment on their part. This belief, incidentally, Metaxas held about many people, especially colleagues and fellow officers until 1920 at least. What is also interesting is the termination of French language lessons in the Academy in favour of lessons in the Turkish language. It is not clear who decided this. Metaxas reports he met many families during the winter of 1900–01, and that he worked very hard thanks to the change in his character – 'I overcame the tyrannical desire for women; I became a moderate person.' And he sent quite a sum of money to his family in the autumn of 1900, and returned to a more regular keeping of his *Diary*.

With the resumption of his *Diary* entries we discover that 1901 was a very busy and interesting year for Metaxas and his two companions in Germany. They travelled widely and visited many museums and major industrial centres in the Ruhr, such as Erhardt and Krupp in Essen. Even more important for Metaxas was his promotion to First Lieutenant, after which he was assigned to a Cavalry Regiment for exercises in Westphalia for two months.

There arrived in Berlin in mid-April 1901 Col. Paraskevopoulos[2] on an official mission to procure arms and equipment for the Greek Army. Metaxas describes him as untrained scientifically, of limited education, verbose and mindless, but polite. He visited several munitions factories. Metaxa, with his two colleagues, accompanied the colonel on his travels, which Metaxas describes in his *Diary*, I, pp.544–8.

In late June Metaxas passed the exams in Weaponry and Topography. Edevig, the woman he was having an affair with, became engaged to a young doctor in July 1901, but she suggested they remain friends. Metaxas asks, 'Friends to what end? I don't like the friendship of women' [*Diary*, I, p.556].

When he resumed only too briefly the entries in his *Diary*, as of August 1905, based on the rough notes he had kept of his activities during his last year in Germany, Metaxas focused his attention on his illness – angina and arthritis – and his affair with a certain Margerethe (Grethe),

about whom he wrote with great fondness, tenderness and sentimentality. After sitting his final examinations at the Academy in
March–June 1902, he moved on to the more difficult and final choice,
the final staff officer examination, the *Generalstabsreise*. His difficulties
were not over though. He left Berlin in early 1903 for Denmark, Paris
and Italy on the way back to Greece.

> Four years had gone by from the time I left (for Germany) poor,
> insignificant, inexperienced and miserable, one rainy autumn. Now,
> accompanied by the same friends in springtime, I leave – not the same,
> how I changed – a different person! Education, knowledge, experience
> of the world, of life, enjoyment, self confident, a strengthened character.
> Yet something was lacking – belief in a Higher Providence. What replaced
> it was a steely will, a determination to acquire power in the world. [*Diary*,
> I, p.648]

So a self-assured Lieutenant Ioannis Metaxas was about to return home.
How does he explain this newly found self-assurance, self-confidence?
Among other things, he had read Shakespeare, Houston Chamberlain
on the Foundations of the Nineteenth Century and on Wagner, and had
become attracted to the ideas about the role of personality in history. In
short, Metaxas ponders over his personal–psychological development
while in Germany and reasserts, 'My feeling for the family was always
my good feeling without qualification or reservation' [*Diary*, I, p.639].
But he also comments extensively on developments in Greece as they
would affect him and his career. 'That I will work for the Crown Prince
and (Col.) Sapoundzakis was already decided, but what I will do exactly
I do not yet know. I was assigned to the Directorate General of the Army,
Strategos to the Military Academy, and Papavasileiou to the Ministry.
In my posting I sensed a certain preferential treatment, the result of
special appreciation, and this pleased me' [*Diary*, I, p.640]. The General
Directorate of the Army was under attack from the Deliyannis-led
opposition and the press. Metaxas was actually shocked at the extent of
the opposition to the Dynasty, if not the monarch himself.

> I was livid … and daydreamt I was there powerful at the head of the Army
> to put down all those demagogues … especially after all the reforms
> introduced by the Directorate. But a leader was needed to lead the action
> against the detractors and critics … I could not countenance such a decline
> in royal authority; I felt its opponents were insignificant little people

(tipotenioi). I noted a lack of principles, and a dearth of ideas, and I was sure action would have expelled the spider's web conspiracy, all those small petty interests and puerile ambitions [*Diary*, I, p.641] … I concluded the reaction against the Crown Prince was great. [*Diary*, I, p.642]

During his visit to the Danish Court in 1903 Metaxas records the Danish King's concern over the position of the Greek monarch, as a result of the political row between Deliyannis and his son, the King, and his grandson, the Crown Prince. Metaxas reassured the Danish monarch of his and the army officers' loyalty to the dynasty in Greece [*Diary*, I, p.652ff.]. In Paris Metaxas visited museums and art galleries. His *Diary* entry for April–May 1903 (recorded in 1906) was the last; he did not resume until 6 October 1910, four-and-a-half years later. Even this last entry came after a hiatus of nine months to a year, for in mid-September he abandoned his earlier attempt to update the *Diary* beginning in August 1905. What intervened to make Metaxas drop everything was his father's last illness and death on 24 September 1905; an event he described vividly fifteen years later when in exile in Florence [*Diary*, I, p.557].

The stop in Paris offered Metaxas the opportunity of a whole 'new' education, and a comparison with Berlin. He even comments how in Germany he learned to judge Napoleon by different standards and criteria as an ideal man. In Rome, the Capitol, the Vatican and St Peter's, especially the Sistine Chapel, impressed him very deeply. He would return to Greece as one of the few Greek staff officers with an extensive exposure to Western Europe, a purveyor and appreciative acolyte of the latest in its culture and science [*Diary*, I, pp.650–63].

At thirty-five then Metaxas had more or less made his most important choices: culturally and militarily he became a determined and serious follower of Western Europe in general and Germany in particular. Socially and politically, he returned to Greece not simply a better trained Staff Officer of the Corps of Engineers, but a committed monarchist too, who had declared his unbending devotion, loyalty and duty to the Greek Crown.

NOTES

1. For example, he sent them 150 Marks.
2. About Paraskevopoulos, see Mazarakis, *op. cit.*, p.465. General Paraskevopoulos was Chief of Staff in 1918–20. See Lt General Leonidas I. Paraskevopoulos, Chief of the Greek Army from 8 November 1918 to 8 November 1920, *Anamneseis* (Memories) 1896–1920, 2 vols, Athens, 1934, 1935.

PART II

Soldiering and Diplomacy:
Rapid Professional Advancement and
Growing Political Involvement, 1910–25

5

The Balkan Wars, 1912–13

Metaxas abruptly stopped entries to his *Diary* in April 1903, and did not resume them until October 1910, a gap of seven years! Although the first 100 pages of volume II of his *Diary* are replete with details of the new post-Goudi Venizelos government and its relations with the Crown Prince, there is hardly anything directly about the Goudi Army coup of 15 August 1909 itself. By this time Metaxas had married Lela Hatziioannou, a match of heart and purse; had been assigned to normal tours of duty as a line engineer staff officer in Larissa for one year. He had lived through the transition to the first Venizelos regime, including the changes and reforms in the army and the administration following the military debacle of 1897. 'The unfortunate war of 1897', General Pangalos recorded in his *Memoirs*, 'wounded in time the pride and aroused the conscience of the nation. It caused the insurrection of 1909 which led the nation to its glorious period from 1912 to 1920.'[1]. But the sorry consequences of the 1897 War also provoked strong opposition and resistance to the Royal Court and the Government. As a soldier relatively at mid-career, Metaxas found himself in the middle of these upheavals, at a critical period of the country's history. He felt the crisis personally. The passionate and intense struggles in Macedonia and in countering the Bulgarian threat were some consolation and compensation for the disgraced Greek Army and humiliated Greek nation; they tended to restore the national morale and prestige of the discredited 1897 War officers who were led by the royal princes. A sense of purpose was slowly redefined with the effort to reorganize and retrain the armed forces, both of which tasks had been neglected since independence. The notable exception was the attempt by the Tricoupis administration and his personal military aide Nikolaos Zorbas (of subsequent Military

League and Goudi Army coup fame). It founded military schools, including reserve officer schools, and purchased three cruisers-destroyers for the Navy (s.s. *Ydra*, *Spetsaia* and *Psarra*), but this was an isolated episode. The successor administration of Deliyannis tended to be demagogic with grandiose schemes when the state was militarily weak and in disarray thus culminating in the ignominious defeat of 1897, international financial control of the State, the eruption of a hostile public opinion against the King and the Princes, including an attempted assassination of the King in Phaliron. The agitation against the Royal Court, its courtiers and politicians, prompted the Goudi Army coup on 15 August 1909.

All of this affected Metaxas directly or indirectly, especially when the most pressing issue of the day was the reform of the armed forces, the invitation of French and British military missions to provide the new training and organization of the armed forces. As he himself admits in his *Diary*, it heralded a new epoch in his career, marked by his close collaboration with Venizelos. The transition comprised his involvement in the GHQ staff of the Crown Prince, and his hostility to the foreign military mission, which he tried to forestall and thwart with all means at his disposal.

Although primarily a Staff Officer in Army GHQ, the role of Metaxas during the Balkan Wars was not confined to his military duties but extended to the centre of Greek Balkan diplomacy. The period from 1912 to 1915, including that of the first two years of the Great War, may well have marked the entry of the young Staff Captain into Greek politics, or at least given him his first taste of political life. To this extent it is important to survey and assess his military–political role in these events – the territorial enlargement of the Greek state and its involvement in the wider European alliance and alignment politics of the Great Powers. And was this experience a consequence or natural continuation of his earlier brush with Greek military politics, albeit limited to the domestic national scene, when he was a young lieutenant during the disastrous Thessaly War of 1897. He was closely associated with the discredited royal princes in the Army and the closed elite of staff officers at the HQ of Crown Prince Constantine, Army Chief Commander, superseded now by another group of Army League officers behind the Goudi Army coup of 1909 which ushered in the 'liberal' political experiment led by Venizelos from 1910 to 1915. How far did his resentment of these changes push Metaxas further into political life.

Most Greeks, including the Royal Court, Venizelos and Metaxas, were agreed in 1912 about one thing, they would have to fight to avoid the triumph of the Slavs in the Balkans – that is, Bulgaria – and the Turks in Thrace, Macedonia and the Aegean – and Western Asia Minor? Thus after Goudi there was a Greek nationalist surge to liberate Greek populated territories – an irredentist expansion – to unite Crete with mainland Greece, secure Thessaloniki, the rest of Macedonia and Epirus, the Aegean islands of Chios and Mytelene. At the London Peace Conference of November 1912, Greece linked Balkan agreements with the wider European diplomacy of the Powers. When at the end of the first Balkan War, there was no agreement with Bulgaria over the distribution of the spoils, and Bulgaria refused to recognize the Greek occupation of Eastern Macedonia, and further demanded its own occupation of Thessaloniki, the outbreak of the Second Balkan War was inevitable; so that in 1913 Venizelos was keen on expanding the territory of the Greek State by securing Macedonia, Thrace, Epirus, and the Aegean islands. Until then of the known 8 million Greeks only 3 million were under Greek rule. By the end of the Great War in 1918, the population of the Greek State counted 5 million Greeks in a territory that had expanded from 64,000 to 120,000 square kilometres. And its army had grown from three to fifteen divisions organized in three Armies, much of this occurring when Metaxas was Chief of Operations from 1913 to 1916.

Metaxas records vividly his summons to meet the new Prime Minister and Minister of Army Affairs in his office on 6 October 1910. Even before he got to the interview Metaxas was convinced he could consider only one appointment, that of Military ADC to the Prime Minister. Venizelos began the interview by reminding Metaxas of the terrible and humiliating state the country was in; that he was asking for Metaxas's contribution to this task; and that he was offering him the post of Chief Military ADC, and that he would be working alongside another officer, Nider, who was already the Premier's personal Adjutant. Metaxas said at the time that the appointment satisfied him somehow, but did not make him enthusiastic. 'I wish I had the strength to decline the post … to appear uncompromising … and insist on a position in the army commensurate with my worth' [*Diary*, II, p.18]. But why did he compromise? Weakness of will, the prospect of a return or proximity to power? Metaxas dismisses all these possible causes and maintains it was his discussion with Dousmanis[2] regarding the extent of the latter's understanding with Venizelos, and the fact that he was really at a loss about his own preferred position when Venizelos's proposition caught him unprepared. 'Furthermore we (i.e., the Greeks) were defeated, and I could refuse the assignment in the new arrangements. But did I have the right and how could I refuse the Prime Minister's offer to save the army? I shall await developments, but remain true to my convictions' [*Diary*, II, p.18]. His first impression of Venizelos was better than he anticipated even though Venizelos did not come across as a 'forceful man' [*Diary*, II, p.19]. And so after a brief tour of duty with troop command (in Larissa) Metaxas left his battalion fearing he would always be mindlessly accused of not having had troop command for very long. And what did the new assignment as ADC of the Prime Minister really offer him, especially when he was not certain he would remain in the Army? On the other hand leaving the Army now that he was newly married and planning a family spelled uncertainty

Having assumed the duties of his new post, Metaxas wondered if Venizelos would take back Dousmanis on his staff, but he very much doubted this: 'I confess Venizelos does not inspire me with confidence' [*Diary*, II, p.19]. It is also interesting that whereas Venizelos justified his appointment of Metaxas because of his 'great military worth, which was recognized even by the *Berlinkriegsakademie*',[3] Metaxas thought Venizelos was not a man of resolution or strong will as was widely believed. He is influenced by the remnants of the Military League … of weak character and perceptiveness; and it would be disastrous if the King trusted him completely, for he may not be sincere, especially as he had already acted against the dynasty before, and remains beholden to the Goudi Army rebels. Such a harsh first assessment of Venizelos suggests that Metaxas was already inclined to play a crucial role in the developing antagonism between Venizelos and the King and Royal Court. He was well placed by virtue of his several relatives close to the Palace to keep abreast of developments. Thus it was Menelaus Metaxas, a cousin, who informed him that Venizelos would appoint Dousmanis to a post in Defence. Equally his close relationship with Prince Andreas, youngest son of the King, was crucial, especially as he could brief Metaxas about the meetings between the new Prime Minister Venizelos and the King: he reported for instance that Venizelos told the King he would appoint competent but politically moderate army officers such as Metaxas and Dousmanis to his military staff. The King was reportedly very happy, remarking subsequently 'He will appoint the friends of my sons.' But the suspicious Cephalonian remained unconvinced and dubious, 'Perhaps we are the shadows only; Venizelos appointed us in order to throw dust in the eyes of the King and the people, in order to calm them down, to reassure them' [*Diary*, II, p.21], and still believed that Venizelos remained under the control of the Military League, the Goudi rebels. What is interesting is the fact that at that time Metaxas worked behind the scenes, his political involvement was indirect through his connection and influence with the royal princes, especially Prince Andreas. He sought to strengthen Venizelos against the Military League cabal, by advising the royal court of the advantages of this policy. What also comes through this early political battle for the control of the Army, the battle, that is, between the old GHQ Staff clique of Dousmanis–Metaxas surrounding the Crown Prince and the Goudi rebels, is in effect the attempt to restore royal control over the Army. The rebels for their part sought to stop Venizelos from appointing Dousmanis, whereas Metaxas saw the new Venizelos regime as a continuation of the Zorba-led Military League rebellion.

The question of the link between Venizelos and the Military League preoccupied Metaxas throughout 1910; this was his first political involvement which revealed his capacity as a consummate intriguer. Thus he worked hard to convince all anti-Venizelist politicians that Venizelos was determined to bring in foreign military missions to retrain and reorganize the armed forces, and that his own appointment and that of other royalist officers was only so much humbug. Critical to understanding and appreciating the decision by Metaxas to engage fully in the developing political rift between the King and his new Prime Minister is his confession, 'Even if I am formally the Premier's Military ADC, my political convictions, including my loyalty to the Reigning House are known. So what is the use? It is time I reconsidered my position.' At the same time he took every opportunity to make clear and known his doubts about the sincerity of Venizelos, the disadvantages of the French Military Mission, as well as his determined support of the Crown Prince and his loyalty to the Dynasty against Venizelos and the rebels, or the so-called New Order. Nor did Metaxas shrink from subtly and consistently undermining the then Chief of Staff, General Sapoundzakis. In the meantime, Prince Andreas remained his most secure contact in the Palace and Royal Court, while officially he cooperated with the Crown Prince in the attempt to reorganize the Army as per the Prime Minister's instructions and brief. Thus he reports several discussions with Venizelos about this matter that also shows his subtle rubbishing of the existing military hierarchy by alluding to its incompetence and the need for competent staff officers, eventually goading Venizelos to point out his differences with the King over this very matter:

The King as you know does not want the French; he does not trust them, and is adamant in this view. He fears it will enrage the Kaiser. So be it, but our national interest lies in our siding with the Triple Entente – the resolution of the Crete problem, for instance, is in Britain's hands, and we are forced by international politics to seek out French financial assistance. I feel the military issue is destroyed, because its evolution depends on the interests of foreign policy. [*Diary*, II, p.39]

And so he intensified his cooperation with the Crown Prince in a desperate attempt to forestall the coming of the French Military Mission. For Metaxas was convinced that the idea of the French Mission was part of the Zorba-led Military League policy to thwart the reappointment of Dousmanis to Staff GHQ, and thus prevent any influence of the Crown Prince and other royal princes in the Army. The internal policy dynamic of the Military League dictated the need of a foreign military mission. There is also throughout this debate the suggestion that if a foreign military mission was inevitable, it should be German for the Army and British for the Navy. What also emerge are the convoluted intrigues of forces active in the contest over the question of the foreign military mission. Thus the Theotokis–Kaiser talks about a 'German Military Mission'; the mix-up over the refitting of the battleship *Averoff*, and the fact that all of this went on through the Court of the Crown Prince, especially his Palace in Corfu. While the Venizelos government was negotiating with France, the leading Corfiote Opposition politician Theotokis, together with the Crown Prince – the Royalist side – was negotiating with the German Kaiser. The contest between France and Germany, two major European powers, for political predominance in Greece was on.

In this contest, it was clear Venizelos was desperate to secure the loan (with French help) needed by the revolutionary regime. Metaxas on the other hand was anxious to cast doubts over the competence of the then Chief of Staff, Sapoundzakis and his associate Zymvrakakis, both of whom were instrumental in preventing the return of Dousmanis to the Staff of Army GHQ. They were also, it was rumoured, political clients of the Prime Minister from his home island Crete. Metaxas rationalized his political involvement by arguing that his professional duty was to advise Prime Minister Venizelos, his boss, on purely military matters; it was not part of his duty to follow the Premier's policy vis-à-vis the King, Crown Prince and royal princes, or the Military League: 'I have a past reputation which imposes duties of loyalty to the reigning dynasty.'

Metaxas was fully aware that Venizelos appointed him his Military ADC in order to gain access to his advice over strictly military matters, especially when Venizelos occupied a double position, that of Prime Minister and Minister of Army Affairs, and thus the highest military counsellor of the King in his capacity as Army Chief [*Diary*, II, p.48]. At the same time, he was the creature of the 1909 Goudi military rebels who were opposed to the Dynasty. In other words, Venizelos was in an ambivalent and therefore a precarious position. He must have double vision and exercise an ambidextrous policy, that of the King's counsellor, keeper of order and discipline, and that of political leader of the Military League that is committed to radical changes in the political–military institutional arrangements of the country – an impossible position to be in? Metaxas, on the contrary, saw himself as occupying a straight-forward and simple position, loyal to King and country while serving his Army Minister loyally. 'Granted my position', he admitted, 'is delicate and morally dangerous.' Venizelos however tried to justify the French Military Mission to the Crown Prince by telling him that it was virtually forced upon them by the demands of foreign policy and economic neces-sity. At the same time, Venizelos insisted the Crown Prince remain Chief of the Army even when the French Military Mission was in the country; he also asked Metaxas if he and other German-trained officers would cooperate with the French Mission. Metaxas confirmed they would, but that the selection of the Mission personnel should be left to the French Government [*Diary*, II, p.51].

Throughout the autumn of 1910 Metaxas was busy trying to have an effective voice in the new arrangements in the Army, in the hope of erod-ing the influence of his bête noir, Chief of Staff Sapoundzakis, and his clique of officers, and promoting instead the greater role of the royal princes in limiting the influence of the French Military Mission. Prince Andreas continued to be his main source of information about the dis-cussions between the King and Venizelos. What becomes clearer by this time are certain personal qualities Metaxas displayed throughout his life: stamina, steadfastness, perseverance and singularity of purpose when fighting or defending his own corner in a political culture marked by the centrality of patron–client relations. He was in fact relentless. In the end though he had to concede that in this battle between the monarchy and Venizelos over the issue of the foreign military mission, Venizelos had won with the support of Britain and France [*Diary*, II, p.59]. The pro-Kaiser old royalist politicians led by Theotokis lost – and by extension, Metaxas too. But he also emerged as a consummate survivor. Thus during the major political clash between the King and his Prime Minister, Metaxas continued to discuss with his boss Venizelos such matters as the reform of training and reorganization, the economics of supply and procurement in the Army, but curiously only in order to suggest that such a vast and major reform programme required a good Staff HQ, led by someone – Dousmanis? – of higher calibre than Gen. Sapoundzakis. Metaxas even sought to exploit the Kaiser's pro-Turkish policy in Crete when the latter reacted against the preference of Venizelos for the French Military Mission, and all the time seeking to restore the princes to the Army.

Towards the end of the year Metaxas had to cope with two persistent rumours, one that Sapoundzakis would become Army Minister, the other that the King was thinking of abdicating in favour of the Crown Prince. The first rumour was unfounded and was quickly dispelled by Venizelos himself when Metaxas told him that under no circumstances would he remain Military ADC to Sapoundzakis. As for the second rumour, Dousmanis at least tended to discount it, whereas Prince Andreas thought there was some truth in it. In the end though Metaxas assesses the year 1910 as interesting and not as disastrous on the whole as it might have been: 'My detractors slowly eased off, my appreciation by others was restored; I erred frequently and sinned too' [*Diary*, II, p.64]. He still entertained doubts about many things, but began the new year 1911 with closer and more frequent contacts with the Crown Prince. Then with Dousmanis he engaged in the exploration of ways by which the Crown Prince could return as Inspector General of the Army, closing the rumoured rift between him and the King, and undermining further the French Military Mission. He was also taken up by instances of ill-ness and death in the family, haunted by his older obsession with family finances, the need to economize, and professionally how he would face the newly arrived French Military Mission and its Chief, General Eydoux. He worried how this matter would affect him personally: his name was already well known to the French Mission as one of the staff officers highly esteemed and trusted by the King and Crown Prince, so that there was no need for him to hitch the fortunes of his career to the Mission, especially since its real objective was to nurture a pro-French policy in Greece. Anyway, the draft legislation for Army reform was ready by February 1911, and Metaxas advised the Crown Prince to reject it, especially as it proposed Sapoundzakis to be Chief of Staff, even though it also provided for the return of the princes to the Army.

The first quarter of 1911 was marked by further family vicissitudes –

illness and death. Metaxas's sister Marianthe lost a child and his father-in-law died from liver and kidney failure. Delicate matters of inheritance figured prominently in his relations with the extended family. Metaxas therefore withdrew temporarily from any direct involvement in the 'politics' of the Army Ministry, and his boss Venizelos seldom consulted him. He did however, once in March 1911, concern himself with the legislation for the reinstatement of the Crown Prince in the Army, the text of which was essentially the same as the one

> I had drafted in the first place. I suspected Venizelos's relations with the Crown Prince had improved, but insisted nonetheless upon my initial views of the Crown Prince's position, rejecting as unfounded and unfair the several charges against the Crown Prince, and making it clear that the form of the legislation under consideration I was briefed about by Col. Pallis, the Chief of the King's Military Office. The outstanding problem was the position of the Crown Prince in the Army in view of the French Mission and its chief, General Eydoux: though only a Major-General in the French Army, Eydoux could become a Lieut. General in Greece, that is, the same rank as the Crown Prince.

This matter constituted the basis of further political intrigue in the Army with Sapoundzakis trying to demote the Crown Prince and prevent him from returning to the Army. The new legislation however gave Eydoux jurisdiction over most matters: finances, procurement, transfers and promotions, and a new Staff HQ consisting of French Mission officers, led by Bousquier as Chief of Staff. Metaxas warned Venizelos that all of this would undermine the work of the Greek Staff, and he continued to relate his efforts to neutralizing Sapoundzakis's intrigues against the Crown Prince, and by mid-May was in full battle involving Venizelos and Nider. He was nevertheless wholly disappointed by the unrestrained enthusiasm for the French Military Mission. In short, a year taken up mostly if not entirely by Army politics that pushed Metaxas at the end of it to withdraw from Army Ministry affairs beyond his professional duties – as Venizelos's Military ADC – only to return to full professional duties as a staff officer in the first Balkan War in 1912. Yet his experience of this period prompted Metaxas to utter more than one general characterization of his fellow-Greeks, viz., 'the worship of the foreign, envy and flattery were specialities of the Greeks' [*Diary*, II, p.56], and 'the Greeks remain a people of slaves' [*Diary*, II, p.56]; that is, with the mentality of slaves.

By late Spring 1911 Metaxas claimed he was withdrawing from Army affairs beyond the performance of the formal duties of his job, and otherwise confining himself to home life and his studies,

> but always getting ready for the future, when my time will come again [*Diary*, II, p.76] … , and then as is always in the back of my mind I will resign (my Army commission). I can imagine how they will beg me to stay on … In any case in three years time I will have completed the number of years needed for me to retire on a Major's pension … I have no future in the Army, nor hope of promotion, and I can expect only further marginalization by the French. My personal relations with Venizelos are excellent: what pleases me especially is the King's appreciation of me, which he repeated to Venizelos, Pallis and Eydoux on several occasions. I owe this to my loyalty, and to Prince Andreas. [*Diary*, II, p.77]

At this juncture Metaxas was still seriously contemplating leaving the Army and approached Aristide Siotis, the representative of a Belgian business firm, about a possible job. In the meantime, the French newspaper *Echo d'Orient* published attacks on the Crown Prince, inspired by the French Military Mission. Metaxas daydreamed about a job with private business firms: he agreed with Siotis that if the Belgian firm made him a good offer he would resign his Army commission. He was elated by the prospect and together with his wife Lela made plans for the future. And yet underlying even this possibility was a streak of revenge against a state that he thought had humiliated him ('Needless to say, I shall continue to serve the nation and if need be sacrifice my life in its service, but I need to take revenge too! It will also be a blow against the regime' [*Diary*, II, p.78]).

By the end of June 1911 Metaxas was convinced the French would fail in their Greek mission, even though in the meantime they managed to push aside all those who had links with Germany. The mutiny on the battleship *Averoff* he considered an ironic consequence of the indiscipline inspired by the Goudi Army coup; and Metaxas was now of the opinion that the Crown Prince should distance himself from his political–military clique of Staff Officers and advisers, as this would increase his popularity, especially when he was seen as being above the political fray. He reminded the Crown Prince that in order to lead the Army effectively he must engage in partisan politics, and argued that the French Military Mission was an instrument of French foreign policy. But his advice to the Crown Prince was that he remain outside the political fray, not to clash directly with the French Mission, but to engage in frequent inspection tours of the Army, and to avoid appointing any of his known close army officer associates to his military office, but to look to people like Gonatas.[4]

Having settled several family matters, including that of property, Metaxas was rather contented and pleased with himself. His wife was expecting a child, and he himself had finally decided to stay in the Army for another three years. But the question of his sister Marianthe's dowry remained unsettled and bothered him. How would he pay it, when his savings were almost nil? He sought a bank loan. His personal finances were precarious. In seeking a loan Metaxas needed the collateral guarantee of his mother-in-law, the rents from the shops they owned in their block of flats, but this too was theoretically part of his wife's dowry, that is, the property of his in-laws. He also sought the help of the Bank of Athens and the National Bank of Greece, and alludes to total assets of 400,000 drachmas, an impressive sum of money in those days, consisting of property in Athens and Egypt, plus his mother's shop in Agrinion.

Metaxas was pulled away from these family and personal pre-occupations by the threat of Turkish mobilization and concern over the defences in Epirus – Yanina and Arta. In view of the consideration of mobilization plans and discussion about the role of the French Mission and its leader General Eydoux, Venizelos sought the advice of Metaxas regarding these matters and asked him to prepare logistical plans in case of mobilization. Actually Venizelos wanted to avoid hostilities with Turkey for he believed the Greek Army, under Eydoux's retraining and reorganization programme, would not be ready for battle for another two years. Impressed by Venizelos's need of his counsel, Metaxas at this point is again full of himself, 'I was in effect the Chief of Staff' [*Diary*, II, p.93]; and yet he was still impatient to leave the Army. 'The more I think of what I offer the Army, the greater the Army's injustice towards me appears to be, and the firmer my determination to leave the Army becomes' [*Diary*, II, p.93]. Metaxas records at this time another instance of sentimentalism when he visits his father's grave in the cemetery on the anniversary of his death [*Diary*, II, p.94].

Metaxas essays an assessment of Venizelos, a kind of revised view of the man whom he now sees not as untrustworthy as before, whose experience in power brought him closer to the King and rendered him more compromising:

Venizelos, … is a big man … and I believe quite sincere in his relations
with the dynasty. He has burnt many of his bridges of course, and is now
determined to march on, go forward with the King. [*Diary*, II, p.95].
Experience of executive power and responsibility of government made
him more conservative … but also passionate for revenge. He was
influenced by the radical trend of our time, but soon discovered he could
not accomplish much with the rebels, and so eventually turned against
the ethos of Goudi, clashing with the Military League and therefore the
Rebellion.

Metaxas conveyed these views of his to Prince Andreas with whom he
continued to correspond and who remained his main link with the Royal
Court. Metaxas was also busy at this time translating articles for the
Army Journal: 'I make money this way which I need to meet my obliga-
tions to Marianthe' (his sister's dowry) [*Diary*, II, p.97]. His daughter
Loukia (Loulou) was born on Tuesday, 18 October 1911: 'I hoped it would
be a male – the rearing of a girl frightens me' (dowry costs?). She was
christened on 9 December with the Crown Prince as godfather.

The fate of General Sapoundzakis was still in the balance in mid-
1912, and Metaxas was keen to have a hand in its determination. Clearly
Venizelos felt he had an obligation to promote Sapoundzakis by finding
him an appropriate role in the military hierarchy. But Venizelos needed
to secure the consent of the Crown Prince and General Eydoux. They
all agreed Sapoundzakis could not be entrusted with army command,
but only with an administrative sinecure: he was finally promoted to General
and made President of the Army Review Board [*Diary*, II, pp.104–5].

Meanwhile a scandal had erupted after Venizelos had publicly criticized Crown Princess Sophia in the press relating to his wanting to be
introduced to the Princess's brother, the Kaiser of Germany, during the
reception at the Crown Prince's palace for the visiting Orientalists. But
the Princess left for Corfu just before the scheduled reception. It was all
linked to the reconciliation between the royal princes and the Goudi
rebels. In his irritation, Venizelos blew up. But the Crown Prince interpreted Venizelos's attack on his wife as proof that his lingering anti-
dynastic sentiment remained deeply embedded in the depth of his soul
[*Diary*, II, p.107]. Metaxas, on the other hand, suspected that Venizelos
panicked as he watched General Eydoux and the French Mission actively
seeking to get closer to the Royal Court. Yet amidst all this gossip and
intrigue, Metaxas continued to discuss the new mobilization plans which
envisaged his appointment as Divisional or Corps Chief of Staff.

The Italo–Turkish War in Cyrenaica was on during the spring of 1912, while domestically the main political issue remained that of the struggle between Venizelos and the Royal Court for the control of the Army. Metaxas continued to be involved in the question of the royal princes in the Army, setting out his views on the special case of Prince Nikolaos in a memorandum to the King via Prince Andreas [*Diary*, II, pp.114–16], and using Agamemnon Pallis, the Chief of the King's Military Office. Then when he accompanied Venizelos to Corfu, Metaxas discussed with him the Turkish threat and the position of various Greek politicians, including those of the Opposition [*Diary*, II, p.118]. The Kaiser succeeded in reconciling Venizelos with his sister Princess Sophia and Venizelos was elated. After extensive Army exercises and manoeuvres, the contest between the Royal Court and the French Military Mission was resumed. Professionally though Metaxas thought the Mission had brought the Army up to scratch. He also kept the Crown Prince informed about the views of Venizelos (see letter to Prince Andreas for the King dated 25 June 1912 [*Diary*, II, pp.123–4]); and he was anxious to defuse the contest between the King and Venizelos, hinting that it could be detrimental to the Army. Finally, his Corfu visit evoked more sentimentalism as Metaxas remembered his earliest posting there after he was commissioned in 1891–93.

Just before the outbreak of the first Balkan War, Metaxas had gone on holiday with his family to the island of Tinos, an annual routine that his family would observe for the next twenty-five years. After a month's holiday in Tinos, Metaxas returned to Athens on his own without the family, and he initiated a month's intense correspondence with his wife Lela in which he highlights his further work for Venizelos on the eve of his diplomatic missions leading up to the first Balkan War, as well as reports on Athenian society. It represents the period of his closest collaboration with Venizelos. It is also significant for Metaxas's own evaluation of its contribution to his future career prospects. Most significant though is the experience gained in the diplomacy, politics and conduct of war at the highest national level. Thus Venizelos sent Metaxas to Sofia to assist Greek Ambassador Panas in the negotiation of the Greek–Bulgarian alliance, and Metaxas was so impressed by his new brief that he wrote to his wife, 'Venizelos has appointed me in effect an undersecretary and chief of staff, a post actually entrusted to General P. Danglis'.[5]

The Greek–Bulgarian defence alliance had been signed in May 1912; what Metaxas went to assist Panas with was the conclusion of a military pact which was negotiated between 24 September and 5 October 1912, when it was signed by the parties. General mobilization began by 30 September and hostilities against Turkey began on 17 October. Metaxas joined the Crown Prince and his GHQ Staff in Larissa directly he returned from Sofia. After three weeks of fighting the Greek Army was about to enter Thessaloniki in triumph. Together with Dousmanis Metaxas received the Turkish surrender of the city.

His letters to his wife as he prepared for his Bulgarian mission and during the first Balkan War are very important for sketching a portrait of Metaxas. Thus he tries to impress Lela with the suggestion that he had to rise to the call of the nation – noblesse oblige – and go to Sofia, describing his preparation for the voyage in great detail:[6] 'They depend on me!', and tried to impress her also with his urgent series of meetings with Chief of Staff Danglis, Venizelos and the Crown Prince: 'I have become, as you see, a great man ...' [*Diary*, II, p.149]; 'I have become a diplomat, and I must wear a monocle' [*Diary*, II, p.152]. But he also thinks of the reward for all of this: on 2 September he writes Lela about the extra work for Venizelos, who is 'scared and leans on me' [*Diary*, II, p.152]. He also claims he told the government he would not go on any mission if he were not paid enough: 'They are paying me 800 francs and 40 francs per diem.'

One must note that Metaxas hoped there would be no war, that it would be forestalled or prevented by the intervention of the European Great Powers: 'The Europeans will stop us.' At the same time he hoped Greece would obtain Crete at least. But he sounded dubious about the whole enterprise, believing that the ambition and fanaticism of Koromelas and his Macedonia struggle comrades pressed for war. Yet he was not beneath reaping any possible benefits of this whole episode to himself: 'Whatever happens, thanks to this mission I will benefit – at least my position will be secure, for it is a great mission indeed of extraordinary satisfaction and perhaps the basis of a better future – who knows?' [*Diary*, II, pp.165–7].

Yet despite all this activity and excitement, Metaxas remained apprehensive and restless, repeating his intention to go into business 'when all this is over'. It is revealing moreover when he confesses in a letter from Sofia to Lela dated 18 September that she helped him overcome his neurosis and impatience, enabling him to become calmer [*Diary*, II, p.167].

Hostilities broke out on 5 October 1912, but the correspondence with Lela continued, with Metaxas reporting a succession of victories in battle, and hinting that all operations were planned by GHQ Staff consisting of Fondas (Strategos), Dousmanis, Pallis and himself. The inflated sense of his own importance in these events and developments, as articulated in the correspondence with his wife, is almost insufferable: referring to an 'Athenian clique' which had arrived in Yanina to celebrate that city's (capital of Epirus) capture from the Turks, Metaxas states wildly that 'it dirties our social class, because we are the aristocracy' [*Diary*, II, p.209], and boasts further on, 'If my trained methodical intellect were not available what would happen to Greece?' And in the following Second Balkan War against Bulgaria, he claimed the planning of operations [*Diary*, II, p.222], and refers to his rapid promotion from Captain to Major to Lt Colonel by September 1913 [*Diary*, II, p.226]. All this boasting and self-congratulation appears in his letters to Lela in which he reports details of his part in the war, followed by his diplomatic mission in London to negotiate the end of the War and conclude a peace treaty. His moment of glory arrived on 27 October 1912, when he and Dousmanis, on the orders of the Crown Prince, negotiated the surrender of Thessaloniki by the Turkish Commander, which the Crown Prince at the head of the Greek Army's First Division entered in triumph on the 29th, taking prisoner 30,000 Turkish troops. The tone of these letters to Lela incidentally is excited, dramatic, triumphant – 'I must dash', he scribbles in haste, 'they are summoning me, and I must leave you now' [*Diary*, II, p.175]; and on 30 October, 'Now we must press on with the conquest of western Macedonia; the whole Turkish army has been destroyed.' 'What do they say about us in Athens?' he asks, but manages to inform her that he has bought for her two furs from Kastoria that he sent on to her with Dousmanis of the Foreign Ministry. Although others (Greece's allies in the War) had signed an armistice, the Greeks by 23 November 1912 had not, he tells Lela, and 'I shall be going with General Danglis to London for the military side of the peace negotiations' [*Diary*, II, pp.175, 176, 177]. At this time, incidentally, Lela was expecting their second child, and the Crown Prince was trying to fix his trip after its birth. Writing again from Paris on 13 December, Metaxas praised the company of General Danglis, and describes several others in the party of accompanying diplomats such as Rangavis, Pappas, Dimaras and Kriezis.

On 17 December Metaxas was describing London where he had arrived the day before, still anxiously concerned about the awaited birth of their child, and refers to his work with Venizelos and George Streit of the Foreign Ministry. Fully excited by the sights of the city on the

Thames and London society, Metaxas in this case too does not fail to mention the envy of others, viz., Dousmanis, who is also in the negotiating party [*Diary*, II, p.182]. On 21 December Metaxas records his happiness over the birth of their second daughter, but does not refrain from alluding to the importance of a male in the continuation of the family name, etc., although he hastens to protest that he is indifferent to the sex of the newborn baby. He regales Lela with details of all the dinners and receptions in London and notes, 'The English character is calm, dignified, not verbose and always polite' [*Diary*, II, p.186], but also mentions his hard work with the mission. Here he hints though that operations in Epirus were not going well due to a mistake by Gen. Sapoundzakis. He remarks briefly about the way the British celebrate Christmas and lists the telegrams of congratulations he received for the birth of their daughter – from Princes Andreas and George, Dousmanis and his other colleagues in Staff GHQ [*Diary*, II, pp.186–7]. By the New Year 1913, Metaxas writes Lela about the plays he attended in West End theatres, St James's Palace, the Carlton and the Savoy, and other well-known London places, such as the Banqueting Hall and the Palace of Westminster. On 11 January 1913, Metaxas warned Lela he hoped to be back by the time she received his letter, for he had been urgently summoned to join the Crown Prince's HQ Staff on a rescue mission in Epirus (the capture of Yanina), as the war with Turkey was still on. On 21 February, together with Fonda, Metaxas signed the Protocol for the Turkish surrender of Yanina and in his letter of 25 February 1913 he describes for Lela the triumphant parade of the Greek Army in Yanina. In an aside he tells her about his long chat with the Turks Izzat and Vehib beys, European-educated and very civilized people [*Diary*, II, p.205]. Then once again in referring to his own role and his promotions, Metaxas tells Lela, 'Whether as Captain, or Major, I have led the Army' [*Diary*, II, p.210].

By 21 April 1913, Metaxas was embroiled in the negotiations with Serbia in order to meet the threat from Bulgaria, their erstwhile common ally in the war against Turkey. Neither country could accept Bulgarian demands, and on 22 April 1913 they signed the protocol of an alliance between them. The specific role of Metaxas in this was to negotiate with his Serbian counterparts the military conditions of this alliance, and these were formally agreed on 1 May 1913; however on 28 April he had already reported armed clashes between Greeks and Bulgarians [*Diary*, II, p.214]. Serbia refused to sign and ratify the Protocol negotiated by Metaxas, and fresh negotiations had to be initiated in Belgrade and

Thessaloniki where a Treaty of Greek–Serbian Alliance was finally signed on 19 May 1913. King George I was assassinated on 5 March 1913 in the newly liberated capital of Macedonia, Thessaloniki, by a demented man, Alexander Schinas. Hostilities against Bulgaria began in earnest on 18 June 1913, and Metaxas resumes his narrative about Staff GHQ in his letters to Lela. But the man simply cannot overcome his persecution complex; once again he regales Lela with reports about the envy of Dousmanis, and warns her to carry on normally in her relations with Mrs Dousmanis in Athens. 'Leave it all to me, when my time comes', he repeats several times [*Diary*, II, pp.220–21]. He is always biding his time, as if savouring an inevitable revenge against all his rivals!

NOTES

1. Lt General Theodoros Pangalos, *Ta Apomnemoneumata mou, 1897–1947: I Tarachodis periodos tis teleutaias pentikontaetias* (My Memoirs: The Turbulent Period of the Last Fifty Years), 2 vols in one; Athens, 1959, p.31.
2. See *supra*, ch.3, fn 2, p.62.
3. Pangalos, *op. cit.*
4. On Stelios Gonatas, see Thanos Veremis, *op. cit.*, pp.420–21.
5. General Panagiotis Danglis (1853–1924). Military Academy, Artillery Corps; further military studies in France. Member of the National Society; 1904–09 officer in newly created GHQ Staff Officer Corps. Introduced the Snyder Gun to Greek Mountain Artillery; 1915 a Deputy in the Parliament Chamber from Yanina; 1916 one of the Thessaloniki Rebel Government Triumvirate; Army Chief of Staff in 1918; a moderate member of the Liberal Party.
6. See my 'Metaxas the Man', Robin Higham and Thanos Veremis, editors, *Aspects of Greece, The Metaxas Dictatorship*, Athens, 1993, pp.179–92.

6

The Great War, 1914–18

On 24 August 1913 the Kaiser handed his brother-in-law, King Constantine, hero of the Balkan Wars, the baton of a German Field Marshal (*Feldmareschal*), and Constantine announced that the victories of the Greek Army were due to his and his staff officers' German military training. Metaxas was promoted Lieutenant Colonel on 26 September, his second promotion during the Balkan Wars.

In September 1913 Lieut. Colonel Metaxas assessed the consequences of the London Peace Convention at the conclusion of the Balkan Wars and identified two major problems for Hellenism: (1) Albania and North Epirus, and (2) the Aegean islands. The problem with Turkey was a territorial one, or a contest over territory in the Aegean and Asia Minor, and to that extent entailed, inevitably, a naval rearmament race with Turkey over the control of the Aegean at least, but actually of contested territory in general. Metaxas became concerned with naval strategy as part of wider defence strategy, and supported the purchase of cruisers in the USA, shortly before the outbreak of the Great War in August 1914. As the new regime of the Young Turks accelerated its persecution of the Greeks in Western Asia Minor in retaliation for the ceding of the islands of Chios, Samos and Mytilene by the London Peace Convention of 1913 to Greece, Metaxas came to believe that war with Turkey was inevitable, prompting him to prepare a paper advocating a surprise attack on Asia Minor, a view in full accord with the position of Prime Minister Venizelos at that time. Metaxas argued that war be waged against Turkey before the latter acquired naval supremacy – with its purchase of dreadnoughts in the UK – in the Aegean.

Despite the signing of the Treaty of Athens on 13 November 1913, relations between Greece and Turkey deteriorated, especially in view of the unresolved issue of the Aegean islands. While Venizelos was on a diplomatic tour of the capitals of European powers to rally support for Greece, and Metaxas pored over his plans for a surprise pre-emptive strike against Turkey before she acquired naval superiority, the public remained apprehensive and restless over the Turkish threat, especially after the Balkan Wars. Thus the Government refitted American naval ships firstly in order to counter Turkey's impending acquisition of two dreadnoughts, and secondly in order to appease the restless Greek public.

Unfortunately, there is a break in the Metaxas *Diary* from 30 July 1913 to the outbreak of the Great War, and it is therefore difficult to reconstruct easily the extent of his involvement. Moreover, his correspondence with his wife was down to a very few letters, and these he mainly wrote while accompanying the King on his inspection tours of army units in the newly conquered areas in Macedonia. It was also during the period from September 1913 to July 1914 that Metaxas drafted his historic expositions regarding military strategy to counter the Turkish threat, including approaches to the Aegean/Turkish problem in complete agreement with the then view of Prime Minister Venizelos. Yet only a few months later, when the Great War had broken out, Metaxas was to find himself diametrically opposed to the Venizelos strategy and political view of entering the War on the side of the Entente Powers, and initiating Greek military operations in Asia Minor.

Even when the two men were in general agreement before August 1914, one could already detect fundamental differences between them over the handling of the problem of naval requirements for defence, and the problem of the transport and deployment of troops in Macedonia and the Aegean islands. Then whereas Venizelos was content to depend on a British alliance, Metaxas insisted on Greece acquiring its own naval force against Turkey in the Aegean even though both men agreed that Greece must avoid finding itself on the opposite side of Britain. They disagreed also over the willingness of Venizelos to cede Greek territory – for example, Cephalonia as a naval base to Britain in return for British protection – a concession Metaxas was vehemently opposed to. He was equally adamantly opposed to any territorial concessions to be made to Turkey. After the return of Venizelos from his European tour and visit to Britain, it became even clearer that the argument of Metaxas in this debate between the two men was gaining ground: Greece could not wholly depend on Britain, and would be well advised to proceed with the purchase of naval ships to strengthen its Aegean defences [*Diary*, II, pp.234ff.].

Throughout this period, especially the winter of 1913–14, Metaxas was primarily, if not wholly, taken up with serious military planning work, preparing strategic and operational plans for the defence of Macedonia and the Aegean islands, the deployment of Greek forces in the event of a war with Turkey. He was professionally wholly engaged and there was a reduction of his political involvement beyond that in the vagaries of the relations between staff officers and his differing views from those held by his boss, Prime Minister Venizelos. Perhaps his great contribution to Greek strategic thinking in Greece at that time was the linking of the defence – and retention – of Macedonia to the Greek control of the sea. He also recommended the fortification of the Saronic Gulf, the approaches to the Attica Coast (Athens and Piraeus). At the same time Metaxas concluded that any military operation to force the Straits – against the Dardanelles – had to possess the element of total surprise if it were to succeed, and that it was necessary for the protection of the Aegean islands against further Turkish encroachments, requiring one Army Corps transported on 70 merchant ships. All of these proposed plans were submitted to Venizelos in the spring, March–April, of 1914. 'Although he did not discourage me and urged me to carry on with my work, Venizelos very much doubted the feasibility of such a plan' [*Diary*, II, p.241]. Venizelos was hesitant and indecisive, in fact, immobilized over these plans, even neglecting the needs of the Navy. In fact, Venizelos had changed his mind about a war against Turkey; believing now that Greece could reach an understanding with Turkey and thus avoid a war. Thus GHQ Staff Officers, led by Metaxas and Dousmanis, appeared in the summer of 1914 as the War Party, and Venizelos as the Peace Party for he now sought a peaceful accommodation with Turkey and further dependence on an alliance with Britain. But if Metaxas is to be believed, he insisted in his reports about this prolonged debate over Greek defence strategy in 1913–14 that Venizelos was indecisive and immobilized at dead centre in the sense that he could not act one way or the other over the matter; and that when it became known that Britain had impounded the two cruisers intended for Turkey, he looked like a man relieved of a great danger; and after that Venizelos would not hear a word about Greek mobilization [*Diary*, II, p.249].

A careful reading of the Technical Memoranda about military operations against Turkey, prepared and submitted by Metaxas in the period from September 1913 to July 1914 cannot fail to detect the dextrous linkages he established between military operations, political and diplomatic conditions and requirements reflecting his high calibre as a staff officer, as well as his historical–political perceptiveness and acumen.[1] They represent a superb strategic–political analysis of the Greek–Turkish confrontation at the outbreak of the Great War. Equally careful and cogent is his Mobilization Plan, based on circumstances prevailing in June 1914, and submitted to the Chief of Staff, including detailed estimates of Turkish strength, as well as a preliminary or tentative Plan of Operations. Metaxas was ahead of the Allies, when he predicted any successful landings in Gallipoli depended on the prior destruction of the Turkish fleet, and the completion of the landings within twenty-four hours.

II

Metaxas met Venizelos who had returned from his tour of European capitals impatient to learn about its outcome. But Venizelos did not report much except to say that he found the British reserved and very cautious: the participation of Greece on their side in a European war was they thought desirable, but inopportune; perhaps later. Britain, Venizelos thought, avoids alliances in principle; Greece was in dis-agreement with Turkey. Despite Britain's sympathy for Greece, it was not prepared to get involved, and if there is an armed conflict, the posi-tion of Greece will be difficult. Consequently, Greece must come directly to an agreement with Turkey, even if it has to make certain sacrifices. Now that Greece is 'bigger' (as a result of the Balkan Wars), it must not risk its situation and position for the sake of minor detail, for its future is great.

This report by the returning Venizelos was a great disappointment to Metaxas. It was immediately decided to purchase any available dread-nought, even one under construction, and Captain P. Tsoukalas was dis-patched to the USA for that purpose. But there was no dreadnought for sale. Everybody was worried. In moments of despair, Venizelos con-sidered wild, reckless (*paravola*) schemes, some imposed upon him by different people, others off his own head. One of these was that if they could not find any ships to purchase they should watch for the passage of the *Rio de Janeiro* from England through Greek waters and, assuming it was headed for Constantinople, torpedo it. But if the crew sailing her was British it would complicate matters. Later it was learned that a Turkish crew had gone to England to receive the ship; that the ship would be fitted out in an English dock, and the Turkish crew would train there;

in short, more complications and new concerns. The view was gradually formed that a pre-emptive war against Turkey was necessary before she acquired her cruisers. About this eventuality the ideas of Venizelos were indeterminate and unclear. He wanted to avoid such a war by all means.

In a handwritten document in the Metaxas Private Papers Archive Metaxas records:

> One evening in the Spring of 1915 Venizelos rang to ask me to stop by his home. When I got there I found him in the small lounge, off the dining room, with a tall elderly gentleman white haired and clean shaven and wearing tails of the old style that were badly pressed. He was introduced as Mr Dillon. After Mr Dillon had offered to act as a go-between with the Turks regarding the matter of the islands; he was going to Constantinople soon. Venizelos agreed with him: he accepted his offer of mediation. Venizelos moreover told me he was prepared to cede sovereignty over the islands to Turkey, allowing even the Turkish flag to be hoisted there, and a small Turkish guard force. I told him that this was a sad step indeed after all our struggles; that if Turkey attained naval superiority she would not stop there – that is, would not be satisfied with these concessions – regardless of how much they massaged her sense of national honour while humiliating Greece; and I added, if we cannot purchase dreadnoughts we must declare war on Turkey before she acquires her superiority, and thus preventing her from getting ships from British shipyards. But then Turkey will declare war on us immediately she gets these ships. Venizelos remained sceptical and disturbed. Then he told me he very much hoped that Mr Dillon will succeed in his mediation effort for he is a very able man and is well disposed towards us.
>
> After his return from Europe Venizelos often reminded me that neither Britain nor France was inclined to intervene on our behalf in the matter of the islands; instead they advise and press us to be conciliatory towards Turkey. Only Germany seemed inclined to help reach an accommodation favouring us. Russia was of course inflexible regarding our evacuation of Imbros and Tenedos and showed no disposition regarding the cession of other islands to us.

Metaxas further reports that he asked to see Venizelos one morning in March–April (1915), and met him in his residence.

> By then it was most unlikely we would find any dreadnoughts to purchase. Summer was around the corner and Turkey would dispose a powerful fleet of cruisers. Meanwhile, widespread persecution of Greeks in Asia

Minor had begun; the rapprochement between Bulgaria and Turkey became clearer daily; and everything pointed to the gathering storm: we could not avoid the war. The important problem for us was its timing; that is why we should preempt its declaration before Turkey secured her ships. In these circumstances, Britain, as a neutral power, could not hand the ships over to Turkey. That left Bulgaria: would she intervene against us? On the basis of a treaty with us, Serbia was duty-bound to support us, and Romania could do the same.[2]

Metaxas comments further that he had studied at length in Staff GHQ the conduct of such a war, and had set all this out before Venizelos,[3] even though he had been already fully briefed about it. And Venizelos agreed: he saw no other way out, but thought they still had time before Turkey received the ships around the end of August. But Metaxas further suggested they might be able to make other favourable connections: thus Russia for some months maintained a kind of partial mobilization of 700,000 men over the basic strength of its army, and to what end? A rumour circulated by Col. Pesicz, Military Attaché of the Serbian Embassy in Athens, had it that a union was being sought between Serbia and Montenegro, and that this would occur during this year (1915), that Austria would oppose it with the threat of going to war. In that case Russia would go to Serbia's aid. Metaxas averred that this was mere rumour, that Russia was actually preparing to resolve the problem of the Straits, and so it had to have a force ready to oppose any Austrian or German attack, or even involvement. Perhaps Metaxas felt, 'we should not ally ourselves with Russia for such an objective, but only time our operation conveniently in order to remove the Turkish threat from the islands.' Metaxas at this point asked Venizelos if he thought it right to explore developments in St Petersburg 'so as to be better able to formulate our stand and make our preparations'. Venizelos recognized the need to pursue this but after much hesitation. He was very reluctant to combine a Greek démarche on the basis of Russian involvement in the Balkans, which in any case was inevitable and not dependent on the actions of Greece. The matter rested there.

As early as September 1913, Metaxas concludes,

I had begun daily extensive work on a plan for the defence of the islands. Col. Dousmanis (the Chief of Staff) assigned to me the task as a staff officer. At first, I thought to fortify the islands to defend themselves against sudden attack (which as per our information from Turkey was not precluded), and to supply them with the means to defend themselves, and to supply them with the means for such defence against a regular war with Turkey even if we had lost naval superiority. So I ordered artillery emplacements along the coasts of Lesbos, Samos and Chios, and observation posts to monitor all movements at sea, connected with each other by phone. The population of the islands were called to arms for rapid training, linked to the wider training of army reserves who served as the local cadre. This way there was a respectable force on each island, and logistical support of stores and supplies. Similar measures were taken on Lemnos. We also prepared studies of troop concentration and deployment in Macedonia.

These lengthy exchanges between Venizelos and Metaxas illustrate Metaxas's mastery of military strategy, as well as the main features of regional and wider European politics and diplomacy. Military deployment and transport were central concerns of Metaxas as a GHQ Staff Officer. They were central to his plans for defence: rapid transport of the army in Macedonia was of the essence especially in view of poor land communications. Metaxas believed that Greece could repel a Turkish attack via Thrace. Without an adequate cruiser fleet, however, he believed Greece's major ports would remain vulnerable to Turkish naval attack, and Greece could lose Macedonia. The fortification of the Argo–Saronic Gulf, commanding the approaches to Attica and mainland Greece was imperative and it would cost 100 million drachmas; but so was the purchase of dreadnoughts imperative. Metaxas may have had great defence plans, but Greece lacked the resources to implement them.

On the other hand, the exchanges portray Venizelos as a hesitant floundering head of government keen to extract maximum political gain from the European crisis and war, and anxious to please the Entente powers. But it is only fair to point to the fact that as a leader of a new Liberal Party or Coalition and a national reform movement, the new Prime Minister Venizelos had to juggle a still chaotic domestic political situation and a complex entanglement in the country's external relations. So there is another plausible version of the background and import of these exchanges between the Prime Minister and his Staff Officer Military Aide Metaxas, which emphasizes the political differences and eventual rift between Venizelos and King Constantine, leading to the Venizelos revolt and formation of an alternative government in Salonica that would bring Greece into the War on the side of the Entente Allies and mark the height of the Greek National Schism. Metaxas features prominently as a key player in this row, one of the King and Queen's closest confidants, leader of the pro-German faction opposed to Venizelos and the Entente.

III

The disagreement and differences between Metaxas and Venizelos can be further recorded and extrapolated from their earliest collaboration as Chief of Operations Staff Officer in Army GHQ and Prime Minister and Minister of Army Affairs respectively in the broad and very important area of national policy, namely, the strategy for the defence of Greece between 1914 and 1915. This particular period illuminates further the political involvement of Metaxas in the struggle against Venizelos, culminating in 1916–17 in his more active and robust support of the monarchy and its wartime stand against the policies of the Prime Minister Venizelos. To the question: What effect the outbreak of a European War would have on the naval superiority of Turkey over Greece, Metaxas reports in a memo[4] that in September 1913, after the Treaty with Turkey, he accompanied HM King Constantine on his inspection tour of the Greek Army in Macedonia, deployed along the length of the railway line from Thessaloniki to Drama. The impatience of troops to be discharged was great; there was a marked restlessness in all units, with one or two serious outbreaks of mutinous behaviour.

The problem which then preoccupied all those involved in planning the defence of Greece was the threatened loss of naval superiority vis-à-vis Turkey. Even if Bulgaria were not involved as an ally of Turkey,

> the latter, safe and secure from any land operation by the Greek army, would initiate a naval war against us. Furthermore full mobilization was impossible as we had very poor transport, and consequently limited mobility: lack of railways and motor roads, limited sea lanes especially for Macedonia and Epirus. Thus the loss of the islands of Lesbos, Chios and Samos was certain, even though this would be the lesser evil because the Turkish fleet could conceivably operate against Piraeus, and blockade our major ports.

Thus wrote Metaxas in his professional assessment of the military–naval situation in 1913, after the Balkan Wars, followed by a recommendation:

The agreed view of our naval officers is that Greece ought to acquire a strong cruiser fleet; and to this end the British Naval Mission under Rear-Admiral Mark Kerr in Athens was approached. The latter believed that Greece should restrict herself to acquiring a submarine fleet, and the construction of submarine bases, so that Britain was opposed to Greece's acquisition of a cruiser fleet.

In view of poor land communication and transport facilities, Metaxas remained anxious about the strategic viability of Greek defence against any attack launched by Turkey and/or Bulgaria in Macedonia and Thrace. Greece could not transport or move its troops fast enough in order to concentrate them in defensive deployment in Macedonia. It was therefore imperative that it be able to transport these forces by sea, from southern ports; and this required the protection and safeguarding of these sealanes by a powerful Greek Navy which could cope with a potentially strong Turkish navy in the Aegean. A strengthened Greek navy consisting of up-to-date cruisers – dreadnoughts – was therefore essential as it would also protect the distant Aegean islands of Lesvos (Mytelene), Chios and Samos, close to the Turkish coast, a deterrent against any Turkish aggression. The British Naval Aid Mission to Greece led by Admiral Kerr was recommending the acquisition by the Greeks of a submarine fleet, which Metaxas and the Greek GHQ Staff considered wholly inadequate for defence of coastal installations, and quite useless for the movement/transport of troops. The Prime Minister, Venizelos, felt secure in the belief that Greece would not wage naval war on its own, but as the ally of a great maritime power, and should expect therefore to be dependent on that power's naval deployment: the British, in short, did not need Greek dreadnoughts. Metaxas reports that by autumn 1913, the Prime Minister was quite indecisive over what to do about the matter: thus he took no steps to purchase dreadnoughts; nor did he order any submarines. 'I have no intention to join a naval race with Turkey', he told Metaxas. 'I concluded that I should take the opportunity of my tour in Macedonia to speak to the King', Metaxas recalls. The King seemed impressed by Kerr's recommendation of a submarine fleet, until Metaxas argued that the problem was not that of Turkish encroachments against Greek coasts, but that the deadlier threat to the security of Greece was the safety of its sea communications, the difficulty of mobilization and troop deployment in Macedonia, two areas a submarine fleet could not protect effectively.

Metaxas was already adept at playing Premier versus Monarch, and vice versa. 'The King', he goes on to record, 'understood the problem clearly, and hastened to reassure me that as soon as we are back in Athens he will insist Venizelos resolve the problem quickly. But he also urged me to see Admiral Kerr and discuss the matter with him.'

The record Metaxas left of his meeting with Venizelos on the evening of 13 January 1914 is crucial both for the differences between them over the strategic defence of Greece as well as the Turkish threat and the proposed Asia Minor venture. He reports in detail on his discussion with the Prime Minister that evening which ranged widely over Asia Minor, the Dardanelles, the territorial promises of the Entente Powers in Asia Minor in return for Greek military operations there. The Prime Minister started the discussion by asking Metaxas about the progress of his paper on Asia Minor operations. 'I replied', records Metaxas, 'it is being continued by Exadaktylos [a GHQ colleague of Metaxas]; and that the overall impression till now is that the Greek population is concentrated on the northern shore of Asia Minor rather than in the western. Venizelos rejected this view offhand, unwilling to accept that the Greek population is concentrated on the northern shore of Asia Minor, which we cannot claim because of Russian interests.' As for the physical–geographical study of Asia Minor and the limits of political division, Metaxas records,

I had prepared studies in the past and was therefore prepared to comment. Venizelos asked me to be prepared to do so the next day, adding that we were being offered parts of Asia Minor and that we must respond to the Triple Entente, and saying further that there is no question of our ceding Kavalla to Bulgaria. 'So, the cession of Kavalla and Drama is excluded', I asked. 'Yes, it is. Only Serbia will make certain concessions, and the only concession on our part is not to oppose Serbia's concessions.' 'Mr Prime Minister', I said, 'as a soldier I am overjoyed by the exclusion of any territorial concessions in the region of Kavalla and Drama, because this allows us to retain excellent frontiers, the detachment of which would otherwise have weakened us strategically.'

Our conversation continued about the south of the Hellespont region in Asia Minor, which I thought we ought to insist be included in any territorial concession made to us in Asia Minor; or at least to insist on the basis of the Greekness of the population there – if they don't compel us to abandon it – or to be compensated elsewhere. Venizelos did not want to hear about such bargaining and did not intend to make any demands in that direction, but confine himself to the limits of the Aydin vilayet. Next, I asked what will become of Turkey, and Venizelos, hesitating, replied, 'Turkey will be destroyed by the Allies, who else?' I told him this was rather difficult, and did he really believe that Britain and France would willingly destroy Turkey. Venizelos believed at that time that they would. As to how it would be done – by forcing the Dardanelles and the Bosphorus – the only way really. But in that case Turkish military power would resist by defending Asia Minor; and who would deal with her and destroy her there? Venizelos became silent briefly, and then added, 'Then we will add ourselves to the conflict, with a military expedition in Asia Minor.' When I asked who will protect our European borders, especially against the Bulgarians, Venizelos offered the hypothesis that the Bulgarians will be allies who will also attack Turkey, and without this assumption we [Greece] cannot participate in the war. I ended the conversation by saying, 'Then we can think about the expedition?'

In contrast to earlier discussions, Venizelos informed Metaxas in their meeting of 15 January 1915,

> On the basis of statements by the English Ambassador, there could be an expedition in Serbia against Austria–Germany for which we [Greece] would receive the whole of Western Asia Minor.

But in Elliot's statements, Metaxas went on,

> I noticed he was referring to concessions on the coast of Asia Minor, and this was official.

He also implied the English would be able to contribute an Army Corps in Macedonia to protect us against any Bulgarian threat. 'But I did not think this was meaningful', opined Metaxas, because the real deterrent against Bulgarian aggression was English prestige. Here Venizelos added that if he needed to reassure the Bulgarians he would not hesitate to cede Kavalla and Drama. To this, Metaxas declared,

> I objected vehemently at length. (My objections and views generally can be read in my Memorandum of 18 January [1915], which covers mainly the military aspects of the matter.) During this meeting of the 15th we explored the political aspects of the matter.
>
> Another evening however returning to the burning issue of the prospect of Turkish naval superiority, I asked him (Venizelos) if it were not possible to solve the problem by an alliance with a great naval power, and reminded

him that last year in London he told me that we should acquire naval power so that we would be useful as allies of England (a great sea power), and because of that he had stopped the conversion of S.S. *Salamis* into a dreadnought, in order to support and get in line with the ideas and recommendations of the British Naval Mission regarding our naval defences. I had the impression then that he was banking on a British alliance. If this is still possible or expected, we must not hesitate to seek or pursue it. Venizelos replied with an expression of disappointment, saying that the subject had been broached at a dinner by two British government ministers, alluding to future collaboration (or joint action) with Greece, and they seemed to favour it. But the British have not returned to the subject since; they only suggested we (the Greeks) should not be too demanding (implying I presume Northern Epirus), and he asked me: 'How would you react Mr Metaxas, if we ceded to the British Cephalonia as a Naval Base?' I replied: 'Surely Mr President you don't mean to cede the island to them; that would be monstrous: perhaps only to give the English the right to use it as a naval base.' He hastened to say: 'Not of course to give away the island, even though you know, Mr Metaxas, they would be willing to exchange it for us with Cyprus', while looking at me with an enigmatic smile. I felt great frustration inside me. Ceding a Greek island in exchange for anything else is impossible. Nor can I comprehend the right to establish a naval facility. If Britain is our ally she can of course use all our naval facilities, and if there is not one in Cephalonia, they can give us the money to construct it. Venizelos thought this would be a good solution. But I did not feel he was being altogether honest with me in the sense that he had dispelled any idea of exchanging Cephalonia.

One can safely claim that the period from 1912 to 1915 was the most glorious for Metaxas, especially in his military career, only to be topped twenty-five years later in October 1940 by his rejection of the Italian fascist ultimatum.

IV

On the eve of the Great War Metaxas was on holiday with his family on the island of Tinos. With hostilities about to erupt in the Balkans – Austria against Serbia – GHQ summoned him back to Athens. He left his family behind in Tinos. The correspondence between Metaxas and his wife covering the period from 30 July to 2 October 1914 is one of the most revealing sources for the reconstruction of his personal and political profile. During this time Venizelos was en route to meet with the Turkish Grand Vizier in Brussels. But decisive events of the war found him in Munich, with the matter of Greece's stand yet to be decided. By mid-September 1914, the Battle of the Marne indicated that the prospect of a lightning German victory was unrealistic; and the war was soon to become a prolonged slog of trench warfare. Venizelos summarily dismissed a German suggestion that Greece attack its erstwhile Balkan ally, Serbia, from the South ('Greece is too small of a country to commit such a great act of betrayal', Venizelos is reported to have said), and he was determined to keep Greece out of the war, albeit oriented towards the Triple Entente. Immediately and vehemently opposed to this general orientation of Venizelos's view, was George Streit, the Minister of Foreign Affairs and well known – notorious, if you wish – royalist and close collaborator of the King and the Royal Court.

The next episode that contributed to the growing rift between the pro-Entente Prime Minister and the Royal Court – the King and his royalist staff officers, including Metaxas – occurred when Admiral Kerr had lengthy discussions with the King about a possible Dardanelles expedition. These talks took place without the knowledge of the Prime Minister who on 7 September 1914 offered his resignation, while Metaxas voiced his objections to the whole project. In the meantime, on 11 September 1914 George Streit resigned as Foreign Minister, and Venizelos whose own resignation was rejected by the King, assumed that portfolio too. These signs of the growing rift between the pro-Entente pro-War Greeks led by the Prime Minister and the pro-neutrality pro-Central Powers (led by Germany) group of Staff Officers and politicians led by the King, and especially the Queen, may be gleaned from the continued correspondence between Metaxas and his wife in the summer–autumn of 1914. During this time Metaxas worked normally in his office, keeping his boss, the Minister of Army Affairs, informed about military matters and developments in the war. His life was nearest to a routine existence than at any other time. Among other things, he wrote his wife about social life in Athens, even about his concern over the King's promised decoration. As for the certain coming of the European War, Metaxas wrote his wife on 17 July 1914: 'In this great calamity, I hope our dear little Greece will be saved, because according to all appearances – I cannot tell you more – we shall stay out – keep out of it – vigilant guardians of our country, and we will let the big ones fight it out.' In passing he tells her he bought Balzac's *Les Courtisans* for his leisurely reading, 'but it's impossible to read in this heat' [*Diary*, II, p.318]. Metaxas repeats his hope that Greece will keep out of the European War in future letters throughout July 1914, and intones against the oppressive policies of the powerful in the colonies to facilitate the enrichment of a European plutocracy. 'This is the civilization of Europe.' 'We remain vigilant but with sword unsheathed', and closes plaintively rueing the passing of 'a grand European order, so dignified and powerful', alluding perhaps to the end of the belle epoque [*Diary*, II, p.316]. Two days later he writes Lela about Italy's treacherous behaviour: 'It is a cowardly nation', and soon he tries to highlight his own role in all these developments and events. Thus reporting the return of Venizelos he assures Lela he hasn't been to see him, because 'they must become accustomed to seek me out' [*Diary*, II, p.317]. In telling Lela what a terrible war it was, Metaxas adds that it was necessary: on the one hand the arms race between the Great Powers created a difficult situation in Europe, without someone powerful being able to keep matters under control and balance the crisis. On the other hand, there had developed in Europe a terrible moral condition – a crisis – marked by ostentation, irreligion, corruption. The War will now clear these things up. 'It is unfortunate that only with disasters and sacrifices can humanity progress', and admonishes his wife, 'Economize and so will I, as we can't be too sure of the future.' So far so good [*Diary*, II, p.317].

V

Shortly after he returned to Athens on 19 September 1914, Venizelos asked Dousmanis and Metaxas for their considered opinion as to who would be the victor in the War. Metaxas confined his answer to the cautious projection that 'Germany will not be defeated.' During this conversation Venizelos did not express his confidence in the victory of the Entente. On the contrary, he was worried about France's ability to withstand the German military onslaught.

At the end of September 1914, Venizelos was still determined not to embroil Greece in the War, and warned Metaxas 'to get any such idea out of your mind' [*Diary*, II, p.320]. Venizelos asserted repeatedly that the best policy is for Greece to avoid even the most limited mobilization – and the War. When Metaxas protested that he was looking at the issues from a narrow military consideration and perspective because the wider political problem was not part of his brief, Venizelos told him he was mistaken: 'The Staff Officer must also have a political mind' [*Diary*, II, p.321]. Revealing though is what Metaxas reports to his wife on 24 July 1914 about his meeting with the German Military Attaché in Athens GHQ: 'Discipline the Turks', Metaxas told the German Attaché, 'or we will hit them, open the Straits, enabling the Russian Black Sea Navy to join up with the French in the Mediterranean. Turkey will die, and you can imagine what will happen to you (Germany).' Again full of himself Metaxas writes his wife in the same letter, 'Venizelos summons the Chief of Staff (Dousmanis) but Metaxas must go along with him, to discuss the situation and the need for mobilization in particular.' He exults in his letter, 'Greece is like a ship on rough seas; at the helm are four people, the King, Venizelos, Dousmanis and I'; and he closes his letter with a bit of Court gossip, such as the replacement of the Pallis courtiers by the Roidis.

Metaxas renews his earlier promise to Lela that after the end of the War he will retire from the Army, withdraw to their homes in Patisia and Tinos (in the summer). He had had enough of glory. But he is still worried by the fact that the Prime Minister and his GHQ Staff boss Dousmanis had yet to accept his proposal of partial mobilization, a peculiar concern for someone who was seriously contemplating retiring or withdrawing from the fray? [*Diary*, II, pp.326–7]. On the following day, on 30 July 1914, Metaxas submitted to the Chief of Staff his Plan for a military expedition against Bulgaria, an ally of Turkey. The mixed feelings and preoccupations of Metaxas at this time over his professional service to the Prime Minister and his personal relationships with him are revealed in his letter of 31 July to Lela: 'Because of a misunderstanding Venizelos came to see me in order to apologize, saying I should not misunderstand him, that we are linked by a friendship of many years, of love and mutual respect; that neither of us should ever believe what he hears about us from others, that he considers me a friend. On the contrary, he told me he had known that Dousmanis did not like him and conspired against him' [*Diary*, II, p.235]. Here one must note the ability and inclination of Metaxas to allow his main rival to allude to the treachery of a presumed close colleague and friend of longer standing (as in the case of Dousmanis) without protest. Treachery was the name of the game at that particular stage of Metaxas's clawing up the political ladder of the Greek Establishment. Thus in his letter to Lela of the following day, 1 August 1914, Metaxas expands on the significance of his own role in the military–diplomatic arena in Athens regarding the Great European War. 'The Foreign

Ministry sends me the dispatches from all our Embassies, Venizelos entrusts me with off the record, secret information in his possession, Dousmanis conveys to me what he learns from the King, so that I hold all the threads in my hands', he writes Lela, and he remains obsessed with the intrigues of the so-called *camarilla* around Venizelos against him, who 'envy the great confidence Venizelos has in me. Yet I no longer depend on Venizelos, or the King, or Dousmanis, but on myself – I stand on my own two feet. I am aware they need me and I need not attach myself to anyone, that is, to any one patron' [*Diary*, II, pp.337–8]. Thus his letters to Lela throughout August 1914 contain a mixture of his developing relationship with Venizelos, occasional if isolated remarks about the War and its possible outcome, and his own feelings. Especially intriguing is the growing ambivalence of Metaxas over his belief that Germany should win the War on land, that England should prevail on the sea, and that Greece must not end up in the camp that is hostile to England. There is some evidence in these letters to Lela that Metaxas was beginning to boast about his own following among Army officers. 'While Venizelos is pessimistic and disoriented, I am attracting the attention of other officers to my view that the salvation of Greece lay in a German victory. He tells Lela he declined the offer to become Governor of Macedonia in order to be near the King. I shall not break with Venizelos, but retain my excellent relations with him' [*Diary*, II, pp.340–1].

One also catches the first glimpses of Metaxas the journalist and publicist. A series of technical articles on the Great War appeared in the newspaper *Athina* between 29 July 1914 and 21 July 1915, ostensibly written by the journalist Pop, but actually inspired by Metaxas. During the rest of his correspondence with Lela in August–September 1914, Metaxas alludes to this involvement, 'Pop visited me last night till 11.30 p.m. when I told him much about the War in case he wished to write about it', he writes Lela in his letter of 14 August 1914 [*Diary*, II, p.341]. Metaxas may have been reacting to his difficulties with the French Military Mission, at a time when Venizelos was sedulously arousing public opinion against the King, something Metaxas was trying to stop and reverse. 'Venizelos', he wrote Lela, 'is a very confused undependable character, and must be watched closely. But you must sing his praises, like I do …' [*Diary*, II, pp.341–2]. He tells Lela in his letter of 15 August 1914 that his real aim is to become independent – that is, not dependent on a patron like Venizelos – and raise his own flag, or standard, '… I have decided to fly with my own wings, that is as a leader, not as a follower (of anyone). I have evidence that it is high time.'

In glossing over the French, German and others matters relating to the War, Metaxas, in a letter to his wife dated 21 August 1914, opines about Greek society: 'The sense of duty and obedience to God is unpleasant for the Greeks, who are spiritually immature' [*Diary*, II, p.348]. Remarking on how public opinion has been misled by the anti-German press, Metaxas writes to his wife on 23 August about the importance of enlightening public opinion, alluding to the A–Z articles by Pop; the fact that many believe their author is Baron von Schenck of the German Embassy in Athens, or the German Military Attaché; and that there are those who suspect him as their author. Metaxas does not deny the charge or dispel the suspicion, comments extensively on the popularity of the French in contrast to his own minority pro-German position, and reveals his objection to Britain as a proven pro-Slav (as per Congress of Berlin in 1878) power. He complains bitterly about the mindless 'Café diplomats and generals who wish to direct state policy' [*Diary*, II, p.354], a version of his more permanent antipathy to mindless 'street politics', especially when based on little more than ignorance.

Metaxas cannot resist comments on the difficulties of Venizelos, including his tense relations with the royalists George Streit and Dousmanis. Streit resigned from the government because of a fundamental disagreement with Venizelos. The latter, Metaxas avers, wants minions – acolytes – and he warns Lela of the looming political crisis arising from Venizelos's pro-French policy and his wish to humiliate others. In this highly charged political atmosphere, Dousmanis succumbed and Streit resigned, 'but I am a tough Cephalonian, not a Corfiote' – like Dousmanis, that is. In several letters he refers again to the envy of others

> because of my (professional) reputation, your virtue, our pride and financial well-being, our health, our family happiness. that is why we must remain aloof, cool, cautious and reticent. God gave us all: glory, strength, wealth, health, harmony, lovely children, and most important deep love. How many people have or enjoy all of this? It is only natural for them to envy us. We must ignore them and appear compromising …

Here one cannot help but notice the nearly Manichean view Metaxas has of society, of the world? Us against them, or them against us. But he soon returns to political events. 'Streit has fallen', he writes Lela on 31 August 1914, 'but only after he managed to resist giving away the concessions demanded by Russia and England in favour of Bulgaria. And I managed to improve my position with the King in time. Both

Venizelos and Dousmanis are identical unchanged characters, they both
tend to use and exploit people. But Venizelos knows that the broad
consensus in the Army follows me, and that is why he looks after me.'
Metaxas tells Lela why he likes the Germans for some of their great
qualities of patience and piety, and tells her they will prevail because
German culture is the culture of the future and the hope of humanity!
He explains there can be no culture and civilization without power, and
proffers in some detail the reasons for his anticipated German victory:

> It demands dedication to the leader, to duty, the evasion of emotionalism
> and the absence of disappointments, great stability and steadfastness in
> decisions, deep religious faith to supply strength in crisis, great patience,
> perseverance and persistence. All of these are exactly the virtues of the
> German nation: they are the virtues of strong men. That is why I believe
> in the victory of the Germans. To be sure though, I am only human and
> could be mistaken. [*Diary*, II, p.362]

Metaxas is however a bit too convoluted when he returns to the gossip
about Venizelos and Dousmanis, and especially his own relationship with
the Prime Minister. He writes Lela on 3 September 1914,

> Here, if they think you guileless, innocent, you are lost; they walk all over
> you … You must sting a little, not too hard or sharply to provoke hostility,
> but enough to get others to fear you. My own power derives from the trust
> of public opinion partly as a result of the recent A–Z articles by Pop about
> the War in the press. Although I did not write them, they have made a
> great impression, and the majority of readers suspect they could be written
> by no other than Metaxas, without anybody being able to prove this, or
> support such a claim. [*Diary*, II, p.363]

So far Metaxas is suggesting that the overall result of intrigue among
GHQ Staff Officers, especially by Dousmanis, coinciding with his clever
inspiration and direction of the series of Pop articles about the War in
the newspaper *Athina* has been his wider popularity among the Army
officer corps and the public. 'Imagine if these articles were actually
written by him who supplied the ideas for them' [*Diary*, II, p.368]. And
he asserts that he has been rewarded by Venizelos who appointed him
Chief of Operations at GHQ, and by the King who decorated him with
the Gold Cross. Why this favour and goodwill in the Army Metaxas
asks rhetorically? Because of my competence and my character. 'Virtue',

Metaxas writes his wife, 'is a great strength', and quotes Caesar on the role of his wife, and concludes 'This has been your part in the history of Greece. If I ever become great enough for history to mention my name, it will also write yours.' This interesting correspondence of Metaxas with his wife stopped in mid-September 1914, when Lela returned to Athens.

The crucial period from October 1914 to June 1917 during which the rift between Venizelos as Prime Minister and the King grew into the famous National Schism – and in which Metaxas played a significant part – is not recorded or documented by Metaxas himself. There is a gap in his archive, no letters to Lela and no *Diary* entries; only what other *dramatis personae* in this national tragedy wrote or were reported to have said, unless of course Metaxas himself destroyed whatever documentation of his own he possessed of this particular period, especially when he was about to go into exile in 1917, or about to flee the country in 1923, or when the Italian invasion of Greece looked imminent in 1940. There are veiled allusions in his *Diary* to 'schismata', sessions of tearing up paper – there were no shredders in those days – as he periodically arranged his library, papers and archives. It is difficult to say.

But one thing is clear: by June 1917 Metaxas was identified as a close ally of the King and the broader royalist camp opposed to Venizelos and his Entente Power supporters and protectors. His exile, along with other monarchists, was therefore inevitable, inaugurating a period of intense and anxious political struggle against Venizelos and his Entente allies, especially the French, which defined and delineated the basic outline and nature of Metaxas's political orientation and future activity, after he returned home from exile at least till 1935–36, and constituting a kind of prolonged prodromi to his 4th August Regime in 1936, and a preparation for his unexpected national role in October 1940, when in terms of both age and health it was rather late for him to realize all his personal aspirations and national objectives for the country. But the saga of his political odyssey was no less extraordinary in its achievements. That essentially is what makes him an extraordinary person whose life deserves study. The lines of battle between the pro-Entente Venizelist camp favouring Greek participation in the War against the Central Powers, and the monarchist or Constantinist camp inclined to sympathize with Germany and therefore retain the neutrality of Greece in the conflict had been drawn. The former camp believed Greece could expand its territory and thus integrate the unredeemed or unliberated Greeks, especially those in Asia Minor, as well as face down the Bulgarian threat in Macedonia and Thrace by a wartime alliance with the Entente

Powers, whereas the latter camp believed that any irredentist military adventure would end in disaster, and would not in the final analysis be supported by the Entente Powers against Turkey and Bulgaria; and that on the contrary, a pro-German neutrality would obviate the Bulgarian threat in Macedonia and Thrace, as well as the wider Slav threat in the Balkans. It would also restrain and deter Turkey of the Young Turks from its wilder aggressive schemes in the Aegean.

It is also fair to note that after the Balkan Wars and at the outbreak of the Great War most high ranking officers in the Greek Army were loyal to the King. The Army had been greatly expanded and better equipped. Greece in 1914 was at the height of its glory, of which Metaxas, as we saw above, claimed a share. But there were also episodes that reflected the growing National Schism. As Commander in Chief of the Army, Crown Prince Constantine was vigorously, vehemently opposed to the French Military Mission; later, disagreements over the war against Bulgaria led Venizelos to submit his resignation as Prime Minister. And all these indications of national differences between the Crown and the Prime Minister were manifestations of the attempt by royalist GHQ Staff Officers to undermine the authority of Prime Minister Venizelos, or as C. Zavitsianos put it, 'We had a GHQ which wanted to be a government, or at least to represent the government.'[5]

It was alleged that after the assassination in 1913 of King George I in Thessaloniki Metaxas and his GHQ Staff Officer colleagues thought there ought to be a special HQ of the new King Constantine XII, as a governing agency, which soon became the venue for the Kaiser's, Baron von Schenk's and Queen Sophia's pro-German propaganda and influence in the country, as well as a centre of pro-monarchist propaganda. The Foreign Minister, George Streit, was the staunch champion of a pro-German neutrality policy, wholly devoted to the new King and Queen. There followed a confused indeterminate interpretation of the alliance with Serbia. Meanwhile, the political plans of Venizelos were undermined by the tergiversating Entente policy especially when the Entente Powers became pro-Turkish and pro-Bulgarian in their rivalry with Germany for clients in the Balkans, and in order to preempt Germany's push to the East and Russia's drive on Constantinople. When, at the same time, came a German–Turkish alliance, the King, without the knowledge of the Prime Minister, ordered Streit to cable the Kaiser in Berlin that Greece would still remain neutral in the War, thus contradicting the government's interpretation of the Greek–Serbian alliance treaty. The King and his Prime Minister were now at cross purposes.

When the Streit cable to the Kaiser became known, the French came to consider the King as pro-German and therefore disloyal, and moved to have him deposed; so that by September 1914, a month or two into the Great War, the King was buffeted by several influences: his pro-German immediate entourage of GHQ Staff Officers, including Metaxas, the older royalist politicians such as Streit, Theotokis and Gounaris, and his consort, Queen Sophia, sister of the Kaiser. These were pitted against Venizelos and his allies or Entente supporters.

Yet throughout this time Venizelos continued to employ Dousmanis and Metaxas as his top military counsellors. But British Admiral Kerr discussed Greece's possible participation in the Dardanelles (Gallipoli) expedition with the King, not the Prime Minister. The King however rejected the British proposals. Venizelos submitted his views on this matter and his government's resignation which the King did not accept. Latent in this exchange though was the future split between King and Prime Minister. There followed a series of proposals regarding territorial arrangements to assist local states in the Balkans to sort out their differences, encouraged by the Entente Powers. But these moves only widened the rift between Constantinists and Venizelists. Thus Venizelos's scheme of a Greater Greece was seen by Metaxas and his cohorts as dangerous, risky adventurism, and a treasonous cession of Greek territory for uncertain return to boot. The enemies of Venizelos were moreover instrumental in leaking confidential communications between Venizelos and the King about these delicate matters to the press in order to portray him as a reckless adventurer and a gambler with the hard-won new territories of the Greek state in favour of Bulgaria – and the Slavs. Greek public opinion of the day was obsessed with its hostility to Bulgaria and the Slavs. Strangely though when the Gallipoli expedition was launched in February 1915, Venizelos nearly got the King to approve Greek participation in it, when he appealed to his pro-Constantinople sentiment. But Metaxas was ready to scuttle any plans by Venizelos in this direction; and when Venizelos ordered him to prepare the staff plan of operations, Metaxas was ready to undermine the whole project. Thus he declined to draft the appropriate military orders, claiming that the plan was dangerous and that if Venizelos insisted he would resign. For good measure he mobilized the Queen's influence with the King against the operation.

Many have wondered why Venizelos did not at that point sack Metaxas or force him to resign. The opposition's pressure was piled on Venizelos. Thus Theotokis insisted Greece must collaborate with Germany in the war against pan-Slavism, yet many others subscribed to and supported the pro-Entente policy of Venizelos. Even the King wavered until his wife and the GHQ Staff Officers got to him forcing him finally to tell Venizelos he could not approve of his Dardanelles policy. Venizelos resigned and Zaimis formed a new government. Round One in the contest was won by the royalists, that is, the King, Metaxas and his cohorts. 'Metaxas, as was shown subsequently, became obsessed with the persistent idea that he must enter politics in order to govern Greece'[6] [Pangalos, p.38]. The King-appointed government of February–March 1915 were intent on destroying Venizelos on the pretext that he had been prepared to make concessions harmful to the territorial integrity of the country; and this suited the political agenda of Metaxas. An encapsulated, highly compressed version of the nature of the debate, the rift and conflict between the King and his Prime Minister Venizelos may be formulated as follows: the King was, on the surface at least, convinced of a German victory and attracted by German promises to Greece; but he remained uneasy about Bulgarian aims and therefore at one point agreed to partial Greek mobilization which however undermined his relations with Berlin. His entourage of military and political advisers, including if not actually led by Metaxas, were pro-German, actively opposed to Venizelos and hostile to the Entente. In short, the King, together with the old politicians and elite of pre-1910 Greece, wished Greece to remain neutral in the Great War and themselves wanted to return to power. Venizelos represented post-1910 Greece, or the 'New Greece' who saw the country's future to lie in an alliance with the Entente Powers, and therefore supported Greece's participation in the Great War. Unwilling or unable to mount a coup to overthrow the monarchy and change the political system, Venizelos helped usher in a three-year period, 1915–17, of Palace-appointed weak governments which perpetuated and widened the rift between him and the King, between the Court and its supporters and the new post-Goudi or post-1909 Liberal reformist politics of Venizelos.

The elections of 31 May 1915 were conducted while GHQ Staff Officers, including Metaxas, were at the centre of pro-German propaganda, and the King's illness was exploited by them for electoral–political purposes. Soon after Parliament reassembled at the end of August, a virtual Palace autocracy clashed with Venizelos over constitutional issues, mobilization and related matters. The monarchists argued vehemently that the invitation by Venizelos of foreign (Entente) troops to Greece violated the Constitution, even though later they themselves surrendered Roupel Fort and other points in Eastern Macedonia to Bulgaria. It was however on the matter of foreign troops on Greek soil that the King forced Venizelos to resign, so that when Allied troops actually arrived in Macedonia in September 1916, Venizelos was out of power. As C. Zavitsianos recorded in his *Reminiscences*,[7] the King believed implicitly that Germany would win the War: it was with him a cardinal belief, a creed. So the National Schism was really over the War. Another witness, General Paraskevopoulos, in his *Memoirs*[8] claims the King told him of the Kaiser's territorial promises to Greece, but also avers that a serious illness had wrought a change in the King's personality and disposition.[9] It is noteworthy nevertheless that Zavitsianos himself left the Venizelos camp over the alternative or rebel National Defence government Venizelos set up in Thessaloniki in 1916. As for Metaxas, who did not waver in his conviction of a German victory in the War, he worked assiduously and diligently to influence Theotokis and Gounaris, the two leading anti-Venizelist politicians of that time, of this and convert them to his view of the situation.[10]

Monarchy by divine right was becoming a widespread notion during this time, especially as part of the campaign for the elections of 6 December 1915. The differences between the two camps were becoming sharper and deeper and the verbal war was more bitter. The Metaxas clique at GHQ urged the Palace to get tougher with Venizelos and his Entente Allies and supporters, going so far as to threaten to obstruct and disarm Allied troops in Greece. Metaxas was probably the prime mover of this approach, especially when one considers his role in launching the *Clubs of Epistratoi* (Conscript and Reserve officers) to spearhead the military thrust of the opposition to the pro-Entente Venizelos camp. These were further radicalized as the Entente Powers threatened tougher measures against Greece, or at least the Athens Government, King and politicians. Metaxas managed to organize the GHQ Staff and the *Clubs of Epistratoi* into a kind of extra-governmental force. Together with his inspiration of the Pop series of articles in the newspaper *Athina*, the heightened activities of the German Embassy against the Entente and having also secured the active support and assistance of the Queen, Metaxas constructed a formidable political camp to oppose Venizelos and his party, including his rebel government in Thessaloniki.

The succession of Palace-appointed weak governments in Athens, especially the one headed by Skouloudis, fell prey to the 'magical influence of the demon Metaxas',[11] who now seemed to orchestrate the fight against the Entente. The pressure on the King leading to his eventual abdication and exile in May 1917 by the Entente Powers was inexorably initiated and relentlessly kept up, beginning with the Joint (Anglo–

French) Note of 21 June 1916 in the form of an ultimatum. In practical terms it heightened the struggle between the two main Greek political camps. Venizelos with his National Defence organization headed by General P. Danglis proceeded to his coup of 16 August 1916 in Thessaloniki, and further into the arms of the Entente. Huge rallies of Liberals that month allowed Venizelos to protest against the control of the King by GHQ pro-German officers who also sought to establish an autocracy. A monarchist counter-rally addressed by leading anti-Venizelists such as Gounaris, Rallis and Dousmanis, and claiming that Venizelos had insulted the King while the crowds sang the Keisaris-composed mesmerizing monarchist hymn '*Tou Aetou o Yios*', inaugurated a long period of blind and sterile partisan political passion, and rendered the monarch the leader of a political party and the symbolic head of one political faction against another, a situation, in fact, deadly to a consti-tutional monarch wishing to survive and reign above the political factionalism in the country. Interesting for the time was the tragic fact that both factions were headed by vain men, Venizelos and the King respectively. The former had surrounded himself with Yes Men, a veritable court of worshippers, whereas the King was at the mercy of determined anti-Venizelist pro-German Army Staff Officers, and equally strongly influenced by his wife, and through her, the Kaiser. The succession of weak governments moreover enabled someone like Metaxas to make full use of his *Clubs of Epistratoi* and take a leading part in the armed clashes that ensued mainly in Athens against Entente occupying troops. They were also used in the intimidation of leading Venizelist politicians. Like the King Venizelos was surrounded by a political clique: 'He loved those who never said no to him, and flattered him.' Or as his childhood friend Aristidis Stergiadis aptly put it, 'He had no judgment of people.'[12]

What is extraordinary about this period is the fact that as Venizelos mounted his revolt against Athens with his alternative, pro-Entente government in Thessaloniki, and as the King's actions were largely dic-tated by his courtiers of soldiers, conservative pro-German politicians and his wife, actual power seemed to fall in the lap of the *Clubs of Epistratoi*, a kind of part-time terrorist paramilitary organization led by Metaxas, or at least under his control. He was 'the man of the hour', all powerful among these Clubs which he founded, and all-powerful in the Royal Court, especially with Queen Sophia, whom by virtue of his pro-German sentiments, he influenced greatly.[13] Thus when on 3 November 1916 a French ultimatum demanded the demobilization of the Greek Army and the handing over of all weapons, Metaxas reacted with a plan to transfer the Greek Royal family to Larissa and join the War on the side of Germany. At the same time, his armed *Clubs of Epistratoi* would oppose Allied landings by force. The bloody battle in a besieged Athens on 17–18 November 1916 was led by Metaxas: he worked closely with the German Military Attaché Falkenhausen and N. Theotokis, the Greek Ambassador in Berlin. He assisted the Central Powers in Macedonia with guerrilla units he had organized. But his major plan to transfer the Royal family to Larissa or the Peloponnese and enter the War was opposed by the German Ambassador Count Mirbach himself; and the practical result of his more intense radical activities in the armed Greek resistance to the Allies was that the Entente Powers increased the pressure on Athens. Their ultimatum of December 1916 demanded the redeployment of all the Greek Army in the Peloponnese, the disarming of all revolutionary bands, the banning of the *Epistratoi Clubs*, the release of all arrested Liberals/Venizelists, especially after the extensive purges of the previous month, November. The French Press moreover intensified its campaign against the Greek monarch as an enemy of the Entente, so that the brief though desperate attempt by the King at a rapprochement with the Entente came too late and to naught.

By April–May 1917 it was clear the French at least wanted the King out of the way. On 26 May 1917 Allied troops landed in Athens, Thessaly and the Peloponnese. The King abdicated in favour of his younger son Prince Alexander, and prepared to leave the country into exile along with several of his closest political associates. But Metaxas, the bad demon, as Pangalos described him,[14] with the Queen's connivance and encouragement, urged the King to flee to Tripoli in the Peloponnese and lead a regular Greek Army there against the Allied troops concentrated in Macedonia; in short, not to leave the country without a fight. Only from his subsequent articles in *Kathimerini*[15] (1934) does one realize the tenacity and cunning of the man in persevering behind the scenes in the royal corridors of power, directing, orchestrating a sizeable operation of resistance against the Entente Powers and largely through surrogates, such as the *Clubs of Epistratoi*, while he himself kept his distance and remained in the background. He even managed huge popular rallies and demonstrations that tried to prevent the King and his family from leaving the country.

Clearly, Venizelos could not have deposed, let alone exiled, the most popular monarch in modern Greek history, the hero of the Balkan Wars, had it not been for the Entente threat of the use of force against the Athens regime. He was moreover careful not to alienate Russia and lose the goodwill of Britain by abolishing the monarchy. That phase of the King vs. Venizelos quarrel was confined to the King's temporary abdication in favour of his younger son and his temporary exile until a political resolution of the national crisis was found. Round Two, that is, went to Venizelos, who with Entente support, was able to exile about 30–50 leading pro-German monarchist politicians and Army Officers, as well as place scores of them in Greece under surveillance. Supported by a 30,000 strong Army recruited mainly in Crete – a kind of Cretan tribal praetorian guard – Venizelos formed a new national government in June 1917, which was to have a clear pro-Entente run until November 1920, initiate the future Greek debacle in Asia Minor, and a web of entanglements in European and Balkan diplomacy, as well as inaugurate a new and bitter era of feuding in Greek politics, still largely controlled by Venizelos and his new political elite; one that saw the rapid decline of parliamentary government and the sudden, unexpected rise of Metaxas to absolute power. Thus while there were two Greek states in 1916–17, the triumph of Venizelos after September 1916 and his return to national power in Athens in June 1917 meant there was again one Greek state. The leaders of the other one had been exiled.

VI

Although Venizelos was now politically supreme in Greece it should be noted that throughout 1915, Prime Minister Venizelos was taken up by the matter of the Dardanelles and Gallipoli, the Turkish and Bulgarian threats to Greece, even entertaining the bargaining of territory for war, and juggling the various views of his military advisers, chief among them Metaxas, and the royal court regarding the options of war and peace available to Greece. January and February were the two months during which Metaxas had submitted to his boss Venizelos and the King as Chief of the Army, his most elaborate papers on the military options vis-à-vis the Turkish and Bulgarian threats, as well as his overall judgment of the best strategy for Greece, including the military option in Asia Minor [*Diary*, II, pp.384–406]. These submissions by Metaxas were to influence not only the rift between the King and his Prime Minister Venizelos, but also to decide finally the King's preferred choices in the matter. Basically they were opposed to the Prime Minister's plans and intentions regarding Greece's role in the Great War, leading the Sovereign to reject his Prime Minister's proposed policy and force his resignation. The paper by Metaxas was the most elaborate, complete exposition and analysis of the consequences of the participation of Greece in the Great War; it was a model of staff work, combining military operations with economic–political and diplomatic considerations.

In the meantime, Turkey had entered the War on the side of the Central Powers against the Entente, with significant effect on the strategic objectives of the belligerent major European powers. Germany, it was now clear, aimed to detach the Eastern Mediterranean and Western Asia from British influence or control, and free the Balkan Peninsula from Russian influence. The Allies in their turn had to counter this German threat to their respective interests in southeastern Europe and the Near East, including their imperial dominions, and therefore sought to woo Greece, Turkey and Bulgaria over to their camp. It is interesting that in spite of the clash of views and opposing assessments between the King, Metaxas and Venizelos, the King actually approved Venizelos's offer of an Army Corps (c. 40,000 troops) to the Allied Expedition in the Dardanelles – the landings at Gallipoli – which had been accepted by the British. To his surprise Venizelos found that his military advisers, including Metaxas, were opposed to his scheme. His Chief of Staff, Dousmanis, had already been suspended from active duty at the end of January 1915 after the publication of his letter to Vasdekis that was highly critical of government policy. His duties as Chief of Staff were carried out temporarily by Metaxas, who when he realized that Venizelos had decided to contribute a Greek Army to the Dardanelles Expedition without consulting his Army GHQ, remarked, 'Venizelos wants subordinates' [*Diary*, II, p.384]. When he submitted his own Memorandum about the participation of Greece in the Dardanelles Expedition to the Prime Minister on 17 February 1915, Metaxas begged Venizelos to study it carefully, adding that he had arrived at a fundamental disagreement with him over an essentially military matter, immediately relating to his duties, and begged that he be relieved of these duties, and to consider his application to retire from the Army. Even over this matter Metaxas justified his application directly to the Prime Minister, instead of through Army channels, by pleading that he wished to retain the utmost confidentiality, secrecy and discretion in the matter [*Diary*, II, p.407].

It is difficult to determine the nature and extent of any military/ political crisis caused by the resignation of Metaxas over such a major Venizelos wartime policy. Although Dousmanis was quickly reactivated and reinstated as Chief of Staff, the King initiated a series of urgent

Crown Council meetings to deal with the crisis over the question of Greece and the Dardanelles expedition. In these meetings on 3 and 5 March 1915, Venizelos compromised by proposing the contribution of an Army Division instead of a whole Army Corps or group to that Expedition. But the King hesitated and asked for more time to decide. The King's counsellors, including the fiercely anti-Venizelist Theotokis, advised him to follow the policy of the responsible – elected – Premier. But on 6 March the King finally turned down the proposals of Venizelos who resigned forthwith. Gounaris formed a government that lasted till August 1915. On the whole however the political situation in Greece began to deteriorate, leading to the Asia Minor Debacle. Meanwhile, Venizelos announced his own withdrawal from active politics. With the costly human losses in the attempt to force the Straits, the Allies were further alienated by the change in Greek policy, even though the Gounaris government repeated its intention to maintain Greek neutrality in the War. There were also efforts on both sides to reach an understanding over Asia Minor, including the terms under which Greece would enter the War against Turkey.

While the slaughter of Allied troops was taking place in Gallipoli in mid–late April 1915, Italy joined the War on the side of the Entente Powers, the Greek monarch dissolved Parliament in Athens just before he fell seriously ill with pleurisy, a condition which enhanced his popularity and was duly exploited by the politicians in the elections of May–June 1915, which gave the Liberals an overwhelming majority (185 seats vs. 122 for all other parties). Venizelos returned to active politics by resuming the leadership of the Liberals, Parliament met in mid-August, elected Constantine Zavitsianos as its Speaker, and later that month Venizelos formed a government in succession to that of Gounaris, which had resigned.

At the beginning of September 1915 the King sounded at his most pro-German,[16] risking a variety of initiatives, fantasizing about Divine Providence in his role as leader of the Greek nation, until Venizelos accused him of believing he was King by Divine Right. The whole nation though was shaken when it learned of the Bulgarian mobilization, and Venizelos reacted immediately: he proposed the proclamation of a general mobilization, and one specifically intended to deter a Bulgarian attack on Serbia. The King approved the mobilization measure, but rejected the accompanying declaration of its intention. Venizelos disagreed with the King but did not resign right away. In the meantime, he had asked Britain and France to deploy 150,000 troops in Macedonia.

At the end of September the HQ elements of these forces arrived in Thessaloniki under General Hamilton. Buoyed by the actual presence of Allied forces in the country, Venizelos at the beginning of October 1915 became adamant in Parliament that Greece must go to the aid of embattled Serbia, and the King demanded his resignation. The bulk of the remaining Allied forces arrived two days later. The fact remains that the presence of Entente troops on Greek soil came to constitute a watershed in the modern political history of Greece in the country's faltering between neutrality and commitment. It sharpened further the differences between Venizelists and Constantinists, leading to the formation of an alternative rebel Greek government in Thessaloniki headed by Venizelos, an organization of National Defence, the destructive and provocative Bulgarian occupation of Greek Eastern Macedonia, and the eventual participation of Greece in the War on the side of the Entente.

Zaimis formed a new government comprising, among others, former ministers and prime ministers, such as D. Rallis, G. Theotokis, S. Dragoumis, and D. Gounaris. It was reported that at that time the King had received German assurances regarding Greek neutrality, territorial integrity, and the safety of the Greek population in Turkey. If true, this in part may explain the King's highhanded direct dealings against his Prime Minister, Venizelos. The latter doubted such formal assurances, beyond personal ones to the King from his wife's brother, the Kaiser. Metaxas however insisted these were official, formal assurances to the Greek state, the documented proof of which was in the archives of the Foreign Ministry until 1917. In its efforts to counter the German thrust towards the Near East Britain tried frantically to lure Greece to the side of the Entente. Thus on 15 October 1915 it offered Cyprus in return for Greece's assistance to Serbia, regardless of the outcome of the War. Greece rejected the deal, and Britain withdrew its offer of Cyprus. The minority Zaimis government (the Liberals had a majority of seats in the Chamber) fell and was succeeded by another headed by the 78-year-old S. Skouloudis. The King dissolved Parliament again in November 1915 and fresh elections were held in December. Venizelos and the Liberals protested against the King's action and abstained from the elections. The incompetent Skouloudis government announced it would disarm, as per the Hague Convention, the Anglo–French and Serbian forces on Greek soil. But the Entente Powers were determined to maintain their military presence in Thessaloniki. With the failure of their Dardanelles Expedition the bulk of Entente forces were redeployed in Macedonia. Metaxas, in the meantime, was proved right in his prediction that the Dardanelles

Expedition would fail. Nor did he fail in a series of subsequent written communications to inform Prime Minister Gounaris about his discussions with former Prime Minister Venizelos about military matters, so that throughout 1915 Metaxas was busy drafting letters and memoranda to the King and other politicians regarding his views on the War, Greece's role and position in it, and his differences with Venizelos.[17]

Nineteen sixteen was a quieter, less active year for Metaxas. While the impressive German military might and performance on the Western Front was beginning to wane, at home the actively hostile conduct and policy of the minority government of Skouloudis elicited the active enmity of the Entente Powers, leading to their ending of their credit guarantees of the Greek loan (400 million francs) of August 1914, and its replacement by a German loan of 40 million marks in January 1916. A number of meetings between General Serail of the Entente Expeditionary forces and the Greek sovereign yielded no significant results, while the German–Bulgarian alliance demanded the occupation of the Greek border fort at Roupel, which occurred in May, marking the first encroachment of the Bulgarians on Greek territory. Simultaneously, the Anglo–French forces began the partial blockade of Greece, and Serail proclaimed martial law in Greek Macedonia.

In June 1916 the Entente Powers recalled their role as protective powers in the Treaty of London of 1830, demanded total Greek demobilization, the dismissal of the Skouloudis government, the dissolution of Parliament and the holding of fresh elections, as well as the retirement of certain institutions and a number of public figures. Skouloudis duly resigned and Zaimis formed a new government. At this point the opportunist Metaxas saw his chance, especially when the Greek Army was being demobilized, to recruit and organize his own paramilitary force that would assist him in the advancement of his political role and position in the prevailing political chaos, in the shape of the *Clubs of Epistratoi*. In the first year after June 1916 until the exile of King Constantine in June 1917, these Clubs were clearly paramilitary, extra-state armed organizations. They reflected perhaps the attempt by Metaxas to lead a popular autocracy based on terror. After the King's exile however these Clubs were disbanded, but in reality went underground.

Acting on widespread rumours that Greece was about to unleash a military strike against Anglo–French forces in the north of the country in order to support German–Bulgarian operations, the French Admiral Dartige du Fournet landed troops in Piraeus, occupied the Post and Telegraph Offices, and expelled Baron Schenck of the German Propaganda and Intelligence Service. The Greeks underwent great political turmoil. Under the pressure of the Entente Powers Dousmanis was dismissed from GHQ and was replaced by General Moschopoulos. Metaxas was already distanced from GHQ. There were armed disturbances and incidents against the French Embassy in Athens. The Zaimis government resigned and the Fourth Army commanded by General Hatzopoulos surrendered to the Germans. The Bulgarians occupied Cavalla. Kalogeropoulos succeeded Zaimis as Prime Minister at the height of the crisis and on 26 September Venizelos and his close supporters such as Koundouriotes and others, left for Crete and thence to Thessaloniki where on 6 October 1916 they formed the rival government of National Defence, formally marking the division of Greece, and complicated relations with the Entente Powers.

Despite the use of the good offices of the King's brother Prince George, a close friend of French Premier Briand, and the talks between the French Deputy Paul Antoine Benazet and the Greek monarch, the latter was still determined to avoid by every means the entry of Greece into the War. Distrust was rampant, and the French especially were anxious to disarm the Greeks for they thoroughly mistrusted the King and his military advisers. The Lambros government rejected a series of French Notes in November–December 1916 demanding this. The Greek crowds were stirred up by the *Epistratoi Clubs* to defend Greek honour, the honour of the King and that of Greek arms. German propaganda agents exploited this public resentment further, followed by the eruption of armed clashes that led to several casualties. An anti-Venizelist regime in Athens celebrated the siege of the French in Zappeion, and proceeded to punish the Venizelist 'traitors' who were, in their view, the main cause of the country's problems as well as those of its popular King. In the early days of December there occurred the bloody episodes known popularly as 'Noemvriana'[18] during which the capital city was controlled by the mob. On 7 December the rebel government in Thessaloniki issued a proclamation declaring that King Constantine was deposed from the throne, and declared war on Germany and Bulgaria. The newspaper *Nea Imera* had just published a letter from Venizelos to General Koraka which portrayed Venizelos as plotting against the King and the Greek people. It added fuel to the impassioned inflammable political situation. The letter was a forgery but nonetheless provocative; Metaxas, incidentally, believed the letter was genuine. In any case, the Allied blockade of Greece began on 8 December 1916, causing great hardship to the Greek population for the better part of a year. The conflict between the

Greek King and the Entente Powers, between Venizelists and Constantinists, Metaxas and Venizelos was now on in earnest. Passions were aflame and kept alight by the anathema of Venizelos pronounced by the Metropolitan Archbishop of Athens, Archbishop of Greece, on 27 December 1916.

Throughout this period and during these passionate political up-heavals in Greece Metaxas was not at the centre of events of either political camp. He had left GHQ Staff in June–July 1916 and had been made briefly Commandant of the School of Army Captains, thus affording him a kind of sabbatical leave from the centre of the political maelstrom. It has been argued all the same that in actual fact his military and political influence upon these events and therefore his share of the responsibility for them was significant. One can readily accept the direct – and indirect – influence of Metaxas on military matters; this is clearly indicated in the series of official memoranda he submitted to the King and the Prime Minister, as well as the record of discussions and corres-pondence with them. The presumed wider influence of Metaxas is claimed perhaps on the basis of his published series of articles in the political debate with Venizelos in 1934 about the National Schism.[19]

Europe in 1917 was moving fast towards the conclusion of the War, accelerated in fact by the entry of the powerful USA on the side of the Entente Powers, and the overthrow of the Romanov dynasty in Russia and the establishment there of a Communist–Bolshevik regime which concluded a separate peace treaty with Germany, effectively with-drawing from the War as an ally of the Entente. It was also the year when the French strengthened their political presence in Greece, headed by the High Commissioner, Senator Jonnart, who demanded the abdication and exile of King Constantine. Entente troops backed such ultimata with the occupation of Thessaly and the Isthmus of Corinth. The King decided to acquiesce despite popular demands for him not to do so and the efforts of Metaxas and his *Epistratoi Clubs* to prevent him from leaving the country. As the Entente Powers strengthened their armed presence in the capital, Venizelos returned from Thessaloniki to govern the country after the Zaimis government resigned in late June 1917. The parliament elected in June 1915 was recalled – indeed resurrected (*e vouli ton lazáron* as it was satirically dubbed),[20] and Venizelos delivered his famous speech consisting of a litany of charges against the King and his entourage including of course Metaxas. By now Metaxas had become one of the most implacable opponents of the pro-Entente policy. Regardless of his earlier conviction in Germany's victory, what pushed him further against the Entente was French treatment of Greece. Even the King, who was now anxious to avoid a total break with the Entente Powers, found Metaxas too rigid and uncompromising over this matter. Metaxas found himself as a result inactive until he went into exile in June 1917.

NOTES

1. Metaxas Private Papers, and *Diary*, II, pp.226–450.
2. Handwritten document by Metaxas in Private Papers Archive.
3. A précis of *Diary* entries and handwritten documents by Metaxas.
4. Metaxas Private Papers, and *Diary*, II, pp.226–450.
5. Pangalos, *Memoirs*, ii, p.12, also referring to C. Zavitsianos, *Reminiscences*, Athens, 1946, 2 vols *(Ai Anamniseis tou ek tis istorikis diafonias Vasileos Konstantinou kai E. Venizelou opos tin ezise, 1914–22)*.
6. Pangalos, *ibid.*, p.38.
7. C. Zavitsianos, *Reminiscences*.
8. General Paraskevopoulos, *Memoirs*, i, p.242.
9. *Ibid.*, pp.62–3.
10. *Ibid.*, pp.63–4.
11. Pangalos, *Memoirs*, p.93.
12. *Ibid.*, p.155.
13. C. Zavitsianos, *Reminiscences*, p.206.
14. Pangalos, *Memoirs*, p.193.
15. Ioannis Metaxas, *I Istoria tou Ethnikou Dichasmou, ke tis Mikrasiastikis Katastrophis* (The History of the National Schism and of the Asia Minor Catastrophe), Athens, Kathimerini, 1935. See also the recent expanded and annotated edition of the same collection of articles on the Venizelos–Metaxas Debate, *Istoria tou Ethnikou Dichasmou kata tin Alilografia tou Eleftheriou Venizelou kai tou Ioannou Metaxas* (The History of the National Schism according to the Exchange between E. Venizelos and I. Metaxas), Thessaloniki, 1994. Generally on this period see the Liberal-leaning journalist George Ventiris, *I ellas tou 1910–1920, istoriki meleti* (Greece of the period from 1910–1920, a historical study), 2 vols, first published in Athens in 1931, this edition Athens, 1970, and the more independent Gregory Dafnis, *I Ellas metaxy dio polemon* (Greece between Two Wars), 1923–1940. Second Edition 1974, vol.1: The Rule of Venizelism; vol. 2, The Rise of Anti-Venizelism.
16. C. Zavitsianos, *Reminiscences*, pp.81ff.
17. See *Diary*, II, pp.414–39.
18. By the reckoning of the old style Julian Calendar, these events occurred in the third week of November, considering a difference of thirteen days between that and the new style Gregorian Calendar.
19. *Op. cit.*
20. Literally the Parliament of the 'Resurrected Lazaruses'.

7

Exile and Return, 1917–20

When Venizelos read in Parliament his list of charges against the King and his supporters Metaxas was no longer in the country. A few days after the King left Greece, Metaxas was arrested, on 20 June 1917, along with about twenty-five to thirty other Constantinists, such as former Prime Minister D. Gounaris, R. Eslin, V. Dousmanis, Sp. Mercouris and his two sons, G. Pezmazoglou, Ion Dragoumis and others. Metaxas with his wife Lela and two young daughters Loulou and Nana, arrived by ship in Corsica on 29 June 1917 as exiles and settled into the Grand Hotel in Ajaccio.

The period of exile coincided with the war coming to its end and to that extent it constitutes a very important watershed in the life and political career of Metaxas. Forced into idle exile along with a group of royalist anti-Venizelist politicians – D. Gounaris, Mercouris, Pezmazoglou – Metaxas abandoned recording entries in his *Diary*. Instead he developed a routine of reading, family outings, tutoring his daughters in Greek and other Greek school subjects, and generally pondering life, the War, and the future of Europe. The gap in his *Diary* for this very important interlude in his life is partly compensated by the general ruminations about the world Metaxas captiously jotted down in a number of small notebooks. At the same time, he was still possessed by an inordinate fear of the hostile French authorities, fear for his personal and his family's safety, and sought to flee Corsica for Italy. Metaxas tried to assess the defeat of Germany in the War – a defeat which he incidentally did not expect – and the broader implications of this defeat for Europe and the world. He also considered the rise of the USA and Japan as world powers and what this meant for Europe and Asia. He feared US hegemony over the states and nations of Europe, as he contrasted the individualistic puritanism and holier than thou moralistic attitude and virtuous posturing of the so-called democracies with the more collective force-oriented

Germany in order to underline the argument that equality had been the dominating ideal of the world until 1919, a kind of creed, a religion. The more of a chimera equality was the more desirable it became. The leaders of democratic states are not considered superior or above the others and their guides, but the servants of the sovereign or ruling mass public. Consequently, superiority, excellence is not the basis of leadership, but the ability to solicit and flatter the masses; so that the best are not the elite or the leaders. In observing that the Great War was prosecuted with great fanaticism, Metaxas concludes that this was because it was a religious–sectarian war: Germany was proclaimed by the nations that believe in equality to be heretical and the enemy of humanity, making it a war of democratic states against Prussian militarism. They wished to liberate today's peoples from the infection of Germanism, and the persecution of the unrepentant is a work of faith, an article of faith, liberating them if they have to by force. The War was a holy war. Germany represents anti-democratic forces just as Luther was the anti-Christ and had to be destroyed. Did Metaxas believe it was an ideological war, or were these thoughts a result of his Freemasonry?

Inequality, Metaxas discovered, was the natural condition of mankind, of society. His remarks about equality, democracy, majority rule, etc., are really part of a diatribe against representative government, against the tyranny of majority rule, characterized in its domestic partisan politics as a form of permanent civil war, causing widespread insecurity, and lack of social cohesion and cooperation. By contrast in aristocratic states the polity reflects a social hierarchy deriving from the natural inequality of man, but they are flexible enough to allow the extraordinary to influence the whole by their worth and merit and yet with a feeling of security; it frees human activity, creates self-confidence and cooperation, solidarity, regime stability and a higher kind of patriotism beyond the banal one of fetichism towards the idol of the fatherland. In such a situation real civilizational advance is possible, and only in such states do citizens experience real freedom.

The victory of the Entente Powers at the end of the War in November 1918 was a time of great anxiety and apprehension for Metaxas. He feared possible French action against him, especially in view of his prominent opposition to the French Military Mission in Greece since 1910, and his leadership of the pro-German neutrality camp in Greece against the Entente Powers from 1914 to 1918. It was therefore urgent that he leave Corsica – French territory – so as to put a fair distance between the French authorities and himself. To this end, he prepared a plan of escape together with D. Gounaris and G. Pezmazoglou. It entailed fleeing overland from Ajaccio to Bonifacio and from Bonifacio by sea to Sardinia. But he and Pezmazoglou had to consider their respective families in this escape plan, and ensure their safety and eventual reunion with them on mainland Italy. They would also have to obtain the acquiescence of the Italian authorities to their arrival and temporary asylum in Sardinia. Such a risky adventure could not have been embarked upon without assistance, or at least the tacit acquiescence of several people who could be trusted by the fleeing exiles, especially as they had been under close surveillance by the local police for seventeen months in Ajaccio. The escape from Corsica was of the utmost urgency for Metaxas himself, in view of the fact that the Venizelos regime in Athens had conducted the trial of army officers and monarchist elements active in the November 1916 clashes against Entente forces and political supporters of Venizelos. Among those tried in absentia was Metaxas; actually he was sentenced to death in January 1920. By that time too Metaxas had lost much of his self-confidence and his morale was very low, especially when his wartime projections, including his prediction of a German victory, proved wrong. Ajaccio was an unpleasant and unhappy experience for Metaxas despite the presence of his wife and children with him. He was possessed by fear, insecurity and depression. In fact, he had lost everything connected with his career; only his family remained. The traumatic experience of exile in Ajaccio and Cagliari influenced deeply the rest of his life and career.

It was difficult for Metaxas to influence the rather unfriendly attitude of the Italian authorities towards his plight and that of his fellow-exiles. He was however a high ranking Freemason,[1] and once in Sardinia, Metaxas sought and cultivated the friendship of the local Freemasons, especially that of Canepa, Master of the local lodge in Cagliari. Canepa it turned out had connections and contacts in the Italian government. Coincidentally, Pezmazoglou was a Freemason too but of a lower rank than Metaxas. It came to pass though that it was largely the sustained and active assistance of the Freemasons that enabled Metaxas and his friends to go from Sardinia to the Italian mainland, and Metaxas was reunited with his family in Sienna.

In addition to his other misfortunes, Metaxas had to endure living apart from his family during the first six months of 1919. This was probably one of the most traumatic sufferings of his life; in fact he was on tranquillizers most of that time. Then in mid-May 1919, mandated by the victorious Entente Powers, Greek forces landed in Smyrna, while

a Treaty of Peace was being negotiated in Paris. The Greek epic in Asia
Minor was on and he, Metaxas, was out of it. He recognized that in his
case the defeat of Germany, which he never expected, had changed everything, that is, thrown off course all of his calculations, projections and
plans [*Diary*, II, p.472]. His *Diary* entries allude to the hostile Athenian
press, the fact that Switzerland denied him asylum, and in February
1919, 'My return to Greece seems impossible' [*Diary*, II, p.478]. In
desperation, Metaxas even suspected a great power like France of making
life difficult for his wife and children as a way of taking revenge against
him. He had difficulty sleeping. In the meantime, he had also enlisted
the aid of Mrs Nazos (Mrs Aspasia Nazou) for the welfare of his family.

Apart from the emotional stress, exile was severing the bond between
Metaxas and his family. He was becoming steadily paranoid, believing
he was pursued by state agents everywhere. What is not quite clear is
the role of Mrs Nazou who offered to assist with the reunification of
the family. Yet amidst all this turmoil and personal emotional upheaval,
Metaxas persevered with private Italian lessons. Clearly though Mrs
Nazou was offering her effective help with the Italian authorities while
exploiting her freedom to travel to France. Metaxas was having serious
stomach trouble, mainly the result of nerves, anxiety and depression. He
believed the French held his family hostage, and persevered with
strengthening his relations with the local Freemasons. In late March he
notes his weeping bouts out of despair, and having learnt about the
sentences of the Venizelist courts in Greece against the Constantinists,
including himself, he worries about his property at home as his feeling
of persecution intensified. He noted that all the concessions of Venizelos
to the Entente Powers were intended to keep Metaxas and his other
political opponents out of the way: Venizelos lobbied both France and
Italy to make their return to Greece difficult. So long as the victorious
Allies considered the Greek monarch a threat to their position in Greece
they supported Venizelos. But the time came when their respective interests
in the East required a rapprochement with Turkey and consequently
their support for Venizelos began to wane. The more this occurred
the better the prospects of the Greek political exiles returning home.
Nevertheless, Metaxas wondered about the soundness of his decision to
flee from Corsica: 'Why not face surrender and trial; what was there
for me to fear? Right was on my side. I only sacrificed my family and
embarked upon an adventure the end of which is unknown' [*Diary*, II,
p.495). And he continued to struggle for his freedom, using everyone in
sight – Mrs Nazou, the philhellene Italian Parliamentary Deputy

Roberto Galli, and the Freemasons. By sheer perseverance Metaxas managed to get his agent in Athens, Rousos, to keep a close eye on his property and finances, and succeeded in renting the shops in his block at home. His wife's brother sold some of his stocks and shares, for by May 1919 Metaxas was in need of cash.

On 18 May 1919 Greek forces occupied Smyrna, but politically Metaxas noted 'we have been defeated decisively ... No matter, so long as Greece becomes greater. We will live in exile, persecuted ... My political life stopped for ever ...' [*Diary*, II, p.506].

> Yet I feel that despite its expansion, Greece has been internally corrupted: the sense of freedom has declined, flattery, envy and the obsession with gain or profit, the mania for advancement by any means are at their peak. It is with hubris, mischief, sycophancy, force and injustice that people struggle today in Greece. This has been the effect of 'Ententism'. I foresaw all this, and the need to rise against it. Time will tell if I was right; the struggle is not over yet. [*Diary*, II, p.507]

Then on 19 May 1919, after nearly two years in exile, the Italian authorities lifted all restraining conditions from the sojourn of the exiles in the country; they could now travel freely about the country. By the end of May 1919, Metaxas was in such despair he believed that had it not been for his worry over the fate of his wife and children, he would have committed suicide [*Diary*, II, p.509]. He went through several days swaying between hope and fear, optimism and pessimism, rendering his nervous condition worse, and thus taking more tranquillizers. One day Metaxas discovered a telegram from Lela which had lain undelivered in his hotel for days – his name had been garbled as Jean Metaux – he still sighed 'patience, patience, I must persevere so that I can take revenge one day' [*Diary*, II, p.512]. The following month, June, his family and that of Pezmazoglou were allowed to proceed from Corsica to Marseilles, the first leg in their journey to join Metaxas in Italy. But Metaxas still suspected the French intended to try him and his fellow-exiles before an international tribunal, and found their continued surveillance humiliating. He was grateful to Italy and the Italians for refusing to turn him over to the French, and for helping to bring his family to join him in Italy. 'We must be grateful to Italy; I shall never forget that it saved us.' Mrs Nazou was all the time pressing the government to speed up his family's transfer to Sienna. However in early July 1919 the European press was already alluding to the exiled Greek monarch's impending return to Greece, and there was the first news of Greek reverses in Asia Minor. In mid-July, Metaxas reported that the people considered Venizelos 'as having destroyed Hellenism in Asia Minor . . .' [*Diary*, II, p.527].

The French authorities finally relented and handed the wife of Metaxas her passport enabling her to join him in Sienna. Before that her passport was available only if she went directly from Corsica back to Greece. Highly instrumental in the transfer of Metaxas to Sienna on mainland Italy was Mrs Aspasia Nazou: she mobilized the help of Galli, Tittoni and many others in the Nitti Government. On 15 July 1919, the exiles were reunited with their families in Sienna, where they stayed for a year. But soon Metaxas found forced idleness in Sienna unbearable; he longed to be active again. The causes of his fears and anxieties remained, viz., the trials of his anti-Venizelist colleagues in Athens, prominent among them the leading staff officers of GHQ, including himself. Strategos and Exadaktylos were acquitted, Dousmanis sentenced to life imprisonment, Metaxas to death. 'I am proud and depressed' Metaxas exclaimed in his *Diary* on 14 February 1920, 'Yes, I am their enemy, and I haven't surrendered.' But what really depressed Metaxas about Sienna was the loss of his freedom; the absence of an ideal. Everything had crashed, and it is this demolition of confidence and beliefs which tortured Metaxas most cruelly. Wholly taken up with his family, and making up for missed Greek school by teaching his little daughters the rudiments of the Greek language, Metaxas had less time to brood over his situation or to think about political developments at home. Within less than a month of the resumption of his freedom of movement Metaxas visited the exiled King in Milan and discussed with him the political situation in Greece.

It is interesting that a contemporary chronicler of these events regretted the fact that Greece offered no other civilian politician as powerful and forceful as Venizelos to counter his influence and policy. This pushed GHQ Army Staff Officers such as Metaxas, surrounding the King, to become deeply involved in politics. According to Philip Dragoumis only the King's personality and moral authority kept them at bay.[2] The diarist Philip Dragoumis incidentally belonged to the extreme wing of Constantinists and Hellenic irredentism, and cultural anti-Westerners: 'We must save our part of the world from Frankish enslavement.' And it was Venizelos who brought about a Western occupation of Greece in the Great War – the treason of Venizelos. Between 1917 and 1920 the Venizelos regime was imposed on the Greeks by foreign bayonets, leading to a regime of terror that conducted an extensive purge of the Army, the bureaucracy and the judiciary. In his Memoirs, Timos Malanos, who had lived in Alexandria for sixty years (1906–66), reports that among the papers of the lawyer George Rousos, a leading supporter of Venizelos and agent of his rebel government (1916–20) in Alexandria was evidence of the pressure brought to bear on the Greeks in Egypt to support the rebel Venizelos Government against that of the King in Athens. The element of blackmail lay in the fact that the Venizelos National Defence Government was supported by the Entente Powers, Britain and France, when the British were also masters of the political situation in Egypt. A comment that tends to support the claim by Philip Dragoumis in his *Diary*.[3] It did though provoke the opposition of the Greeks who turned to the support of the King, especially when they suspected Venizelos was undoing the accomplishments of three generations of Greeks, and they became worked up about saving their civilization from Frankish control. By then in any case the Entente Powers were veering towards the support of Atatürk's new Turkey, the Italians pressed for their interests in South-west Asia Minor, Albania and Epirus, and the Bulgarians were demanding plebiscites for autonomy in Macedonia. In short, the Greeks as well as Venizelos himself felt hemmed in on all sides. Dragoumis concluded by describing the situation in Greece as one of tyranny,[4] while popular support for the King grew. And so finally the Greeks preferred the return of their King from exile to the throne over the promises of Venizelos. These conditions converged with the Allied pressure for the release by the Venizelos regime of political detainees.

Metaxas held a central position among the anti-Venizelist forces, led by the King and including George Streit, D. Gounaris and S. Mercouris. Some in fact considered Metaxas the brains behind the whole constellation, with Queen Sophia, sister of the Kaiser, his main ally and supporter. This array of forces held, incidentally, throughout the Asia Minor debacle. Some claim Metaxas had a mephistophelian strategy, especially when he launched his small political party (*Eleftherophrones*) for he foresaw the fall of Gounaris and his close collaborator Stratos when he could construct his favourite stratopolitocracy against both Venizelists and the old, discredited political parties and thus have a free hand in promoting German interests throughout southeastern Europe and eastwards to Suez (Germany's *Drang Nach Osten?*).

Metaxas had lived in a twilight period from 1915 to 1917 and again from 1917 to 1920, mainly in exile. During this period he had no military function or role, and was not engaged politically. Upon returning to

Greece after the elections of November 1920, Metaxas was bitter but free to act politically. He was unpopular among his erstwhile fellow exiles, Gounaris and others, who managed quickly at first and only temporarily to marginalize, if not neutralize him politically. Restoration to his old military status was typical and perfunctory since he himself sought retirement from the Army with the rank of Major General almost immediately. It seems though that Metaxas sought to detach himself from the rest of the main body of anti-Venizelist politicians too, including the Gounaris government for he insisted that his quarrel with Venizelism went beyond his opposition to Venizelos the politician himself; it was complemented by concrete positive views about and perception of the great problems of Greece. After all, he did disagree fundamentally with the continuation of the doomed expedition in Asia Minor under the leadership of the post-November 1920 royalist governments. Metaxas plainly opposed his erstwhile political allies who were now in power and in control of a war against Atatürk's Turkey in Asia Minor which he was convinced would end in a national catastrophe and said so publicly.

NOTES

1.   He joined the Hesiod Lodge in Athens in 1917. In a typewritten memorandum in the Metaxas Private Papers, G. Rammos comments about Metaxas the Freemason, as well as his spiritual world. He notes that Metaxas became a Freemason in 1917 when he was a Colonel in the Engineer Corps. He advanced rapidly up the Freemason hierarchy of degrees, and was soon a 'Most Reverend' in the Hesiod Lodge in Athens. Rammos judged Metaxas to be an optimist, with encyclopaedic knowledge and a strong will; someone who believed the world can become better through struggle that overcomes obstacles. In his view Metaxas was an intellectual who believed 'perfection, not happiness, was the aim of life'. He carved out his destiny: he did not know the end, but believed in the route he had carved to it.
2.   P. Dragoumis, *Diary: Alexandria 1916*, Athens, 1984, p.48.
3.   T. Malanos, *Memories of an Alexandrine*, Athens, 1971, pp.54–5.
4.   P. Dragoumis, *Diary: Dichasmos, 1916–19*, Athens, 1971, p.447.

8

Entry into Politics and Second Exile, 1920–24

I

In order to enumerate the baggage of apprehensions Metaxas carried back with him to Greece from exile it is necessary to go back briefly to his life in Sienna. Although happy that his family was with him, Metaxas found Sienna a medieval town, and in July 1919 was already fretting about moving on. He sought the assistance of Theotokis in order to move to Switzerland, explaining that he wanted to come out from the narcosis of the past and to enter a contemporary town with a new exciting life. Quietude and filial happiness he felt created a kind of ambivalence and uncertainty. He also thought long about injustice in society, and how the working classes sought a more equal distribution of goods. At that time he believed that it was in the interest of the bourgeois classes which represented the prevailing political system to encourage nationalist ideas and the presence of a bogy, a major threat, to them – in this case, Germany. Throughout that summer and autumn of 1919 Metaxas followed the courts martial and other trials of his colleagues and friends in Greece, and kept in touch with Rousos and his wife's brother Babis regarding the protection and management of his and Lela's financial and property interests. He discovered too that he would not be granted a pension if he retired from the Army then; and records in his *Diary* on Sunday, 17 August 1919 his trial *in absentia* for high treason along with Dousmanis, Strategos and others, and worried about the confiscation of his property and other assets. By September though Metaxas was leading a normal family life: 'Tonight we dined together as a family for the first time since October 1916' [*Diary*, II, p.546]. He was receiving mail regularly from Greece, perusing Greek and other newspapers, frequenting the theatre and enjoying sightseeing tours. He was buoyed too by the waning star of Venizelos. In late September 1919 however Metaxas was unwell with a bout of pharyngitis, tonsillitis and fever. But on the last day of September, Metaxas confesses that in spite of Lela's and the children's comforting presence he saw a dark future ahead of him. Medieval Sienna depressed him and he wanted to leave [*Diary*, II, pp.551–2]. He was again worried over finances, and adds, 'I have become cowardly, hesitant and inactive' [*Diary*, II, p.555]. In October–November 1919, Metaxas received visits from relatives and political friends who reported growing popular opposition to Venizelos's tyranny.

While following reports in the Greek press of his own trial in Greece, there was occasion for Metaxas to comment on his erstwhile boss and mentor Colonel Dousmanis, who was also on trial for treason, hinting at his envy and petty rivalry, and the testimony of others against him. He also commented on the elections of November 1919 as marking the defeat of the bourgeois class and the death of the old society. On the whole, though, 1919 closed with a depressed, thoroughly demoralized and discouraged Metaxas in exile, albeit one content with his family life. Events in Europe and Turkey were to affect indirectly the greatest shift in the political fortunes of Metaxas. The success of Atatürk in Turkey influenced the relations and growing differences between the major Allies in their respective policies in the East. Venizelos expanded Greek aims in Asia Minor, the Treaty of Sèvres of 10 August 1920 vindicated his territorial or irredendist ambitions, and therefore his policy since 1914. And yet the divisions among the Greeks persisted as deep and sharp as ever. Thus the ostensible success of Venizelos pushed his rivals and opponents to acts of extreme desperation, culminating in the attempt on his life at the Gare de Lyons in Paris. The Venizelists reacted with great fury, their punishment of anti-Venizelists culminating in the cold blooded execution of Ion Dragoumis.[1]

Then came the disastrous defeat of Venizelos in the elections of 14 November 1920, and the Greek public was in utter political confusion. But it is suggested by the *Diary* of Metaxas that the political exiles in Italy may have had a major role in this electoral result. One must be careful though and treat any such suggestions with caution, for they are no more than conjecture and speculation. What is more certain is the emotional–psychological condition of Metaxas during that time: he was not only depressed, but also deplored the lack of interest of Gounaris and others in him: 'They all forgot me; I have been wiped out – erased – from Greece' [*Diary*, II, p.631]. Yet come 23 November 1920 and Metaxas is back in Greece, only to discover that the new Prime Minister Gounaris does not intend to use him, and he is now therefore completely disillusioned, and intends to stay away from the centre of politics. On 25 December 1920 his promotion to Major General is gazetted and his retirement from the Army is published.

But nothing was quite as simple with Metaxas in those days. The previous April he was already referring in his *Diary* to the prospect of standing for a parliamentary seat [*Diary*, II, p.591]. At the same time his concern for his property and income continued. He remained in frequent touch with the leading conservative politician Theotokis, even though it was also a time of recurrent illness in the family. To be sure it was clear he did not like Sienna: 'Sienna has shattered us' [*Diary*, II, pp.600, 630]. It was in Florence in the autumn of 1920 that Metaxas recorded yet more of his ideas and random thoughts about Greece. Starting off with his condemnation of political parties for seeking power for egotistical reasons, he remarked that ever since 1821 the Greek people had never been sovereign, only a small minority of which till 1909 came from the national masses and was linked to the people by personal ties; only one class served the national cause, or interest. But after 1890 the ties of this elite or ruling class with the people were loosened, until it was overthrown in 1909 by a new class or elite based on professional skill and merit, not on its record in the national struggle as the previous one had been. Now this ruling class had become tyrannical, and the people have no close links or ties with it, and they are therefore alienated from the exercise of sovereignty. When in 1916 the people wanted, for the first time, to become sovereign again, the ruling class sought the assistance and protection of foreign power allies and friends and maintained its position by force. Most interesting in this connection is the assertion by Metaxas that there is only one political party in Greece, the 'bourgeois party', which is national and liberal. 'It is the only party in Greece since independence; there is no other. The Greek worker is not by nature inclined towards socialism, rather he is a candidate for a petty bourgeois rather than a proletarian' [*Diary*, II, p.638]. He insisted that the only difference between any parties was the personality of their leaders. And still he remained ambivalent: 'They have all forgotten me', he recorded on 16 November 1920. 'So much the better for it is a time to be morally rechristened and to remain clean, untainted by the tumult of the mania for glory' [*Diary*, II, p.640].

II

What really preoccupied him upon his return to Greece was his financial situation – pension, property, investments. With no faith in his State employment and political prospects Metaxas assured his wife that his first priority was the rearrangement and management of their finances [*Diary*, II, p.645]. While a passionate public hatred of Venizelos permeated the country, Metaxas told anyone who would listen that he would not return to active Army duty under any circumstances, nor would he accept appointment to any public office [*Diary*, II, p.646]. In a subsequent letter to Lela at the end of November 1920, Metaxas reported his visit to his father's grave as well as the graves of several politicians, such as those of Gounaris and Eslin. He wrote her that there was no talk whatever about jobs or a parliamentary seat, and he felt that all that there was left for him to do was to take care of their personal–family affairs, and assured her that the monthly pension of a Major-General would be 700–800 drachmas, and outlined his plans for the building up of their property holdings and assets portfolio, including his collaboration with a German business firm, and finally totted up their potential monthly income as follows: pension, 800; shop lets, 700; house let, 1,700; income from stocks and shares, 900; making up a total of 4,200 drachmas, a respectable monthly income. In considering how they might settle down and retire in Athens, Metaxas referred to the very high cost of living there and outlines the options of rented accommodation available to them. He considered it the right time in their married life to think of arranging their estate matters in such a way as to secure their financial future. On his first visit to his family in Cephalonia since his return from exile, Metaxas reassured Lela that he made it clear to his political friends and well-wishers on the island that he was not interested in contesting a parliamentary seat. He did however vote on the referendum for the Restoration, and repeated his belief that financial security was a prerequisite for any future political plans, conceding in this connection his mother's inordinate ambition that had influenced his own life and career [*Diary*, II, p.655]. He told Lela in passing that he hesitated settling down in Europe because of a devalued drachma. On the whole, his letters to his wife at this time are arguably the most political. Thus in describing the enthusiastic reception of the returning King and princes Metaxas for the first time openly confesses that he had founded the notorious paramilitary *Clubs of Epistratoi*, 'to my eternal glory', and what good material the simple people are [*Diary*, II, p.664].[2] In another letter he tells Lela that the three main matters that occupy him, home, pension and employment, will be resolved after the return of the King. And yet while in Cephalonia he went on a tour of the island and founded a Popular Political Club in the capital Argostoli. In his letter to Lela in early January 1921 however Metaxas sounds more withdrawn and detached from the company of his old colleagues, from the royal princes and Athenian society in general. His main concern at that time remained that of maximizing his income. He affects a new determination not to be as amenable with royalty and colleagues: 'I am no longer the good old Yannakis, the good boy who never denied favours to anyone. This is all behind me' [*Diary*, II, p.677]. And yet profound contradiction characterizes his behaviour: having secured a house to rent in Neon Faliron, and arranged to rent his own existing property in Patissia, Metaxas does not cease to cultivate his contacts especially with the industrialist Kanellopoulos (a member of that family was later to become an Executive Director of the Metaxas National Youth Organization, *EON*) and his political and Army cronies as if he were still job hunting and politicking [*Diary*, II, pp.676–8].

III

On 17 November 1920, a week after the elections which Venizelos lost, Dimitris Gounaris, the recognized leader of the anti-Venizelist camp, cabled Metaxas summoning him back to Greece from his Italian exile in Florence. Metaxas was back in Athens in a matter of days, only to discover after several hours of discussions with Gounaris, his erstwhile fellow-exile in Corsica, Sardinia, and mainland Italy and now Minister of Army Affairs in the new Zaimis Government that his expert professional military services were not required after all. Perhaps this was just as well since Metaxas was, in any case, opposed to the new government's – and Gounaris's – policy of persevering with the military expedition against the Turks in Asia Minor. Moreover, he had just retired from the Army with the rank of Major-General, marking the end of a thirty year long military career. Metaxas was forty-nine years old and about to embark on a fitful, controversial and contentious political career. Nor was Metaxas too enthusiastic about this 'new beginning' in his life. Upon arrival in Greece from his three-year exile, he hazards an immediate comment, 'The Greek people is great indeed, but the ruling class is inept and ridiculous, and deserves to be booed' [*Diary*, II, p.641].

For the next fifteen years or so, from 1920 to 1935, Metaxas will, after some hesitation, and tergiversation, as well as a very serious illness, play an active, often leading role in the parliamentary and party politics of the country, in the struggle for the capture of the new constellation of social forces in Greece, the control of the military establishment and Army Officer Corps, including the recriminations over the National Schism, the contest between Republican Liberal Venizelists and Conservative Monarchist Constantinists.

The new year, 1921, began inauspiciously. He had spent the months of November and December 1920 in Greece without his family, who had stayed behind in Florence. In January 1921 he complained of persistent dizziness – the first or earliest signs of cardiovascular trouble? After a preliminary exploratory visit to Germany he failed to find a satisfactory job in private business, and he was still trying to sell his house in Patisia. The Popular Political Club he had founded in Argostoli in December 1920 was gathering momentum and generating typical political problems. It constituted the earliest indication that Metaxas planned a political career, especially as it was followed by the launching of the *Epistratoi Clubs* and finally the *Eleftherophrones* political party. He developed a close relationship with Nico and Angelo Kanellopoulos who were in private business. He sold the family home at 152 Patision, the main part of his wife's dowry, where they had lived as newlyweds and till his first exile in 1917. The combination of a bout of illness (Metaxas complained of stomach trouble again on 14 February 1920), the sale of his first family home and the renting of new residential premises for the family at Neon Faliron elicited some sentimentalism in Metaxas – a recurring feature with him – recalling all the family events since his marriage associated with the Patision home [*Diary*, III, p.65] which had just been sold to a certain P. (Peter?) Goulandris – probably of the shipping family by that name from Andros. And still he found time to revive and strengthen his ties with the Royal Court: 'In the evening at 7 we were received by the King and the Queen, proof of their goodwill, kindness and benevolence' [*Diary*, III, p.67], and attended the wedding of Princess Helen to the Crown Prince of Romania (subsequently King Carol of Romania).

The steady relentless process of the greater involvement in politics of Metaxas is reflected in the series of talks to the Popular Political Clubs he had founded and the repeated efforts of his political friends – e.g. Theotokis and others – to draft him into political office. The Group of Radical Reformers (*Metarythmistes*), one of the forerunners of the *Eleftherophrones* party founded by Metaxas in 1922–24, was the occasion for a frantic spate of letter writing and other pieces by Metaxas in the press. Worthy of note is the use Metaxas made of old acquaintances and contacts going back to his early Army days, including the *Berlinkriegsakademie*, as well as those he acquired while in exile. He did though successfully resist all attempts to lure him back to the staff of GHQ so long as the disastrous Asia Minor campaign lasted. What eventually defined the rough outline of his future political career were the dramatic–tragic events of 1922–23, the scuttle from Asia Minor and the military revolt led by General Plastiras to defend the deteriorating Venizelist position against the Constantinists, using the charge of treason against the leaders of the latter, the political leaders and military commanders who took over the direction and management of the Asia Minor adventure from the Venizelists after the elections of November 1920; trying and executing several of them.[3] The King in the meantime had reinstated the old mentor of Metaxas, Victor Dousmanis, as his Chief of Staff during this catastrophic adventure. Metaxas did fret over his moral position in declining to serve his country as an army officer, but he was convinced he was right in recommending a policy of reconciliation with the Turks. Gounaris however attacked Metaxas in the newspapers – such as *Protevousa* – for refusing to take part and share in the responsibility for the Asia Minor military operations. But Metaxas on the surface at least remained unconcerned and instead increased his visits to his relatives, his extended family in Athens and Cephalonia; while despite his doubts or misgivings, he carried on with his political contacts behind the scenes. An important link for Metaxas with the Establishment at this time continued to be that of Prince Andreas, Dr Yeroulanos (later Professor of Medicine and Surgery at the University of Athens, and his personal physician), and George Kouratos, subsequently Private Secretary to Metaxas. The month of May 1921 was crowded with a fierce debate in the correspondence columns of the press between Metaxas and his main critic Gounaris and his clique. Amidst all of this he records his impression that the main strength of the Greeks is their intelligence, not their character [*Diary*, III, p.108], and he still found politics personally unattractive, even offensive, and complains, 'When instead of national dreams, fantasies, the Greeks acquire national objectives, only then will they be able to create a lively state in the East ...' (30 June, 1921) [*Diary*, III, p.116]. In July 1921 he already knew Nicoloudis at the newspaper *Politeia*. Nicoloudis served as Minister of Press and Publicity in the Metaxas 4th August Regime.

Clearly though Metaxas was undergoing yet another life crisis: with the loss of gainful employment after his resignation and retirement from the Army, he was unsure if a political career was right for him. 'About to finish reading Carlyle', he records in his *Diary* on 1 September 1921, 'I have had such a great book around me for so long and did not realize it' [*Diary*, III, p.125]. (One wonders how many other Greeks of that period or since then were aware of, let alone have read, Carlyle). He watches the national economic and political difficulties looming large on the horizon, 'and yet people refuse to abandon the Byzantine dream. How can I intervene? Would not public intervention lead me to ruin?' [*Diary*, III, p.126]. In mid-September 1921, Metaxas noted the weakening of the government, the failure of the Asia Minor policy of all governments since January 1915, and yet the allure, the magic of the Byzantine dream continued to possess the public and the masses. Yet, he claimed public attention was turning to him as he became active via Rallis and others in ending the Asia Minor adventure as soon as possible, and continued to write in the correspondence columns of *Nea Imera* and *Chronika*. Kouratos, one of his closest aides, encouraged him to consider launching a new publication, a newspaper with the backing of the Group of Radical Reformers in order to counter the opposition of such politicians as Theotokis and others, and to get closer to Kotzias with his *Chronika* newspaper. But he was also in financial difficulties and therefore seeking to encash more of the dwindling family stocks and shares.

On 9 November 1921 Metaxas reports a gathering of his party's nucleus, comprising, among others, C. Kotzias, owner of the newspaper *Chronika*, Alex Vamvesos, lawyer and politician from Trikkala, G. Haritakis, Professor at the Higher School of Commerce, Y. Septsiotis, Director of Merchant Marine in the Ministry of National Economy, Yannis Sagias, politician and government minister, D. Rediadis, lawyer and later government minister (Minister of Finance) in the 4th August administration of Metaxas, and Speros Stavropoulos, a lawyer. George Vlachos, founder and publisher of *Kathimerini* newspaper, approached Metaxas with a view to some kind of political collaboration, but Metaxas further intrigued with his political friends in the Freemasons Lodge, especially with Radical Reformers and Rediadis. He also established a publication line and connection with the media, especially *Nea Imera* and *Chronika* which undertook to support him. Kotzias meanwhile pressed Metaxas to open a political office in Athens, but Metaxas found it would be too costly – 36,000 drachmas per annum. Throughout the last week of November 1921 Metaxas was busy fixing political deals with the Radical Reformers, while the Popular Political Clubs remained the nucleus of his political programme for the moment. On 11 December 1921 Metaxas mentions a report about his political party in the Free Press (*Eleftheros Typos*), and at a meeting with Rediadis he puts the finishing touches to his political programme, and *Nea Imera* publishes more

1. Ioannis Metaxas as boy of about nine or ten.
(Source: D. Kallona, *Ioannis Metaxas: Student, Soldier, Politician, Fighter, Governor-Ruler*, Athens, 1938)

2. Metaxas with fellow students, Ippocratis Papavassileou and Xenophon Strategos at the Berlinkriegsakademie, Berlin, 1902.
(Source: ELIA [Hellenic society of Literary and Historical Archives], Athens)

3. Portrait of Metaxas when he was a staff captain with his wife Lela Hatziioannou.
(Source: D. Kallona, *Ioannis Metaxas: Student, Soldier, Politician, Fighter, Governor-Ruler*, Athens, 1938)

4. *Above:* Formal portrait of Metaxas as a Captain, 1910.
   (Source: *Diary of Ioannis Metaxas*, Vol. 2, Frontispiece).

5. *Below:* Metaxas and Greek delegation at the London Peace Conference
   with Turkey in 1912. Metaxas is on the extreme right in the second row
   from the top.
   (Source: *Diary of Ioannis Metaxas*, Vol. 2, p. 192)

6. *Above:* Metaxas (second from left) with Crown Prince Constantine at Emin Aga, 1913.
(Source: *Diary of Ioannis Metaxas*, Vol. 2, p. 200)

7. *Below:* Siege of Yanina, 1913. Metaxas, who was one of Crown Prince Constantine's staff officers, is standing on the right.
(Source: *Diary of Ioannis Metaxas*, Vol. 2, p. 200)

8. *Above:* Grand Hotel, Ajaccio, Corsica, where Metaxas and family lived in exile, 1917–18.
(Source: *Diary of Ioannis Metaxas*, Vol. 2, p. 456)

9. *Below:* Family picture of Metaxas, his wife and two daughters in exile in Corsica, 1918.
(Source: *Diary of Ioannis Metaxas*, Vol. 2, p. 456)

10. *Above:* Metaxas with King George II during manoeuvres, 1937.
(Source: *Diary of Ioannis Metaxas*, Vol. 4, p. 267)

11. *Below:* Metaxas with King George II (a rare photograph of a monarch who never smiled).
(Source: ELIA, Athens)

12. *Above:* Metaxas with his Minister for Athens, Costas Kotzias, on his left, inspecting Ilisos River public works in July 1937. Standing behind is the Minister Elias Krimbas.
(From the private archive of the late Elias Krimbas, kindly made available by his son, Professor George Krimbas)

13. *Below:* Group photo of the Council of Ministers after the occupation of Argyrokastron in 1940.
(From the private archive of the late Elias Krimbas, kindly made available by his son, Professor George Krimbas)

14. *Above:* Laying the foundation stone of the Children's Sanatorium for Tuberculosis in Pendeli, 19 October 1940.
    (From the private archive of the late Elias Krimbas, kindly made available by his son, Professor George Krimbas)

15. *Below:* Metaxas with members of his government, National (Independence) Day, 25 March 1940.
    (From the private archive of the late Elias Krimbas, kindly made available by his son, Professor George Krimbas)

16. Return from Thessaloniki, 7 February 1940.
(From the private archive of the late Elias Krimbas, kindly made available by his son, Professor George Krimbas)

17. Portrait of Metaxas as Prime Minister in his office.
(Source: ELIA, Athens)

18. Last photograph with the 'Leader', 1 January 1941.
(From the private archive of the late Elias Krimbas, kindly made available by his son, Professor George Krimbas)

about it. Metaxas is now politically detached and separate from the anti-Venizelists in government. Actually the whole of the second half of 1921 was full of frantic political activity, while he kept in touch with Prince Andreas, especially about Asia Minor. Thus the reader of the Metaxas *Diary* entries for December 1921 gets the impression of intense political activity on the part of Metaxas. He himself describes 1921 as a 'strange year'. On the same day of the previous year, he recalls, 'I was returning from Florence politically marginalized, but determined to follow my honourable course. The government's policy to carry on with the doomed expedition in Asia Minor forced me to take a stand, and my course has been anomalous ever since, yet I enjoy total family happiness' [*Diary*, III, p.148].

It was Metaxas himself though who the moment he felt forgotten or ignored tried with all means at his disposal to relocate himself in the attention of other politicians and the public, mainly by a campaign in the press. 'I feel I am being forgotten, so I wrote an article in *Chronika*', and from his *Diary* entries in January 1922 Metaxas appeared up to his ears in national as well as Church politics (given that the election of the new Ecumenical Patriarch Meletios Metaxakis, a known Venizelist and Freemason, was one of the juiciest, and most controversial, political issues of the day), and continued to weave his web of political alliances even though he wondered if people wanted him. Thus he records in his *Diary* on Tuesday, 18 January 1922, 'political matters morning and afternoon' [*Diary*, III, pp.151, 152]. He came under fierce attack in the newspapers *Embros* and *Protevousa* for his alleged sacrifice of Asia Minor in order to save Thrace. Metaxas answered his critics in *Chronika* and *Estia*, and continued to lobby politicians and government ministers for his preferred policy of military withdrawal from Asia Minor. In doing so, Metaxas also tried to alienate Theotokis from Gounaris, and became part of active conspiracies to topple the Gounaris government, either under Theotokis or others. But at the end of the week on 5–6 February 1922, Metaxas was again rueing not having kept his distance from all of this, especially as he took to reading fiction and went through a bad patch over his younger daughter's illness with a suspected heart condition but actually a case of tuberculosis. He still considered the national situation had deteriorated, but thought he could not really get involved with the politicians in power he considered crooked (*apateones*) and who conducted a national policy he had no faith in. 'I was forced on to the road of politics by people and events, not by my own impulse or passion, for at this moment I am doubtful' [*Diary*, III, p.155]. He found that the public still chased after nationalist fantasies, dreams, and his own doubts and reluctance in that respect rendered him unpopular, unwelcome, bad news. On 14 February, Metaxas reported that he was criticized as indecisive because he had no political party. But 'it seems my friends are in a great hurry, especially the newspaper *Chronika* which hopes through me to increase its circulation'.

When at the end of February Stratos sought his participation in a new government, Metaxas demurred because there was no support in parliament for it, and suggested that the government should either resign or be succeeded by one of national unity, or an all-party one. But Metaxas gives his fully fledged political game away when he reports that after consulting his political supporters in *Chronika* and the Radical Reformers – i.e., the nucleus of his new *Eleftherophrones* political party, he concluded he could not collaborate with the Gounarists, as some of the anti-Venizelists came to be known [*Diary*, III, p.159].

What Metaxas considered to be a political crisis continued in March 1922, and he expressed his revulsion at the state of the political world he was living in; he wished he had no political party – a regret expressed almost immediately after Metaxas founded *Eleftherophrones*. Many of his followers and supporters now considered the latest proposal of a movement for an autonomous Greek entity in Asia Minor as a political salvage operation following military defeat – a scheme thought out initially by the organization 'National Defence' in Constantinople,[4] but which came to naught. Stated differently, the Greeks there already saw the catastrophic end of Greek military policy and sought to limit the damage to themselves. But Metaxas himself was very cautious and circumspect about the plan, despite his claim that his popularity was rising. Then the last hurrah of the Gounaris government for a military operation to grab Constantinople failed, as it was partly thwarted by the Allies themselves, who called for a Peace Summit in Venice in August 1922,[5] after Kemal Atatürk had launched his attack on Afion Karahissar. 'Dreadful catastrophe', Metaxas remarked on Saturday, 20 August. 'The tragic end of our military acme which began in 1908, reached its zenith in 1912–13, and was buried today; it is all my history' [*Diary*, III, p.185]. Atatürk entered Smyrna on 27 August 1922.

In connection with the rout of the Greek Army in Asia Minor, it is odd indeed, albeit interesting, that while Metaxas insisted that the defeated Army should remain loyal to the State, and the Greeks in Asia Minor should proclaim their own autonomy, he was also 'studying Einstein', reading Homer's *Iliad*, and the modern poetry of Costis Palamas

[*Diary*, III, p.163]. In his meetings with Army officers Metaxas discovered they were anxious for a more active involvement in politics, and they complained about his own circumspection and hesitation in this respect. He explained that if Stergiadis, Greek High Commissioner in Smyrna, was dubious about the plan of Greek autonomy in Asia Minor and the British were opposed to it, he remained opposed to it too. Furthermore, he advised the officers to keep quiet especially since the Greek Army could not evacuate Asia Minor until and when the security of the Greek population there was guaranteed by serious and firm international agreements. He told Army officers that only then would he consider becoming a minister in a National Unity or All-Party Coalition government, but not one of a political party; and then only if he agreed with that government about events and developments [*Diary*, III, p.167].

As the political crisis worsened and the prospect of a National Coalition or an all-party government seemed likely, Metaxas carried on with his political manoeuvring behind the scenes during the following month. Gounaris and Stratos formed a government with twenty ministers. It was reported to Metaxas that when he was proposed as a minister Gounaris became furious; the antipathy between the two men had really grown. Metaxas all the same carried on with further political jockeying, especially as regards the possibility of cooperation with Stergiadis over the Greek occupation of Constantinople and the creation of an autonomous Greek entity; but he was also urgently concerned closer to home with the autonomy of Thrace and Smyrna [*Diary*, III, pp.171–3]. His machinations, his activities, reached further into the Royal Court, assuming the King might impose him upon the new government. His Cephalonian friends were also active in promoting the funding of a newspaper and raising funds in the UK, Egypt and the USA for the Metaxas cause.

In mid-June 1922, Metaxas reports yet another stomach complaint, which tended to recur during periods of intensive political activity and anxiety, including intense debate in the media [*Diary*, III, p.175]. Later in the month, on 20 August 1922, there were rumours the King would entrust Metaxas with the formation of a government. 'I saw Prince Andreas who told me the King was influenced in favour of Stergiadis, and asked me for my reply – if I agree or not – to convey back to the King. I answered that I accept, but the King must dispatch Papoulas to the front.' At the same time Kotzias urged Metaxas to use force to implement policy, but Metaxas ruled out any disturbances: 'Above all else I am a Greek' [*Diary*, III, p.185], bearing in mind the unseemly sight of a split party in power earlier in the spring, and everyone looking after his own personal interest. On top of all that Gounaris accused Metaxas of having destroyed the Army's morale. In reply Metaxas got busy preparing the media and other grounds of his own defence. In order to prevent his being asked to form a government, the Gounaris, Stratos, Protopapadakis group put it about that the French and other Allied powers would sever relations with a Metaxas government. Metaxas however got Bentinck, Political Counsellor of the British Embassy to deny any such intention. Still the political moves against Metaxas persisted. At this point the number and pattern of frantic contacts and exchanges between Metaxas and his supporters and others is too great and complex. He is busy countering charges of Germanophilism and other accusations regarding Thrace and Asia Minor. The fact remains that the political crisis was moving quickly to some kind of climax, and that there was a concerted effort to prevent Metaxas from acceding to power, while he himself was engaged in a parallel effort to retain his independent political role in any new developments, including Army coups.

The Plastiras-led revolt broke out in Mitylene the morning of 13 September 1922, accompanied by a vehement attack on the King and the arrest of the political and military leaders of the anti-Venizelist government during the closing phase of the Asia Minor debacle, Gounaris, Stratos, Protopapadakis, Theotokis, Papoulas, Hatzianestis, and others. Metaxas advised the King to abdicate quickly. The rebels, he believed, were determined to force the King out ('The Crown Prince keeps me near him for he feels the need of my counsel') [*Diary*, III, p.198]. Metaxas and his supporters were now faced with the clear intention of the rebels to expel the King, and to try and execute several of the monarchist politicians and soldiers. Metaxas published his reaction to the Plastiras-led revolt in the newspapers with wide repercussions. General Stylianos Gonatas, one of the Revolution Triumvirate, warned Metaxas he was under suspicion. Actually that autumn Metaxas was accused in the Venizelist press of pro-Italian leanings; in that tense political atmosphere, Metaxas feared for his life and believed some plotted his assassination, but continued to consider arrangements for an election, writing virulent pieces in the press which also publicized his own political programme. But the new revolutionary regime proceeded with the arrest of the so-called traitors: 'I am prepared to die for the freedom of the people', Metaxas scribbled as he was still threatened with arrest [*Diary*, III, p.202].

The impression from the entries in the *Diary* for October 1922 is one

of a greatly agitated, apprehensive, really scared, Metaxas in the face of
the new revolutionary regime's threatened purge of the Gounaris–
Stratos administration and the deposition and exile of King Constantine.
With Men on Horseback in control and on the rampage, Metaxas slept
badly, sought consolation for his years in exile, and tried to ensure his
privileged position with the Royal Court through the new monarch,
King George II, and his uncle Prince Andreas. He faced difficulties in
financing his new small political party, especially as Kotzias was no longer
able to afford the use of his paper *Chronika*, and sighs revealingly, 'If it
were not for the Cephalonians', who clearly bankrolled his political
programme and activities [*Diary*, III, p.204]. He was looking for office
space for the party. In the meantime, he published an article in *Politeia*,
'The National Crisis and Tomorrow's Electoral Problem', in which he
argued the need for a new anti-Venizelist political constellation, not
linked or tied to the class-bound political parties of the past. Metaxas
was actually after three things: (1) to establish his credentials as leader
of the only credible opposition to the Venizelist forces; (2) somehow to
get accepted as the leader of a constitutional political party, a credible
parliamentarian who though a known erstwhile monarchist was now
committed to a constitutional parliamentary republic; and (3) that he
stood for compromise and reconciliation between the two major feuding
political camps of the National Schism, especially over the control of the
Army Officer Corps, for the sake of the restoration of political normality,
stable government, and a democratic state.

The programme of the new *Eleftherophrones* party founded by Metaxas
after he returned from his first exile was published in the newspaper *Nea
Imera* on 13 October 1922. It was prefaced by a critique of Greek political
life before and after the elections of November 1920, a condemnation
of the governing and administrative record of the past. It emphasized
the promotion of the interests and ideological orientation of the agrarian
and petty bourgeois classes, as well as the interests of the working class.
It accepted the retention of the monarchy as essential to the national
interest, but at the same time also strengthening and promoting the
popular character of the political regime of the country. Interesting in
this published Manifesto is the party's intention to expand and secure
individual civil liberties, and the economic well-being of all the Greeks.
In its foreign policy the party undertook to continue to strive for the
liberation of the as yet unredeemed Greeks, strengthen the country's ties
with its Balkan allies, and so on. The Manifesto then went on to list
detailed programmes of its agricultural policy, its support for the

professional classes, employees of the public and private sectors, shipping and industry; its approach to labour legislation, its taxation, public finance and public economic policies, education and the Armed Forces. There were already in this published Manifesto several indications of concrete reforms and changes Metaxas believed were necessary. Thus under education, he proposed to introduce six forms of secondary schooling and to increase the number of vocational schools in middle education, by reducing those of the classical curriculum.[6]

The charges against those arrested by the Revolutionary government were drafted and published by Pangalos in the press on 26 October 1922. There was also an attack on Metaxas who now felt seriously threatened and yet continued his political activity. He remained dubious about British help over this crisis. The execution of the so-called Six caused widespread horror in Europe and a revulsion against Greece. Prince Andreas, who was also tried and sentenced to death, made the position of Metaxas even more precarious. Luckily Captain Talbot commanding a British warship snatched Prince Andreas and his family from Corfu and carried them off to safety, away from the gallows or the firing squad. There was further radicalization of the Revolution fanatics and the wider spread of fear while Greece was trying to negotiate the end of its quarrel with Turkey. Britain was seeking closer relations with Turkey, and Venizelos was losing support, especially after the executions. Metaxas felt isolated, 'How can I cope against the Capitalist states as well as the old party politics of Venizelism and its tyranny?' [*Diary*, III, p.213]. King Constantine died in Palermo on 23 December 1922. Metaxas immediately appealed to the Gonatas government to return the King's remains to Greece for burial.

During the first half of 1923, Greece was in a twilight period between war and peace. The radicals of the Revolution headed by Pangalos, were still clamouring for war using the newly constituted Army on the Evros River. Army officers remained restless, conspiring against the new Revolutionary regime. Thus in July 1923 General Othonaios founded the Army League with a view to displacing the original leadership of the Revolution, and proclaiming an 'Uncrowned Republic'. By June 1923 it was clear the Revolution regime was aiming at elections even in the face of the obstacles presented by the conspiracies of the Army League towards unconstitutional extra-parliamentary solutions. Metaxas had to cope with both of these trends and phenomena. It was, in other words, a struggle for the nature of the regime in Greece that was to be decided by an elected Constituent Assembly. In fact by autumn 1923 Metaxas was alienated from the more traditional anti-Venizelist politicians, such as D. Rallis, with their press baron friends and allies such as George Vláchos, Aristos Cambanis, Georgios Pop and others. Their aim in any case was to prevent Metaxas from becoming leader of the anti-Venizelist camp.

Although Gonatas announced a change in the electoral law – from a proportional to a straight 50 per cent + 1 majority one – Metaxas was determined his party should contest the elections whereas other anti-Venizelist leaders declared their intention to abstain from them. There was even confusion over the purpose of the elections.[7] Among the Venizelist camp, Plastiras and Venizelos were not keen to transform the regime, but rather to restore and retain the monarchy, whereas the fanatic radicals, including officers of the Army League, wished to change the political system. However, the anti-Revolution coup led by Generals Leonardopoulos and Gargalides intervened on 20 October 1923. At this point it is difficult to determine the actual role of Metaxas, the extent of his involvement in it, especially when he was campaigning very hard for political reconciliation over the return to normal parliamentary government. Much has been made of his letter dated 4 March 1923 to one of his closest party colleagues, the lawyer and government minister Y. Spetsiotis, a founding member of the *Eleftherophrones* party, in which Metaxas set out in great detail the domestic situation, including the intrigues among politicians of the Revolution, the Revolutionary government's security and police measures; he mentioned how they did not dare arrest him, but would try instead to assassinate him, as well as the outline of his own policy, and the division between those who wished to retain a revolutionary government and those who wanted to proceed to elections of a normal parliamentary government[8] [*Diary*, III, pp.230–6 for the text of the letter]. It is significant that this letter was allegedly stolen by the security police along with other documents. There is no indication in this letter, as some have argued, that Metaxas was the actual leader of the anti-Revolution coup of 20 October 1923. He may have had prior knowledge of it as he was in touch with so many Army officers, and frequently received information about impending or aborted coups. At the time of the coup he was on an extensive election campaign tour of the Peloponnese. The more open, intensive and articulate political activity of Metaxas and his party in opposing the Revolutionary regime and aiming to make a serious dent in the promised elections may have encouraged the Army officers to mount their coup, especially as a counterweight to the emerging Pangalos/Kondylis military cabal with clear dictatorial prospects and intentions.

IV

During the last week of October 1923 Metaxas hoped against hope to
evade and survive his relentless pursuit by the Pangalos and Kondylis
forces in the Peloponnese. But the counter-revolution coup itself had
already failed in Macedonia. Lieut. Colonel G. Ziras who led its forces
there fled to Bulgaria. It was sinking fast in Athens and elsewhere too.
It was alleged by the anti-Revolution camp that the military leaders of
the counter coup ignored or refused to take Metaxas's advice and failed
to initiate their rebellion in Athens instead of in the provinces. In fact,
they were not all that keen on Metaxas, and were loath to allow him the
leadership of the coup. Metaxas was duly shaken: 'I think of flight,
escape.' Only two to three people were privy to his flight plans. As the
rebel army was defeated by Pangalos and Kondylis, Metaxas considered
escape by sea. And on 27 October in Corinth he boarded a Norwegian
cargo ship, the *Belize Soltenhof*, along with his wife Lela, his aide and
secretary George Kouratos, arriving in Messina at noon on 29 October
where they were not allowed to disembark.

Worried about the children they had left behind Metaxas considered
again withdrawing from public life. In the meantime, as a fugitive without
money he docked in Messina from where he wired his cousin Virginia
Colp in Palermo (daughter of his father's rich brother). But he was also
worried about his estate! With the help of a local Greek, Metaxas and
his party slipped away in the dead of night by boat to Paradiso further
north on the coast, where they were put up at the Villa Trompetta. From
there Metaxas decided to cross to Palermo to prepare for a move via
Naples to Rome, where he would attempt to contact Mussolini. Very
soon though on 2 November Metaxas reported that the news from
Athens was bad: he thought his party had been destroyed, and noted
that several anti-Venizelist leaders were opposed to him. When they
finally arrived in Rome on 4 November, Metaxas's main concern was
over how they would manage. It was also difficult to find suitable accommodation because landlords feared trouble with the police. Having
managed to outfit himself Metaxas got busy with one or two Greek
journalists in town as a means of maintaining continued contact and
communication with the Greek political world – e.g., Manos Vatalas and
Chalcokondylis. Once the authorities granted him a visa to stay in Italy,
Metaxas was very keen to meet Mussolini. A week later he was joined
by George Streit, and his efforts to reach Mussolini continued. In the
meantime, his old crony and agent Spetsiotis urged Metaxas to travel to

France. On 10 November, Metaxas succeeded in getting as far as Gianini, minister in Mussolini's office, from whom he requested some kind of diplomatic intervention on his behalf. The trip to France at the invitation of the newspaper *Le Matin* became attractive, and the funds he needed to make it were borrowed from Maximos. Spetsiotis was to arrange for the needed travel documents.

After a day or two of touring Rome's archaeological sites, the French Embassy issued Metaxas and his wife with laissez-passers. Although he was in poor health, troubled by boils, and burdened with heavy expenses, the situation was not desperate or dramatic for he remained in close touch with his associates and supporters. On Monday 19 November Metaxas met with another of his agents, Frangoulis, in Paris and spent the next few days agreeing a modus vivendi with Jouvenal of the *Matin* newspaper in preparation for his interview with it about the political situation in Greece. But he also remained in touch with the royals, namely, Princes Andreas and Nikolaos in France. In a series of interviews with Greek and French journalists, Metaxas tried to achieve a reconciliation with France and maintain himself in the forefront of Greek politics.[9] The attacks on him by the Venizelists continued, especially his association with the *Berlinkriegsakademie*, the Kaiser and his stand over the Dardanelles and Roupel. Metaxas rebutted these attacks in his interviews and statements in the French press, and his talks with French political leaders. His assistant Kouratos urged him to return to Rome in order to be closer to the grave developments in Athens. And then suddenly during the first week in December, threatened by the so-called Republic extremists, Generals Kondylis, Othonaios and Pangalos, General Plastiras sought an understanding with Metaxas, even pleading with him the need to return to active Greek politics in view of the anarchy that prevailed, and offered close collaboration between them. Plastiras claimed he wished to save the monarchy from its enemies, Pangalos, Othonaios and Kondylis.

After the elections of 16 December 1923 which formally ended the Revolution, the new Army League sought the ousting of the reigning dynasty, and inaugurated the endless series of Army coups which undermined the new Republic itself and finally buried it. It also forced the original Revolutionary leadership, as well as Venizelists in general, back to more conservative considerations such as the return to normal parliamentary government, the stabilization of the political system even if that meant an autocratic regime, a policy not so very different from that of Metaxas. But the Revolution still retained strict censorship, and rigorous police and security measures. And it was in this political atmosphere that the new party of Metaxas experienced its early participation in politics – that is, surveillance, and arrests. At the same time the Army League had forced King George II to leave Greece on 19 December 1923.[10]

NOTES

1. See the interesting book of fiction *I Ektelesi* (The Execution) by Freddy Germanos, Athens, 1987.
2. On the *Epistratoi*, see also Pangalos, *Memoirs*, pp.95–100.
3. See I.A. Peponis, *Nikolaos Plastiras sta gegonota, 1909–45*, Athens, n.d.; and *I diki ton Ex, Ta stenografimena Praktika* (The Trial of the Six: the Transcript in Shorthand, 31 October–15 November 1922), Athens, the Proia newspaper edition, 1931.
4. See General Anastasios Papoulas, *I Agonia Enos Ethnous* (The Agony of a Nation: the Military Expedition in Asia Minor according to the private papers of General Papoulas, Commander of the Greek Expeditionary Forces) by the journalist Ioannis D. Passas, Athens, 1925; and Xenophon Strategos, *I Ellas en Mikra Asia* (Greece in Asia Minor), Athens, 1925.
5. See C. Zavitsianos, *Reminiscences, op. cit.*, vol. 1, pp.134–9.
6. See text of the published Manifesto, 'The Political Programme of the Party of the Eleftherophrones', *Diary*, III, pp.778–82.
7. See Stelios Gonatas *Apomnemon evmata* (Memoirs), Athens 1958.
8. The anti-revolution coup was led by two 1922 Revolution officers of Venizelist origin, Generals Leonardopoulos and Gargalidis. Several of the younger captains involved had contacts with I. Metaxas, among them C. Maniadakis of subsequent 4th August Regime fame or notoriety. See P. Kanellopoulos, *I zoe Mou* (My Life), Athens, 1985, p.27.
9. See *Diary*, III, pp.219–24, 280–9.
10. See P. Pipinelis, *George II*, Athens, 1951.

The National All-Party (*Ekoumeniki*) Government

In the dozen or so years before his assumption of dictatorial powers, a recognizable pattern of Metaxas's political strategy was emerging. He exhibited consummate political dexterity and acumen in deliberately positioning himself to negotiate safely the treacherous shoals of the country's shambolic political chaos, to swing between monarchy, military revolt and republic, and to surface eventually as the supreme arbiter of state power, order and stability in the country.

By 1923–24 though it was clear the Army was back in politics.[1] This, in a way, was the most shattering consequence for Greek politics of the Asia Minor debacle and the October 1923 abortive coup inspired if not led by Metaxas. It is significant nevertheless that his second exile pushed Metaxas deeper into the maelstrom of Greek politics; and this at a time when his great rival, Venizelos, had been forced by revolutionary army officers and radical republican politicians (e.g., Papanastasiou and his allies) to withdraw from active politics and leave the country. Noteworthy is the decision by Metaxas to engage fully in the traditional forms of Greek political activity, use his small *Eleftherophrones* political party, his supporters among the press and other connections in order to pit his wits and political instinct against those of both Venizelos and his opponents from the older political parties of the Right. Many have thus dubbed the five-year period 1923–28 in the political life of Metaxas as his realist phase, when he himself concluded that the surest and safest road to first, political survival and later political power lay in a reasonable, moderate and active participation in the parliamentary system as defined by the world of the old political parties in the context of the new republican regime. Thus from Italy he had gone to France where he courted and used intensively the press in order to maintain a high profile in Greek politics, to explain his view of the events and developments of 1922–23, to recruit support among the French and Italian establishments, to negotiate an amnesty for the perpetrators of the abortive coup of October 1923, and to return to Greece on 6 April 1924.[2] Henceforth his political conduct is impeccably correct. Not only did Metaxas take part in the Referendum of 13 April 1924, but he also recognized the Republic, declaring his intention to conduct his political activities within its framework (*politiki tou plaisiou*), immediately eliciting the ire of the monarchists who accused him of treachery.

His party experienced its first minor success in the elections of 7 November 1926, when it secured 54, or about one-fifth of the total (250) seats in the Chamber. Many of the speeches and public statements by Metaxas during a very active period of his political life soon after his return from his second exile in Italy in 1923, and at least as of 1924, culminating first in his participation in the All-Party (*Ecumenic*) Government of Alexander Zaimis, 1926–28, later in the Demertzis government of 1935–36, and ultimately at the head of his own 4th August Regime, are reproduced in his *Diary*, vols III and IV, in the documents' appendices.[3] These invariably represent Metaxas at the height of his participation in the arena of Greek party and parliamentary politics as the leader of a new political party. They also reveal many of his views as he offers his own gloss on the events in Asia Minor, the reasons for the Greek military failure there, the faults of the Venizelos policy, but also an explanation of why he had urged Venizelos to avoid a military adventure in Asia Minor [*Diary*, III, pp.799–802]. It is clear Metaxas used this intensive political exposure in the media to clarify and justify his position vis-à-vis anti-Venizelist political leaders such as D. Gounaris, but also in order to project his own vision of the political future of the country. Prominent and significant among these is his speech in Thessaloniki on 24 October 1926, in which he emphasized again his own and his party's concern over agriculture and shipping, the armed forces and the defence of the country, as well as education and culture [*Diary*, III, pp.831–4].

A month later Metaxas was sworn in as a member of the All-Party government (*ekoumeniki*) headed by Alexandros Zaimis. This was the first time the party of Metaxas shared in power and it did this for about eighteen months, or the summer of 1928, when Venizelos returned and set Greek politics in a tizzy. These were by the way a crucial eighteen months for Metaxas who as Minister of Communications became engaged in the execution of a number of public works, especially a road network for the country's transport and communications infrastructure.[4] He was also responsible for the negotiation and granting of contracts for land reclamation, railway construction and irrigation projects. All this represented valuable administrative experience for Metaxas, but also an opportunity to observe at close hand the workings of political party government. Overwhelmed and discouraged by calls and visits of politicians to the Ministry for favours Metaxas confided in his *Diary* on 18 February 1927, 'I believe it is impossible to make progress under the parliamentary system.' The unresolved issue of the Army List – of dismissed officers and their reinstatement – continued to exercise Metaxas, as well as his old enemy General Plastiras, and that ironically brought the two together with a view to cooperating for its resolution.

Although Metaxas had opposed the short-lived dictatorship of General Theodoros Pangalos with its 'praetorian guard', the fact that it lasted for over a year tended to undermine, to weaken parliamentary politics even further. Another soldier, General George Kondylis, over-threw the Pangalos interlude with the prospect of a return to political normality. The reappearance however of Venizelos seeking to lead again the Liberal camp tended to undermine whatever balance was being established after the Pangalos anomaly or digression. And while Metaxas may have been lulled into complacency or political contentment with his return to the Greek political fold, the elections of August 1928 shattered his confidence. Even his compatriots did not vote for him, and he lost his seat in Cephalonia; but five other candidates from his party were elected. The coalition government of Liberals and Radical Democrats that succeeded the All-Party government of Zaimis did include *Eleftherophrones*, but not Metaxas himself who decided to leave active politics for the second time.

NOTES

1. See *Diary* of Penelope Delta, entry for Monday, 5 November 1923, Vol. A of her Private Papers, *Eleftherios Venizelos*, p.145, edited by P.A. Zannas, Athens, 1983, where she refers to the pressure exerted by General Kondylis and Pangalos, as well as Admiral Hatzikyriakos on General Plastiras to proclaim a Republic.
2. A report of the Metaxas interview in the Paris newspaper *Matin*, was published in *Chronika* on 30 March 1924, where Metaxas expressed his preference for the prevalence of the spirit of moderation in Greek political life, for the restoration of political normality in Greece, after decades of domestic strife. See *Diary*, III, pp.788–9.
3. See for instance, texts reproduced in Documents Appendix, *Diary*, III, pp.777–82.
4. Interesting and illuminating for example, is the record of the introduction by Metaxas, as Minister of Communications, of new legislation in Parliament regarding the construction of a national road network, its importance for national

economic development, and the parliamentary debates that ensued. See *Diary*, III, pp.836–41, 847–53, and 865–95, 902–5. The strength of Metaxas in parliamentary debate is also reflected in his interventions to explain why he agreed to participate in the All-Party (*Ekoumeniki*) Government, as well as his 'Swan Song' on 28 June 1928 in Parliament when ironically he warned of the threat of dictatorship: 'absolute power is always messy', Metaxas concluded [*Diary*, III, pp.899–912].

PART III

Prelude to Power:
The Momentum of Leadership

10

Greece in the 1930s

Greece in the 1930s was still a country of merchants and sailors; its economic culture was overwhelmingly privateering and commercial. Considering the fact that less than one-fifth of its land area was cultivated, and industrialization was in its very early stages, this is not surprising. To be sure, over 50 per cent of Greeks were occupied with agriculture, producing enough tobacco, wine, raisins, currants and dried figs to account for 70 per cent of the country's cash exports. But one must also remember that in the foreign trade markets, these were luxury agricultural products. Despite the country's considerable mineral wealth, it had very scarce energy resources to fuel, and fewer raw materials to develop, a manufacturing industry. The costs of such development would have been so high that the scope for industrialization in Greece remained limited. Hence the more natural link between commerce and a seafaring nation: by 1939 Greece had the third largest merchant fleet in the Mediterranean (after the French and the Italian), ranking ninth in the world, with an annual revenue of £8 million for the Greek state from shipping.

The country's economic survival was managed thanks to a static population (seven–eight million) maintained by immigration to the North American continent, Australasia and Africa (1898–1920), less than seven million in 1938–39; and dependence on foreign capital in the form of loans and investment in capital works for the country's basic infrastructure ranging from electric power and other public utilities to roads and other transport, water, drainage and sewerage. About half a million Greeks had emigrated over a period of a century, or since the rise of the modern Greek state (1830–1920), and the remittances of immigrants by the 1930s had reached on average a rate of $25–30 million per annum.[1]

It is noteworthy that as mass migration to North America, especially during the period 1897–1920, was curtailed with the introduction by the United States of the quota system in 1924, the Asia Minor refugees arrived in Greece. The Balkan Wars (1912–13) and the Great War may have doubled the area of independent Greece, but the refugees who inflated its population had to be absorbed into the country's poor economy.[2] Beginning with the Agrarian Reform in 1917–24 which, among other things, redistributed land to farmers and compensated the big landowners in Thessaly, by 1923 refugees from Asia Minor were settled in ex-Bulgarian and ex-Turkish lands; the arable and cultivated area expanded greatly. The newly settled refugees developed further the cultivation of cash export crops, like tobacco, while the state, especially in the mid-1920s, executed major land reclamation works which added yet more arable areas to the country's agricultural economy, especially in Macedonia.

Together with other major public works projects, including the draining of marsh and swampland, and road construction, the problem facing the Metaxas regime in 1936–37 was partly the aftermath of the Great Depression, partly the security of dependable export markets for Greece's luxury agricultural products, the servicing of a growing external debt, initially incurred over the importation of basic food commodities, such as grain (wheat etc.) and fuel, and made more acute by the regime's crash rearmament programme. There was also the as yet incomplete accommodation of certain long-term changes over the previous fifty years (1885–1935) which could have transformed the Greek economy. This period saw the rise of a benighted national bourgeoisie, the mainstay of the famous Harilaos Tricoupis liberal administrations, followed by the republican experiment of Eleftherios Venizelos, and the supporters of the 1911 Constitution. The ranks of the bourgeoisie were swollen by the rapid development of shipping, banks and a nascent industry, when its leaders proceeded to form so-called modern political parties which dominated Greek politics for half a century. After the Young Turk Revolt around the same time (1908) Greek capital began to be transferred to Greece; and there was an influx of British and other foreign capital in a high growth, rapidly developing though dependent economy.

The sway of West European liberalism as first championed by Tricoupis in his state administrative reform programme, subsequently embodied in the 1911 Constitution and the Venizelos Republican experiment (1924–34) allowing Greece access to foreign aid, especially from France, and the vast borrowing in order to meet the cost of modernization and reform, all helped accumulate a burdensome external debt for the country. In fact, sixty years earlier Tricoupis was removed from office, essentially because his government foundered on the rocks of economic difficulties created by his rapid state reform and modernization programme. Opposed as he was by the Palace, its courtiers and other clients, as well as the Banks, the imaginative and bold founder of the modern Greek administrative state died in exile. The euphoric Venizelos, at the head of the first modern Greek republic since the ancient ones in Athens, added to the financial burden with costly French military missions to help with and supervise the modern reorganization of the Greek Army, with British missions doing the same for the Greek Navy.

Inevitable too were the social consequences of rapid economic growth, frequent wars and population movements. These manifested themselves early in the Army, where an Army League led a coup in 1909, emulative perhaps of the Young Turk (CUP) led coup in Turkey. Syndicalist and labour movements surfaced among the increased number of agricultural and other workers among the Asia Minor refugee and other communities, demanding state social legislation, based on notions of state welfare benefits and borrowed socialist ideology.

Over a period of fifteen years (1917–32) Greece's foreign or external debt had grown from 360 to 790 million dollars. Servicing this debt was equal to two-thirds of state expenditure; and to make matters worse, the country could not secure or attract foreign capital easily during the Depression.[3] Nor was the country food-sufficient, especially in grain or cereals and huge amounts of these had to be imported from North America, Australia and Latin America. The need for capital was, by the mid-1930s, desperate. At the same time the country's agricultural cash export crops faced stiff competition: tobacco was always threatened by American Virginia, as was the raisin with the rapid development of the wine growing industry on the West Coast of the United States.

The annual per capita income in Greece of that period was about £50; and the diet poor. Most farming families were on a subsistence level as they scratched a living on small farms. Endemic disease and illness was widespread; whereas the scourge of malaria was being gradually eradicated as a result of the draining of swamps and marshes, tuberculosis was rampant. State health services were meagre.[4]

All these factors influenced Greece's public economic policy as well as the course of its foreign relations – at least on the surface – under Metaxas. The 4th August Regime in 1936 was confronted with a vast range of social and economic problems, the treatment of which forced it into a tricky area of political decisions including sailing through treacherous shoals of foreign policy. Thus Metaxas faced the need for social and economic reform, dealing with a huge external debt, finding markets for the country's luxury agricultural cash crops, and raising capital for his reform and rearmament programmes at a time when the Fascist–Nazi challenge to the democratic powers in Europe was stronger than ever. It was in fact the desperate need to secure export markets which forced Greece and especially the Metaxas regime towards closer economic relations with Nazi Germany to which country Greek exports had risen by nearly 20 per cent in the 1930s. Coinciding with the Reich's new scheme of a 'clearing' system in its foreign trade, especially with the Balkan countries, Greece was more or less compelled into accepting imports from Germany under the new system (a kind of dumping), especially in view of its rising exports to that country, tantamount to an exchange or barter system of trade.[5] At the same time a wave of economic nationalism which grew with the regime, that is as a result of greater state control of the economy, pressed Metaxas to erode the influence of such foreign monopolies as Cable and Wireless in telecommunications and the so-called *Power* (the Electric Transport Company) in transport, as well as lesser British insurance companies by seeking to renegotiate their contracts or if need be threatening to nationalize them.

Greece, in short, faced a difficult economic problem: it had to sell even more luxury agricultural products, such as tobacco, olives, currants, liquorice roots, in order to pay for imported necessities such as wheat, fuel and arms. Even if there were a chance of becoming self-sufficient in wheat by growing more at home, tobacco was ten times more profitable and it was given priority over arable land. However, a drop in tobacco exports and other agricultural luxury products was accompanied by a drop in their world market prices.

Even though there had been universal male suffrage in Greece ever since the new (post-Otto) Constitution of 1864, Greek society remained mainly or largely agrarian and political organization one of patron–client relations. Nationalism exerted a major influence on the country's political life.

The rise of political parties after 1910 was marked by a division between a liberal Venizelist and a populist conservative royalist camp.[6] Both camps tended towards the pursuit of popular autocracy. A revolutionary leftist challenge spearheaded by the Communist Party developed slowly in the early 1930s, drawing by far its greatest support from the large Asia Minor refugee population, especially in the north of the country, and a new generation of town and city 'intelligentsia'.

Before 1936, change had been slow albeit relentless. A traditional agrarian economy was being slowly transformed into a modern indust-rial, mercantile and urban one. Nevertheless, Greece was a Medi-terranean society still influenced by tradition and religion. But there was also a perceptible move away from the elite liberalism of the late nineteenth–early twentieth century of Tricoupis to an incipient democ-ratization under Venizelos and his cohorts, but also tending towards authoritarianism and autocracy and a flirting with social democratic notions. If this shift can be dated from the 1909 Goudi Army coup and the first Venizelos government, the process was accelerated rather disastrously. Without a civil society at its base, Parliamentary government soon broke down making way for transient though persistent forms of semi-authoritarianism and autocracy, fostered in part too by the National Schism which promoted internal strife and attracted frequent foreign power interference. One of the consequences of the Great War and the Asia Minor Debacle, was the revolt of General Nicolas Plastiras and his colleagues in 1922 and the abortive counter-coup of Generals Leonardopoulos and Gargalides in October 1923, which marked the increasingly intense deleterious politicization of the Army Officer Corps from 1922 to 1967, a period of nearly fifty years marked by political and governmental instability: 1936–41 and 1955–63 stand out as exceptional periods of relative stability and development.[7]

In external relations generally Greece was a weak southeast European state that had experienced humiliation at the hands of stronger foreign powers. It had not quite resolved its national problem, viz. the integra-tion of the Greek nation.

NOTES

1. See Mark Mazower, *Greece and the Inter-War Economic Crisis*, Oxford, Clarendon Press, 1991, and Ioanna Pepelasi-Minoglou, *The Greek State and International Finance*, unpubl. doctoral thesis, LSE, University of London, 1993.
2. See G. Mavrogordatos, 'To Anepanalypto Epiteugma', *Deltio* (Bulletin, Centre of Asia Minor Studies), edited by P.M. Kitromelidis, Athens, 1992, pp.9–12.
3. See Mark Kazower, *op. cit.*, and Ioanna Pepelasi-Minoglou, *op. cit.*
4. In his dispatches during 1936–37, British Ambassador in Athens, Sydney Waterlow, referred to a 'Socio-Economic New Deal under Metaxas', while H.E. Finlayson referred to the Metaxas Rearmament Programme (FO371/21146, 35271) with supporting figures about its finances and Reform Programme. In an aside Waterlow remarked significantly, 'any sort of planning [is] a new departure'. See also Sydney Waterlow, 'The Decline and Fall of Greek Democracy, 1933–1936', *Political Quarterly*, vol.18, nos. 2 and 3, 1947.
5. Figures regarding drachma balances are reported in the Sydney Waterlow dispatches from Athens.

6.   On political parties in Greece, see Hariton Korisis, *Die Politischen Parteien Griechen-lands, Ein neuer Staat auf den weg zu Demokratiem 1821–1910*, Nurnberg, 1966; Greek transl. *I Politiki zoe stiu Ellanda*, Athens, 1974, and George Th. Mavrogordatos, *Stillborn Republic: Social Conditions and Party Strategies in Greece, 1922–1936*, Berkeley, California, 1983.

7.   See Thanos Veremis, *I Epemvaseis tou ellinikou stratou stin politiki, 1916–1936* (The Intervention of the Greek Army in Politics, 1916–1936), Athens, Exandas, 1977.

11

Political Party Leader, Prominent Member of Parliament and Rivalry with Venizelos

Despite his protestations to the contrary and notwithstanding his contrived and apparent serenity, in actual fact Metaxas was quite agitated and restless. He was really deeply hurt by the election defeat, but his decision to leave politics was not irreversible. He conceded he needed to be active, especially as he found inactivity soul-destroying. This allowed him to conclude in plain demotic, 'I have the right to offer myself whole, with my own ideals and aspirations, without retreats or compromises. I must be whole and real, without nepotism for the incompetent' [*Diary*, 27 and 31 August 1929].

Fortuitously, one must say this was just as well because the next two years, 1930–32, were difficult. Not only did Metaxas himself suffer serious illness, but he became obsessed with his younger daughter Nana's prolonged illness which in the end turned out to be an indisposition due to a kidney disorder (probably a kind of *albuminuria*, *lefkoma* in Greek). Nana Foka herself told us in November 1996 that she had tuberculosis. By then though and as a result of having been plagued by illness in his own family – brother Costakis and sister Marianthe – Metaxas was a master hypochondriac who thought the worst of every medical diagnosis and treatment; so much so that he accompanied Nana to Switzerland for several months in search of a cure for her condition. But before accompanying his daughter to the Sanatorium in Lugano in July 1930, Metaxas himself had undergone a dreadful period of illness earlier that spring. He entered the Yeroulanos Clinic on 8 May and underwent surgery for an infected appendix on 11 May. The complications that followed kept him in that clinic till the beginning of July [see *Diary*, III, pp.664–86]. At the same time he was tortured by the chances of both his daughters, Loulou and Nana, gaining university places. Loulou especially aspired to enrol in the Polytechnic and her father struggled to improve her maths. He described the following year,1931, as the worst year of his life [*Diary*, III, p.696]. Politically though there was still life ahead of him.

Meanwhile, Venizelos was losing his grip over the Republic he helped create, and his control over his more impulsive political allies and supporters, such as General Plastiras. At the same time, his allies and supporters in the Liberal Party such as G. Kafandaris lacked his own nerve, spirit of adventure and decisiveness; in short, his qualities of leadership, not to mention his charisma. Equally outside and beyond his control were the difficult conditions of a world economic depression and his own inadequate administration. By then Tsaldaris, the bland leader of the Popular (*Laikon*) Party, had finally accepted and recognized the Republic, especially after the elections in September 1932 in which Metaxas also participated. Tsaldaris formed a government in which Metaxas held the portfolio of the Interior. In January 1933, pushed by General Plastiras, Venizelos brought down the Tsaldaris government. He succeeded with his own government to dissolve Parliament and hold fresh elections in March 1933 in which anti-Venizelists secured 136 seats against 110 for the Venizelists, with Metaxas's party securing five or six seats. At that point General Plastiras mounted his coup to neutralize the election result, and impose a Venizelist dictatorship by force. He even invoked the Mussolini model, suggesting the failure of parliamentary government in the face of the Communist threat. Venizelos himself recommended amending the Constitution by introducing a provision parallel if not quite similar to the *Diktatur Paragraph 48* of the Weimar Republic Constitution, so that Venizelos too was considering the path of a stronger Executive. The Opposition rejected all of this, but Venizelos refused to relinquish power without guarantees for republicanism. Tsaldaris recognized the Republican regime but, helped by the Plastiras–Venizelos combination, Parliament dismissed the Tsaldaris government. Unfortunately for Venizelos he lost the very elections he chose to hold very soon thereafter.

It is clear that from 1932 to 1935 Venizelos sought to retain power even unconstitutionally if need be, whereas Metaxas at least part of that time was not ostensibly too interested in politics. It was really the Plastiras coup of March 1933 that revived in him the desire to neutralize his rival. He now sought to fight a double duel, one with Venizelos and the other against Tsaldaris. By then, however, Parliament had lost its credibility and the orientation towards some form of autocracy was shared by most political leaders, especially the contenders for power.[1] Although Metaxas did not participate in the new government, he became nonetheless the focus of political attention, especially in the Chamber. It was possibly the most prominent interlude and illustration of the politics of revenge by Metaxas against Venizelos.

Having drafted and presented in Parliament the charges against the role and ultimate moral responsibility of Venizelos for the Plastiras coup against constitutional legality, Metaxas wondered if he should have got involved in bringing Venizelos to heel. 'Can I put down this giant?' he wondered. And was it his duty to do so? By the summer, however, it was no longer a matter of choice or rumination for Metaxas, but one of implication in the worst kind of political contest, that of the alleged use of violence against the person of a political opponent. On 6 June 1933, three months after the elections there was an attempt on the life of Venizelos in Athens.[2] The Venizelists alleged the attempt was planned and ordered by Mrs Lina Tsaldaris, wife of the leader of the Popular Party, and her political friends and allies, and carried out by the recently appointed Chief of General State Security Polychronopoulos. Implicit in these charges was also the indirect participation of Metaxas in the assassination attempt. Needless to say the Venizelists were furious with him.

Enamoured by Venizelos, Penelope Delta never missed an opportunity to denigrate Metaxas. On this occasion, keen to emphasize the role of Metaxas in the attempt on Venizelos's life, she alleged that the newspaper *Elliniki*, a semi-official organ of the Metaxas *Eleftherophrones* party published an article saying that Greece would not find peace so long as Venizelos remained alive, and claimed that Polychronpoulos paid 1 million drachmas to each of the contract hit men from the Army recruited to carry out the assassination of Venizelos, described in this instance by Delta as the 'creator of Greater Greece'. She also quotes Leonidas Spais's allegation, cited elsewhere in this text. Elsewhere in the same volume (p.231) Delta claims that the Metaxas regime issued a special decree in October 1937, granting Polychronopoulos an extraordinary pension arrangement in order to avoid a scandal, when the latter threatened to spill the beans, about the March 1933 attempt on Venizelos's life. The special pension arrangement, the Metaxas regime contended, was mainly for health reasons.[3] Delta relished any disparaging comments about Metaxas; thus elsewhere in her Venizelos volume, she quotes V. Dousmanis about Metaxas in 1909 '[Metaxas] who had lived near the monarchs all his life remained, unlike Venizelos, corrupt, petty and lowly.'[4] Yet much of all this commotion and furore was an attempt by the Venizelists to rationalize and cover up their unexpected humiliating defeat in the March elections as well as to debarrass themselves of the abortive coup to scuttle the election result by General Plastiras which incidentally was highly embarrassing for Venizelos himself. What is also interesting about this rather complex episode – elections, assassination attempt, and the furore it generated – is that it never had a clear-cut end or conclusion; strictly speaking, it was never quite resolved. The actual perpetrators of the attack on Venizelos were never caught and brought to justice. Everyone seemed to know who they were and rumours were thick and fast regarding the identity of their backers and political masters. Leonidas Spais in his memoirs,[5] *Fifty Years a Soldier, in Service of Nation and Democracy*, noted that in 1937 when he and Polychronopoulos were exiles of the Metaxas 4th August Regime in Skopelos, Polychronopoulos told him that the assassination attempt was with the prior knowledge of ministers, especially I. Rallis, I. Metaxas, Admiral Hadjikyriakos, and General George Kondylis.[6] Special pension arrangements were legislated for by the Metaxas regime as a pay-off to Polychronopoulos who might otherwise have testified before a court of law or other public inquiry body. Writing some sixty years later G. Rallis offers an interesting extensive comment on that past era and its events when he writes, 'Generally the climate of political life at the beginning of 1935 was not pleasant at all. There was a press campaign in favour of a "Crowned Democracy" – really the grotesque notion of a "crowned republic".' But Metaxas was in favour of an iron but honest dictatorship that would save the country. The Prime Minister, Tsaldaris, was caught between two fires, the Democratic Defence and the Monarchists, i.e. the radical republicans and the royalists; and he was a weak, indecisive man.[7]

Metaxas was a minister without portfolio in the Tsaldaris government formed after the March 1935 coup. By then people were generally fed up with Army coups and thirsted for the imposition of order. This in a way marked the beginning of a trend favouring a dictatorship, one incidentally not confined to Metaxas and his followers, but gaining in popularity among the ranks of Liberal and other politicians. Metaxas was inevitably and naturally upset over the continued popularity of the 'Man on Horseback', the actual suppressor of the Venizelist coup of March 1935, General George Kondylis. He was also contesting the leadership of the anti-Venizelist forces with I. Rallis and P. Tsaldaris, a committed parliamentarian, a man of compromise in politics. Along with G. Stratos and Metaxas, I. Rallis founded a convenient political alliance, the 'Union of Monarchists', in order to contest the elections of June 1935 in which members of Metaxas's party, e.g., T. Tourkovassilis and Philip Dragoumis, won parliamentary seats. But Tsaldaris, leader of the Popular Party, was at that time opposed by monarchist Generals Papagos and Reppas and Admiral Economou, while the political fortunes of Metaxas took a sharp upward turn when General Kondylis objected to the King's amnesty (initially recommended by Metaxas). The King dismissed him and his government, and invited Professor C. Demertzis to form a new one. Before all the excitement over this latest episode and the turmoil it caused in the Athenian political world had time to subside, and quite out of the blue, a new sideshow appeared to consume the fractious leaders of the political world. Probably as part of his efforts to relocate himself in the centre of the political world and in order to capture the attention of a grateful public as its elected leader and saviour of the country's Liberal forces Venizelos published a series of articles in the newspaper *Elefthero Vima* about the Asia Minor affair and the causes of the National Schism back in 1915–16. Equally committed to prevailing as the new star of Greek politics and the man of destiny over Venizelos, Metaxas could do no less than publish his own version in response to Venizelos's in a series of seventy articles in the daily *Kathimerini*. The whole year was taken up by this public debate between the two great rivals for the political soul of Greece, representing an older version of the antagonism between Republicans and Monarchists, made even more riveting at least for the newspaper readers by the burning issue of the Restoration. (It was the nearest thing then to the televised debates between politicians today competing for the US Presidency; it was like the riveting soap which grips a whole nation as its audience awaits the next instalment.[8])

One must note the mutual regret and respect over this protracted duel in the respective interventions of the two men in the debate, suggesting a lingering, lasting fondness between the two erstwhile collaborators, especially in the period from 1910 to 1916. And yet the accusations by Metaxas were sharp, concise and without pity. Thus the then Premier Tsaldaris, a moderate conciliatory politician sought an amnesty for Venizelos in order to end the clash between him and Metaxas. But even after the March 1933 fiasco, Venizelos persisted with his conspiratorial politics. Thus in July 1933 he held a conference in Thessaloniki which, among other things, founded a new Army cabal which two years later in March 1935 launched the most serious republican coup against the Right and rehabilitated parliamentarianism. It is not inaccurate to suggest that the Venizelos–Metaxas debate in the press was not strictly historical but mainly apologetic on both sides. In an interesting Epilogue to his series of articles Metaxas wrote on 23 January 1935,

Venizelos and I invited you to look backwards to the past. Now I urge you to look forward to the future; and since you cannot live without ideals, the only suitable ideal is that of the Hellenic Idea. *The Great Idea (I Megali Idea)* itself did not fail; only the attempt at its territorial implementation. The Greco–Byzantine perception of it has failed, but not its ancient classical form of Hellenism. Our [my] disagreement with Venizelos, in the final analysis, is over the understanding, the meaning, significance and form of the Hellenic Idea.

What also emerges by the way in these debates is that the main pre-occupation of Metaxas in foreign affairs was with the 'Slavic threat', and the fact that Greece was unprepared for war. The man simply could not resist: he used the occasion of the debates to put forward his own leadership of the future.

Another political reality Metaxas, as well as all other politicians, had to contend with was an Army willing to interfere in the politics of the country with great alacrity, and by implication to bring undue pressure to bear on politicians in general, political institutions and their political masters in particular. The Big Noise in that respect at that time was General George Kondylis, a kind of arbiter of political power, a moralist and frequently a threatening potential political redeemer and saviour, a 'knight on horseback'.[9] Kondylis was not simply a threat to the parliamentary government, he also represented a deadly danger to the political future of Metaxas himself. The problem for Metaxas now was how to avoid being swept away by this 'tornado', this hurricane and dynamo of a man, this self-proclaimed restorer of the monarchy. Here too Metaxas, all his caveats to the contrary notwithstanding, proved to be a consummate politician and strategist. The practical situation facing him and the country then was the Venizelist coup of March 1935 which finally put paid to the Republican cause, and ended Venizelos's political career rather ignominiously. It revived the divisions in the Army Officer Corps and fanned the virulent antagonism between the two old political camps, and pushed the fleeing General Plastiras into exile in France. Having collaborated with Kondylis in suppressing the coup, Metaxas now shrewdly identified the priority of immediate Greek political activity, namely, the restoration of the monarchy. The Republic was tried and failed; the restoration of the monarchy was now essential, vital to the revival, reconstruction and rehabilitation of the Greek State. As a minister without portfolio Metaxas worked for the strengthening of the government in Athens, the strengthening of the Armed Forces, and proceeded to clear out the Venizelists from both of these institutions as a prerequisite of political stability. But even in the pursuit of this objective Metaxas faced a powerful rival, Kondylis, who was laying equal claims to leading the movement for the restoration of the monarchy. To make matters worse, in the elections of 1 June 1935 Metaxas's party secured five seats only, not an impressive performance at the polls.

It is important to recall that 1935 was a decisive year insofar as the Restoration reflected the dramatic resolution of the Greek political impasse and the acceleration of the rise of the Metaxas autocracy. But it was also a momentous year for critical developments in the wider European and international contexts. Thus Mussolini made his aggressive imperial intentions quite clear by attacking Ethiopia and ignoring League of Nations' attempts to restrain him, thus challenging further two major powers, Britain and France. Then, while Hitler embarked upon his massive rearmament policy, and the reoccupation of the Rhineland, Comintern 'Popular Front' policies had their effect in Spain, France and Greece. But the gravest threat to Greece was Italy's aggressive policies and intentions, its threat in the Eastern Mediterranean and northeast Africa. The inevitable Anglo–Italian rivalry in these strategic areas in turn influenced Anglo–Greek relations.[10] Two years later, in October 1937, Hitler and Mussolini signed the Axis Agreement, the Civil War was on in Spain, and as some Greeks, including Metaxas himself, averred, the threat of war was on the doorstep of Greece.

Metaxas had his own doubts about his political career which he recorded in his Diary on 26 June 1935 [*Diary*, IV, p.153]: 'I have the impression the Greek public does not want me. It recognizes my worth but does not want me' and yet throughout 1934 and 1935 he battled in debate in Parliament against Venizelos and Kondylis repeatedly pointing to the failure of the parliamentary system to deal with the nation's problems, reminding his interlocutors that the deep causes of the National Dichasmos rendered the reconciliation between old and new Greece, between natives and refugees after 1923 difficult, and insisting on the need for a new system that allowed for a stronger Executive. He considered the matter of dictatorship vs. parliamentarism when he argued that the force of political conditions decreed the system of government, and observed that the old capitalist laissez-faire liberal democratic system of the nineteenth century was being overtaken – or in fact had been overtaken – by more state intervention, and the loss of political control by the middle classes. In view of the additional problem in Greece of political integration, a more powerful interfering central government

was needed. The real issue was how Greece was to abandon parliamentarism – via the Communist Door or that of the National State?
Metaxas had embarked on a series of public statements and speeches in
and out of Parliament about the bankruptcy of the prevailing parliamentary system, while he carried on his duel with Kondylis. But the
culmination of all this political debate and war of partisan political words
was the *Epilogue* by Metaxas that concluded his debate with Venizelos in
the *Kathimerini*, published on 23 January 1935, where he offered at least
the youth of Greece his vision of a different political future, a different
Greek state and society, a new nation.

After reminding his readers that the most shattering impact of the
War and its exploitation by Venizelos was the squashing of national
ideals and the destruction of Hellenism beyond the frontiers of the Greek
State, he was considering ways of dealing with the Venizelos calamity,
and countering the apathy of an older generation satisfied with seeking
a comfortable existence without adventure or struggle. He was concerned with ideals for Greek youth, since without ideals or faith in them
youth tends to atrophy and wither. The *Megali Idea*, or Greater Greece,
earlier generations believed in was the *force motrice* behind the struggle
for independence, the liberation and integration of the unredeemed
areas of Thessaly, Macedonia, Epirus and Crete, as well as the integra-
tionist nationalist movements for unity with mainland Greece of the
(Seven) Ionian islands against British rule in the mid-nineteenth century.
In short, the *Megali Idea* was the standard-bearer of Hellenism, of Greek
national identity. It represented the historical right of Hellenism in its
cultural predominance in the Balkans and the Eastern Mediterranean.
When it acquired a territorial irredentist dimension and form it met with
setbacks and failure, especially as it had no control over its territorial–
political evolution in the other provinces of the unravelling Ottoman
Empire which the newly independent Greek nation-state was too weak
to influence or control. At the same time Greece succumbed to the
onslaught of certain European ideological and political currents of the
time, highlighting a combination of rationalism, positivism and historical
materialism, all of them alien configurations. But as the Greek governing
elite adopted or emulated these, the hold and sway of the *Megali Idea*
declined. It remained mainly as an instrument and subject of domestic
political conflict, while it was attacked by the more extreme Westernizers
as an irrational contrivance and great madness, especially when it was
widely believed that logic and faith, rationalism and idealism were not
easily reconcilable opposites.

The reaction to such an arresting, mesmerizing Ideal was powerful as expressed in the National Society at the turn of the century, in which Metaxas the young Engineer Lieutenant back in 1896–97 was a member, and which pushed the unprepared young country into a disastrous war against its erstwhile Ottoman occupier in 1897, followed by the inauguration of the Macedonian struggle at the turn of the century, aiming at the retention of that province's Hellenic identity. There followed the Balkan Wars which expanded the territorial sway of Hellenism. After the Great War and the Asia Minor adventure that ended with the exchange of populations between Greece and Turkey, the proposition that Hellenism was confined inside the territorial limits of the modern Greek state was virtually the kiss of death of the Greek National Ideal. In fact, there was hardly a national ideal of Hellenism left, and youth cannot live without one. There were some who turned to humanitarian ideals that other peoples with a different mentality and culture adopted. Leftism, for instance, abstract and obscure, became fashionable among them. Others turned to the Fascist backlash after the Great War; still others became internationalists, pan-Europeans and cosmopolitans. There was in other words total confusion and disorder in the ranks of the youth, but no unity or unifying ideal: their life is devoid of a great national objective. The educational system contributed to this chaos, especially the new theories that the purpose of education is instruction, whereas its purpose is not and cannot be other than to educate Greeks by rudimentary elementary and essential education towards the great Goal of the National Ideal, the only ideal capable of inspiring the Greeks, and giving purpose and meaning to their lives and uniting them.

People are zoological beings, that is living animals. But spiritually they are Greeks, Turks, French, English, Germans, etc.; that is, ethnic, racial groups and tribes. Man acts through his nationality, and Greek youth must understand this. With the decline, nay, the demise of the *Megali Idea*, the National Ideal will inspire Greek youth. But the *Megali Idea* did not really fail; only the attempt to realize it in territorial form. What failed, in other words, is its Greco–Byzantine meaning, but not its ancient perception, that of the domination or prevalence of Hellenism wherever it is and acts. The genius – the gift, the talent – of our nation is that it has no boundaries. Hellenism has tentacles that cannot be confined by boundaries Only 50 per cent of Greeks live within the frontiers of the Greek state; so that Greek civilization and culture has no boundaries either. Thus the task of the modern Greek state is to reconstruct the Hellenic culture. This was the essence of the *Megali Idea* of ancient Hellenism.

The Byzantine state was or became an instrument of Hellenism too, but constructed as per medieval perceptions. Our *Megali Idea* therefore is not of the Byzantine–Medieval territorial conception but of the ancient or classical Greek perception – the predominance, the prevalence of Hellenism beyond geographical Greece. We must accept historical continuity, the fact that we are not simply residents of a particular country, inhabited at other times by different people, but that we are Greeks through the ages: the language is proof of that continuity as an evolutionary development of the ancient–classical one. The *Megali Idea* of Hellenism lives on as an illustration of our nation's talent and genius. Metaxas justified the *Epilogue* to his series of articles by the argument that Venizelos and the National Schism had transformed national values, and they needed to be restored: he wished to restore the pre-Liberal Age values of Hellenism.[11]

The *Epilogue* really suggested in summary form the objectives, policies, and 'state ideology' of Metaxas if he ever acceded to state power. But it also indicated not simply his disillusionment with bourgeois parliamentary values and political principles, but very much his clarion call too for the restoration of more pristine notions of cultural Hellenism under his own radical version of the National State, to be governed by his own highly personalized rule. Cultural Hellenism was incidentally a widespread movement among the literati and intellectuals of the period from 1880 to 1910, including those among the Diaspora Greeks in Istanbul and Alexandria. Prominent among these were Ion Dragoumis, his younger brother Philip, his brother-in-law Major Pavlos Melas, P. Yannoipoulos, K. Sokolis, C. Cavafy and G. Seferis, N. Papadiamandis, C. Palamas in literature; I. Sykoutris and Fotos Politis in national, social and political ideas. This is not to mention the men of the military establishment, such as Generals Plastiras, Kondylis and Pangalos, all of whom were influenced and attracted by the more militant and apparently effective totalitarian and militaristic states and regimes rising in Europe, many of them under the banner of Fascism. Radical National Socialism was a widespread trend, Mussolini's fascist state in Italy an attractive model of administrative efficiency, disciplined youth organization and internal order to be emulated. Ideas of Corporatism and the Corporatist state were in the air distinctly different from both Capitalism and Communism or Socialism. Thus the enemies of the new National State were Parliamentarism and Communism. And yet the new National State was essential for national renewal, regeneration and national unity. The Metaxas *Epilogue* was on the whole a notice of political intent and the barest outline of the ideological position and orientation of his future regime, his potential rule of Greece. Some Western historians of Greece still argued that 'with all its faults by no means peculiar to Greece, the parliamentary system is the only possible form of government for so intensely political a people'.[12]

During this time Metaxas suffered a great blow to his personal life, the death of his schizophrenic brother Costakis, an event that plunged him into deep depression.[13] Having avoided any clash with the powerful Kondylis and distanced himself from the wider ranks of the monarchists in or out of the Popular Party of Tsaldaris, Metaxas waited patiently, uncommitted to precisely anything in particular – beyond the suggestion that the Republican regime had failed and that the restoration of the monarchy was essential to the political wellbeing of the country He stayed on the periphery, waiting for his rivals to make mistakes so that he could resurrect his own old links with the restored Royal Court, untainted by any political sins of commission in the preceding five years, and as the strong man of the hour. In other words, the shrewd Cephalonian played it long, a rather complicated hand, but one that was to reward him with state power. His giant rival, Venizelos, was a spent force, and his supporters in disarray; the soldiers or swordbearers were equally confused and lacking political support having played out their 'last hurrah' in March 1935. One must underline the fact that the attempt by Venizelos to establish a single party state that would guarantee his permanence in power via the coup failed. He recognized the failure and fled to Italy. In contrast, the government stood its ground thanks largely to Metaxas, who was vindicated in his concern with conditions in the Army, and the rapidly mounting crisis in Europe and the Mediterranean; in short, the Italian Fascist threat. The collapse of the Venizelist Army coup was one of the several indications of the abject failure of the Republic and the impending change of regime. The simultaneous campaign for the restoration of the monarchy begun by the Greek National Society (*Elliniki Ethniki Etaireia*) of Ath. Filonos (founded in February 1933) and its publication *Hellenism*, became more pronounced and plausible only after Metaxas adopted its aims and commended it to the government and the public. He was also instrumental in the launching of the 'Newspaper of the Hellenes', edited by I. Diakos, as the principal organ of the 'Union of Monarchists', an organization now headed by Metaxas.[14] It was a period described by Metaxas as one of '*Rayadosyne*', the feeling of the Ottoman Sultan's subjects, and also one of total disillusionment of Metaxas with the political world.

In fact the years 1934–35 were rather unpleasant and unhappy, not only because of the turn in his political career but more so because of the problems with his daughter's health and education as well as the death of his brother Costakis. For the first time in his life Metaxas came closest to being a fatalist, and if the cheap fiction he read is anything to go by, also an escapist.[15] Thus he could not even enjoy Nana's wedding on 23 September 1935. Was it simply a case of melancholy, of depression, that accompanies ageing? In any case Metaxas made a new Will and last Testament at that time.

In October 1935, a Palace coup led by Generals Papagos, Platys and Reppas brought the Tsaldaris government down. The Republic had been abolished by a stroke of the pen, and a referendum, in November, brought King George II back from eleven years of exile. Two days later the stocky but shrewd Cephalonian was received in audience and decorated by the King with the insignia of the Grand Cross of the Saviour, but only after he had advised the King to proclaim a general amnesty. General Kondylis, the source of many of Metaxas's fears, a tired and sick man, resigned at the end of November, making room for a new government headed by the law professor C. Demertzis. The first elections under the restored monarchy were held on 26 January 1936 on the basis of proportional representation, and yielded seven deputies from Metaxas's party. But the KKE (the Communist Party) with fifteen Deputies betrayed hitherto unknown strength in the country. The lion's share of Deputies or seats was shared between the Popular Party of Tsaldaris and the Liberal Party of Venizelos.

By now Metaxas concentrated his efforts on strengthening the throne, and used his standing with the Army to free it from political intrigue. The way Metaxas practically insinuated himself into the monarch's confidence by putting himself forward as the one, if not the only, man capable of restoring discipline in the Army Officer Corps was dramatic – some might aver dramatic farce. While discussing a rumoured Army coup by Papagos and other generals with his crony I. Diakos on the morning of 5 March 1936, Professor Theodoros Angellopoulos, Chief of the King's Political Office, rang Metaxas to report the Palace's difficulty in reacting to the rumoured move by General Papagos. The shrewd and calculating Metaxas replied that if the King were to make him Minister of Army Affairs immediately, he would undertake to neutralize any Army conspiracies, seditious coups or demonstrations [*Diary*, IV, p.185]. And he was soon invited to the Palace, where he got his appointment almost immediately.[16] As Generals Papagos and Platys were dismissed on the same day, the politicians, including Venizelos abroad, rejoiced.[17] An erstwhile opponent General Plastiras was urging Metaxas openly to proclaim a dictatorship on condition he reinstated all the purged, i.e. Venizelist, army officers. When after the 6 March 1936 elections the King invited C. Demertzis to form a government to include Metaxas as Army Affairs Minister, Metaxas made the ironically interesting statement to the press: 'We are a transitional (*metavatiki*) – interim or service – government which if it fails to secure a vote of confidence in Parliament will give way to one formed by the political parties. Personally at least I believe Greece cannot leave the parliamentary system: it would be disastrous for the country to become detached from parliamentarism,' he confided in his *Diary* [IV, pp.198–9]. Bold adventurism, audacity and drama were followed by the lucky concatenation of fortuitious, fateful events. The dreaded Kondylis had died on 31 January 1936 – the other strong man of anti-Venizelism, of monarchism, was no more. Metaxas became Army Affairs Minister and Deputy Prime Minister in the Demertzis government after the 6 March elections. On 18 March Venizelos died.[18] And on 13 April Demertzis died. The King swore in his deputy Metaxas as Prime Minister on the afternoon of the same day. The clever Cephalonian quickly announced there would be no policy change, and that actually his government would be prepared to hand over power to one formed by the political parties, a declaration he repeated three days later. Frightened by the Metaxas premiership, the Communists agitated and sought to foment disturbances against it. Ioannis Theotokis and other politicians of the Right sought to bring the Metaxas government down. Tsaldaris turned hostile over the question of purged Army officers. All bets were now off: Metaxas repeated his warning that the only military question now was the defence of the country, the reequipping of the Army, and sought and quickly received a Vote of Confidence in Parliament [*Diary*, IV, pp.201–2].

Fate granted him even more political space in the purview of Greek politics when the leader of the Popular Party, Tsaldaris, died on 12 May 1936. Venizelos, Kondylis and Tsaldaris who could all have been formidable obstacles to the political advancement of Metaxas were out of the way. Metaxas may have managed till then to have impressed on everybody his run of bad luck but good fortune seems to have got to him at last.[19]

NOTES

1. Mazarakis, *Memoirs*, pp.360ff; Daphnis, *op. cit.*, ii, pp.150–5 and 290ff.
2. See P. Delta, *Eleftherios Venizelos*, edited by P.A. Zannas, Athens, 1979, pp.195ff. See also Metaxas *Diary*, IV, pp.27–65.
3. *Ibid.*, p.231.
4. *Ibid.*, p.235.
5. Leonidas Spais, *Peninta Chronia Stratiotis* (Fifty Years a Soldier), Athens, 1970.
6. Cited in G. Rallis, *Koitazontas Piso* (Looking Back), Athens, 1993, p.101. See also P. Delta, *op. cit.*, p.232.
7. G. Rallis, *Ibid.*, p.118.
8. See Ioannis Metaxas, *Istoria tou Ethnikou Dichasmou* (History of the National Schism), Athens, *Kathimerini* newspaper, 1935), and the larger more recent edition, including the complete debate, i.e., the articles by both men, E. Venizelos and I. Metaxas, *I Istoria tou Ethnikou Dichasmou* (The History of the National Schism), Thessaloniki, 1994, with an extensive preface and the relevant correspondence of other contemporaries.
9. See two so-called biographies, but in fact hagiographies by admirers and acolytes, Stamatis Mercouris, *Georgios Kondylis, 1879–1936*, Athens, 1954; and P.J. Kapsis, *O Georgios Kondylis en Polemo kai en Irini* (George Kondylis in War and Peace), Athens, 1934.
10. See Dafnis, *op. cit.*, ii, pp.281–369.
11. *I Istoria tou Ethnikou Dichasmou, op. cit.*, pp.523–9, and *Diary*, IV, pp.611–15.
12. William Miller, *The Ottoman Empire and its Successors, 1801–1927*, London, New Impression 1966, p.172.
13. Early in July 1935, Costakis, the younger brother of Metaxas, was diagnosed to be suffering from lung cancer; and it was soon clear the condition was terminal. He died on Saturday, 14 September. Metaxas records the event in his *Diary*, IV, pp.154–60.
14. On I. Diakos, a strange and mysterious figure, highly influential in the government of the Metaxas 4th August Regime as the major rival of the other strong personality in that government C. Kotzias, see Fivos Gregoriadis, *4 August – Albania, 1935–41*, 4 vols, Athens, Kedrinos, 1972, vol. 4, pp.265–90, where he is alleged to have been an agent of the British Secret Intelligence Service.
15. 'I feel I am not worth anything. I don't work any more. I only read murder mystery novels', *Diary*, IV, p.158.
16. See report of hastily arranged secret swearing-in ceremony of Metaxas at the Royal Palace as Minister of Army Affairs in *Diary*, IV, pp.184–6 and 197. In a rare typewritten document commenting on the Metaxas 4th August Regime, Chief of State Security C. Maniadakis described 5 March 1936 as a crucial day in the rise of Metaxas to power. He was referring to the Palace Incident when the King, in a hurried secret ceremony, swore Metaxas in as Minister of Army Affairs in order to neutralize the pressure of a threatened coup by Generals Papagos and Platys. Metaxas Archive of Private Papers.
17. See letter from Venizelos to L. Roufos, expressing satisfaction and delight over latest developments in Athens, including restoration of the monarchy and the appointment of Metaxas as Minister of Army Affairs, cited in Daphnis, *op. cit.*, ii, p.406 and p.432ff.
18. See text of the (Obituary) 'Farewell' to Venizelos by Metaxas in Parliament, *Diary*, IV, pp.203–04.
19. Evangelos K. Zavitsanos, *I dio Megaloi Kefallynes genythendes en Ithaki Odysseas kai Ioannis Metaxas* (The Two Great Cephalonians born in Ithaka, Ulysses and Ioannis Metaxas), Athens, 1939.

12

Metaxas becomes
Prime Minister

I

Ioannis Metaxas became Prime Minister of Greece in April 1936 at the age of sixty-five, ten years after he himself had conceded that he was an old man with no prospect of accomplishing anything (significant) in his life, and nearly twenty-five years after he had voluntarily taken early retirement from the Army with the rank of Major General. On 17 March 1926, Metaxas confided to his *Diary*, 'My life is over; it is approaching the end and I have done nothing ... I have been forgotten by everybody' [*Diary*, III, p.451]. Yet within two weeks of succeeding to the premiership he secured a vote of confidence for his government in Parliament, a reflection perhaps of his personal prestige as the 'man of the hour', his moral authority, and of the fatigue and despair of the bickering ineffectual politicians, as well as the anguish of a nation longing for some semblance of political order and stability.[1] At the same time, Metaxas lacked any broad-based public support; he led a small party (*Eleftherophrones*) that had lost practically every election since 1933.[2] The founding of the party itself was piecemeal and hesitant; in the absence of any other solid evidence in the form of written records what one can say about this matter with relative certainty is that the party sort of emerged from the group of disaffected, royalist officers and his own political cronies in Cephalonia as well as known royalist political figures in Corfu which Metaxas had brought together, after 1918, to oppose the rebel Plastira officer-led republican regime in 1922–23. An important element in the dissemination of the new party's views was a faction of the royalist press. One may also add with relative confidence the suggestion that the party and its composition were not a surprising consequence of the National Schism.

For ten to fifteen years the party served Metaxas's purposes so long as he acted within the purview of a parliamentary system; what is interesting is the fact that Metaxas never depended heavily on his small political party for the further development of his political activities and career. Significant perhaps was the fact that in June 1935 along with I.M. Rallis and George Stratos, Popular Party ultra monarchist MPs from the Athens district, Metaxas founded the 'Union of Monarchists' to press more effectively for the restoration of the monarchy. They succeeded at least in forcing Tsaldaris, leader of the governing Popular Party, to promise a referendum soon, once the issue of the political system had been clearly set before the electorate by the Union.[3] In fact, once he imposed a dictatorship with the support and approval of the monarch, the party became superfluous and, for all practical purposes, disappeared from the scene. One ought to remember that his accession to the premiership in April 1936 owed nothing to the party. Soon he was looking for a different popular base for the support of his regime, mainly the National Youth Organization (*EON*), modelled after the fascist youth organizations in Italy, Spain and Portugal, as well as popular labour and agricultural organizations, a kind of corporatist representation. And all the time the stability of his regime depended on the creation of first-rate state security, censorship and agencies to watch and control educational, cultural and artistic institutions in the country, in effect partly a police state.[4]

Metaxas lacked the political talent and charisma of Venizelos in communicating with the masses. But he possessed rather great moral authority as one of Greece's most competent staff officers in the past, one of its fiercest and most formidable political debaters in and out of Parliament; a man of strong character, determination and executive ability. A known elitist and royalist he abhorred the 'street politics' of the average Greek politician, and deplored the country's economic, social and cultural backwardness. He was determined to change all this by the force of his personality, dint of hard work and strength of will.

When Metaxas assumed the premiership the monarchy had been restored to the country barely six months earlier, and a large proportion of the public and the politicians were still smarting from the failure of the Republican experiment (1924–34), and the eclipse of their 'idol-hero-saviour' Venizelos. They could hardly be expected to be thrilled by the triumph of Venizelos's principal rival, a stern disciplinarian who had nothing but contempt for them and who would surely railroad them into a new style regimented polity and social order, a new autocracy.

Given the World Depression, the country's economic situation was parlous, a devalued drachma and a huge external debt of $800 million, its social order threatened with destabilization by the new radical forces of the Left, especially the KKE (Greek Communist Party), its armed forces in disarray after their prolonged and debilitating involvement in politics, and its traditional political leadership and elite thoroughly discredited.

II

International conditions, especially in Europe, were no more auspicious for the Metaxas new Greek State: 1933–34 saw the end of the shortlived peace after the end of the Great War. With the accession of Hitler to power in Berlin in January 1933 the old European balance of power based on a system of alliances and alignments became a thing of the past. The new principle of self determination had led to and accelerated the dissolution of empire, the masses entered politics under new banners and slogans with new high expectations and thus receptive and readily available to be recruited by sundry saviours and redeemers. America had abandoned the League of Nations and retreated into a barren isolationism, and there were the continuing effects of the Bolshevik revolution in Russia. The dissolution of the Austro–Hungarian Empire left Central Europe in a deep and dangerous state of chaos. Fascist Italy with its Duce's ambitions of empire in southeastern Europe, North and East Africa, became an element of dangerous instability in the Mediterranean. A victorious but shattered France was the only, rather weak, guarantor of the post-war security system in continental Europe.

The critical period of the early 1930s left Greece with two unresolved problems: that of the Army, and that of national unity. Much of the difficulty arose after Venizelos lost the 25 September 1932 elections. He simply would not accept the verdict of the polls. Presumably in order to protect his republican regime Venizelos proceeded to revive all the old passions of the National Schism, encourage the revival and reconstitution of the Army League as a guarantor of his political party and its programme. He brought down the shortlived Tsaldaris government, dissolved or prorogued parliament, amended the Constitution and the electoral system, and arranged for new elections on 5 March 1933. His opponents, the anti-Venizelist constellation of parties and factions won 136 seats in Parliament, the Venizelists 110. At that point General Plastiras mounted his coup to install a Venizelist dictatorship, which failed. But whatever the fortunes of that adventure, the coup itself left a strong impact on the political plans of Metaxas henceforth. The announcement by General Plastiras giving the reasons for his coup set the pattern for that of Metaxas in August 1936.

Metaxas was now at the pinnacle of power, 'Chief of the Greeks', and 'The Great Governor' (*O Megalos Kyvernitis*). There could be no excuse for any abject or dismal failure. There were no elected deputies in a Parliament, no politicians to question or otherwise hinder his schemes; in other words, Metaxas was not accountable to a popularly elected legislature, only to the sovereign, the King, who at Metaxas's recommendation had suspended certain articles of the Constitution, essentially those defining the citizen's liberties or rights vis-à-vis the State. Theoretically, Metaxas was now in a position to introduce as many radical reforms as he wished or thought necessary. A prominent leader of a political faction in the pre-1935 Parliamentary system of a Republic that had succeeded a relatively short-lived monarchy, Metaxas overthrew the system by attacking it from inside its citadel, that is, as a respected 'insider' and supplanted it by a classical, personal dictatorship.[5]

The 4th August Regime was seen by its founder and chief as 'an anti-Communist Greek state that was totalitarian with an agricultural and labour basis and therefore anti-plutocratic. It did not depend on a governing political party: the whole of the Greek people, the nation, constituted if any, such a political party, excluding of course the Communists and reactionary old political parties or factions' [*Diary*, IV, p.553].[6] He maintained moreover that Greeks who still believed in Hitler's or Mussolini's ideologies were foolish and dishonest. Thus German designs on Yugoslavia were really aimed at Greece. Metaxas interpreted noises emanating from Berlin via the Greek Ambassador Rangavis to the King through the Crown Prince Pavlo and his wife Frederika as meaning that Greece should give in to Hitler. The reaction of Metaxas to all of this was, 'It is better that we die' [*Diary*, IV, p.555]. His suspicion of the really hostile German intentions in Greece prompted and informed his careful policy of not provoking an early German attack, even going to the extremes of not allowing the presence of a weak British force in Thessaloniki as proposed by General Wavell during his visit to Greece in November 1940 and January 1941. Support for the correct interpretation of German intentions by Metaxas came later in the *Goebbels Diaries, 1939–41*. Goebbels admits Italian difficulties and corroborates the fact that Hitler was well disposed towards Greece, but the whole Balkan operation was to act as a prelude to the invasion of the Soviet Union; so that the invasion (of Greece) was really inevitable sooner or later.[7] Metaxas was therefore accurate in his assessment of the situation and his conclusion: whatever concessions Greece made to Berlin, the German invasion would still come because of the wider Axis strategy in the Balkans, the Soviet Union, and the Middle East.

III

The 4th August Regime was launched when at the first meeting of its cabinet Metaxas informed his government ministers of the suspension of a number of articles of the Constitution and the dissolution of Parliament. Except for two who resigned the rest of the ministers co-signed the relevant decrees. Threatened strikes in Piraeus and Kalamata to protest against the new dictatorship were stopped, but a general atmosphere of threatened disturbances worked up by the Communist Party hung over the country. Yet all such attempted reaction to the first steps of the regime were muted by the fact that on the surface at least nothing had really changed, especially when the Prime Minister of the country had been the same since the preceding April. This in itself facilitated the imposition and acceptance of the new regime. In Athens itself the apathy, the immobilization of politicians towards the new dictatorial regime was further secured by the strict censorship which made it difficult for dissent to be expressed or voiced. More concretely the leader of the old Liberals, Sophoulis, refrained from any adventurous opposition for he feared a repetition of the previous year's (1935) fiasco, and the parlous security situation. At the same time, Maniadakis had excellent state security arrangements already in place, and quickly arrested and/or banished those involved in any opposition moves. A. Michalakopoulos, the most credible potential opponent among the so-called old parliamentary and political party camp, with excellent foreign connections, especially in Britain, died in 1938.

The controversy surrounding the death of A. Michalakopoulos in the Spring of 1938 was one of the most difficult and delicate political episodes in the Metaxas dictatorship. It was not simply a 'hot potato' but one impinging upon the precarious state of Anglo–Greek relations, the relations between Metaxas and the King, as well as the very legitimacy of the 4th August Regime. There was never any suggestion that foul play was involved or that the Metaxas government had any part in it. What was difficult to accept or explain is why when the government knew of the politician's serious illness, Metaxas still insisted on applying security measures against him by banishing him to one of the islands, where the condition of his health deteriorated. Metaxas insisted on receiving detailed reports about his death from Dr Lorandos, Director of the Evangelismos Hospital in Athens, and from Dr Eppinger, the German Consultant on the case, and somehow managed to dispel much of the controversy.

Opposition to the new regime took three forms: domestic, military and foreign. The manifestations of domestic opposition were weak, consisting of stencilled proclamations by individual – at most very small groups of – politicians. Early examples of this ineffectual opposition were the young academic Panagiotis Kanellopoulos, nephew of the late prominent anti-Venizelist politician executed in 1922; Dimitris Gounaris, in January 1937; the liberal Al. Mylonas in October 1937; Papandreou, Kafandaris and Theotokis among the older, better-known politicians in January 1938. They were all promptly and effectively silenced and exiled to different parts of the country away from Athens. Most attempted coups by soldiers were unsuccessful too, and the only serious challenge in Crete in 1938 was also suppressed. Attempted conspiracies abroad, mainly with the aid of the French, also came to naught, as did those that tried to use the Royal Palace as their main base.

The clashes and reshuffles in the Regime's administration occurred early during its first two years, in 1936–38. The most significant resignation from the government was that of C. Zavitsianos, Finance Minister, Deputy Premier, and close collaborator of Metaxas himself. Equally, the most dramatic and important legislation of the new Regime was passed early in the first two years: on 17 May 1937 the law for the regulation of agricultural indebtedness came into effect; and on 5 November 1938 the law abolishing tax on olive oil came into force.

When Metaxas assumed the Education Portfolio after he sacked Georgakopoulos, he proceeded with his other equally radical reform policy which included the introduction of Demotic Grammar into the schools in December 1938.[8] His serious illness in December 1937 [*Diary*, IV, p.290] led to wild rumours in the press that Metaxas was at death's door, or that he had committed suicide. A stroke was suspected; others spoke of eye trouble. Metaxas did incidentally give up smoking in February 1938 [*Diary*, IV, p.293]. The fact remains that despite his illnesses Metaxas weathered several crises, including the Chania challenge to his rule in Crete, and the challenge to his authority in Athens over the election of a new Archbishop [*Diary*, IV, pp.14, 311–14]. He even managed to settle the prickly matter of the strategy for the country's defence, in case of an

Italian attack, with his Chief of Staff General Papagos. A strategy of flexible defence in the initial stages of such a conflict was agreed upon until mobilization was complete, to be followed by an offensive aimed at throwing the invading Italians into the sea.[9]

The first two years of the Metaxas Regime was a productive one, full of frantic activity regarding domestic social and economic policy, regime security, and external and foreign relations: Greek–British relations, for instance, were crucial. After that Metaxas and his regime were taken up more or less completely with the *EON* (National Youth Organization) and war preparations. And all this time Metaxas himself was plagued by illness.

The only serious and final domestic challenge to the regime before the War, the uprising in Crete in the summer of 1938, failed. More important, the public was unwilling to follow political parties that had lost their credibility, whereas Metaxas had already shown his sympathy towards the urban and rural working classes, by freeing the latter from burdensome debt, and alleviating the lot of the former with a series of social legislation over minimum pay, working hours, paid holidays, social and health insurance, housing cooperatives and property taxes.[10] His Deputy Premier and Finance Minister was already discussing publicly the bankruptcy of laissez-faire capitalism, the abolition of the parliamentary system and promising the rudiments of a corporatist state.[11] The earlier Agrarian Reform of Venizelos broke up big estates and helped settle the Asia Minor refugees. It left no landless peasants so to speak. Unfortunately, the richer rural classes as well as small entrepreneurial provincial families from which so many able and disinterested politicians and public servants had come were submerged. After the War, merchants, industrialist–financial groups – Benaki, Averoff, Bodosakis, Syngros – were practically eliminated by a combination of the Nazi Occupation, the Civil War, as well as the earlier levelling by the Metaxas 4th August Regime. In effect, the elite – or at least the recruiting sources for one – had been decimated. Metaxas may have eliminated factionalism and extreme partisanship by suppressing politics. 'He thereby removed one of the principal impediments to his aims, namely, internal or domestic recovery, stability and preparedness for war.[12] But he also eliminated one of the main sources of politicians, of leaders, of a desperately needed political elite.

By 1938 or within two years of his new regime, Metaxas managed to instil fear, demand abject obedience and attract solicitation from his ministers. The case of Th. Turkovassilis illustrates this. In June 1938, he protested against the false accusations that he opposed the 4th August Regime. But he was arrested and banished, for the error he committed was damning: he had cooked his goose with a letter to General Reppas in Paris about the Chania uprising, dated 18 August 1938, when Turko-vassilis thought Venizelists were strong against Metaxas, and that this particular episode in Crete isolated Metaxas. Another was the case of Navy Chief Admiral Economou, also in 1938, who was dismissed, and the curt response of Metaxas to the solicitations of his Propaganda Minister Theo Nicoloudis. These all suggest the evolution of an ever more personal control by Metaxas over the 4th August Regime, and illustrate one aspect of the relationship between Metaxas and his minions; they are instructive about the Greek vocabulary of political solicitation of a dictator. Thus in thanking the Prime Minister for his congratulations from recently captured Korytsa, General Tsolakoglou referred to Metaxas as the 'embodiment of the Nation'. Metaxas himself records his satisfaction after a quick, triumphant tour in the Peloponnese in May 1938 [*Diary*, IV, p.302].

There was naturally much petty politicking and soliciting of Metaxas, based partly on jealousies among inferiors. Examples of this are the reporting of overheard conversations among suspected conspirators against Metaxas. Thus to be found among the papers of Metaxas are security reports from the Commander of the Athens Garrison alluding to the Kotzias 'treachery' in November 1938, as being at variance with government policy. Here one notices how centralized such policy was in the hands of Metaxas; there was hardly any delegation of power. In fact, Metaxas was also in complete charge of the *Neolea*; senior officers in it like Kanellopoulos and others were only his executive assistants or agents. This is very well shown and expressed in the correspondence between Metaxas and his Press and Information Minister Theologos Nicoloudis in August 1939. One also surmises from that correspondence the thorough censorship of cinemas and theatres. A year before he died Metaxas was still consolidating his hold on rule when he received reports from a diplomat named Kosmetatos in Paris dated 8 January and 1 February 1940 about the likely seditious activities of a senior diplomat like Politis, and the anti-government activities of General Plastiras in France. There are also confidential reports about Slavophone Western Macedonia, Romanian propaganda there, and efforts to Hellenize these Slavophone minorities in Greek schools, etc.

Such security episodes are also mentioned in the correspondence between Metaxas and the King over the issue of the British bondholders of the Greek national debt and related questions of currency reform, and generally economic relations between Greece and Britain. The King approved all the measures by Metaxas, ranging from the appointment of Cabinet ministers to the compulsory law for the protection of the currency, and the rentals law. More serious in this correspondence was the Tsouderos affair, who allegedly passed on secret information to conspirators planning a coup in March–April 1939. In one exchange about this affair, Metaxas told the King, 'I gave him (Tsouderos) an hour to resign.'[13] The tone and confidentiality of the exchange of cables between Metaxas and the King suggest, by the way, a comfortable, even intimate, working relationship between the King and his Prime Minister. By 1939–40, despite everything else, Metaxas felt comfortable about his relationship with the Monarch, and the latter seemed content to leave the government of the country to his forceful Prime Minister with his highly personalized and autocratic style of government. The highly personal style is attested to by the numerous requests for patronage in *EON* or the government.

The Minister of Justice, Logothetis, resigned in July 1938 ostensibly for health reasons, but actually because Metaxas had set up an inquiry into the work of the Ministry after repeated complaints from the public. But as in any long-lived but unaccountable regime, there were by 1938 a crop of rumoured scandals involving ministerial shortcomings, nepotism and skullduggery, and consequently a spate of resignations, including that of the Undersecretary of the Merchant Marine and of Communications. Interesting among these instances was the resignation of Alex. Koryzis, Minister of Public Health, in July 1939, in order to return to his post at the National Bank. That is when Elias Krimbas was recommended to succeed Koryzis in the Ministry. While Metaxas acted as Minister of the Air Force, Undersecretary Passaris had introduced certain changes without consulting him. Metaxas promptly replaced Passaris with Papadimas: he was swift and sharp in reacting to any slighting conduct by his ministers.

The Metaxas 4th August Regime was notorious among the Greeks for a repression comprising censorship, secret police surveillance, for having banned strikes and public association, all of them features of totalitarian rule. And yet Metaxas did not create a one-party state.[14] The 4th August Regime was for the most part relatively benign, closer to the Italian – I would say the Portuguese – than the German model.[15] There were no executions, no military courts and tribunals, no purges. Around a thousand Communist and other internees represented the bulk of repression against individuals. The government was almost wholly composed of civilians (including long-retired senior military officers) who did not prove to be less capable or competent than any others. The regime built schools, organized and reorganized social security schemes, adopted a new civil code by 1940 and encouraged the adoption of the demotic language.[16] Perhaps the most alarming aspect of the regime was its indoctrination and propaganda programme, the mass demonstrations of the *Neolea*, the National Youth Organization, with its slogan of the 'Third Hellenic Civilization', and its promotion of a Metaxas personality cult, who was now the 'First Worker', 'First Farmer', 'First Warrior', etc. Or did Metaxas have a perverse sense of humour, or a mighty sense of the ridiculous? Order and discipline became his primary concerns. The whole national economy became geared to building the Armed Forces; special subsidies and protective tariffs favoured the development of the local munitions and related industries. Trade unions were 'coordinated' as practically administrative adjuncts of the state and government (a Metaxas corporatism) with laws protecting workers, providing unemployment benefits. Extraordinary taxes were collected from industrialists and the more affluent for the war effort. There was a substantial economic recovery, but what there was of the national wealth was diverted to military and other – mainly nonproductive – expenditure. There was inflation and a higher cost of living as wages were not adjusted to rising prices. Clearly, in these circumstances the regime was never popular. It relied on the Army and the police to combat conspiracy and sedition, and to maintain itself in power.

The important thing for Metaxas was to maintain himself in power. He had been able to persuade the King that extra-constitutional powers were necessary to contain a mounting seditious condition, and so on 4 August 1936 the King signed the decree to that effect, conferring dictatorial powers on his Prime Minister Metaxas. The Chamber was dismissed, the Constitution of 1911 suspended. The rest is history.

NOTES

1. George Papandreou, leader of the Democratic Party, voted against Metaxas. See his *Politika Themata*, Athens, 1941.
2. See Apostolos Alexandris, *Politikai Anamniseis* (Political Reminiscences), Patras, 1947, pp.130–5 and 155ff., regarding the dilemma of Metaxas upon assuming power over holding early elections.
3. See George Rallis, *op. cit.*, p.134.
4. See D.H. Close, *op. cit.* A most interesting narrative of how Metaxas formed the first government of his 4th August Regime which shows his dextrous use of people, his touring the country during his first six months in power, and his handling of the country's defence strategy is given by Fivos Gregoriades, *4th August – Albania, 1935–41*, 4 vols, Athens, Kedrinos, 1972.

5. See W.H. McNeill, *The Greek Dilemma, War and Aftermath*, London 1947, and S. Waterlow, 'The Decline and Fall of Greek Democracy', *Political Quarterly*, Vol.18, nos. 2 & 3, 1947.
6. *Tetradhio ton Skepseon* (Notebook of Thoughts) in *Diary*, IV, pp.552–4.
7. *Goebbels Diaries, 1939–41*, transl. and edited by Fred Taylor, Sphere Books, London, 1982, 1983, pp.302ff.
8. See Manolis Triandafillidis, *Demotikismos kai Andithrasis* (Demoticism and Its Opponents), Athens, 1957, pp.61–2 (The Preface to the Report by Metaxas himself), and *Diary*, IV, p.281.
9. See the controversial Ath. Korozis, *Oi Polemoi tou 1940–41* (The Wars of 1940–41), 2 vols, Athens, 1958, and Dion. Kokkinos, *Oi dio Polemoi, 1940–41* (The Two Wars, 1940–41), 2 vols, Athens, 1945, 1946.
10. *Op. cit.*, pp.161–70. See also Babis Alivizatos, *Kratos kai georgiki politiki* (The State and Agricultural Policy), Athens, 1938; Ch. Evelpidis, *I Georgia stiu Ellada* (Agriculture in Greece, an Economic and Social View), Athens, 1944. Metaxas and his regime have been accused of laying their hands on 50 million drachmas of IKA funds, ostensibly for defence expenditure.
11. In a public lecture by C. Zavitsianos at Parnassos. See also Th. N. Anastasopoulos, *To Ergon tis Ethnikis Kyvernyseos* (The Work – Programme – of the National Government On Social and Health Policy); a State Propaganda Tract published by the press and Tourism Ministry, 1938. See also *Tessau Chronica Diakyvezruseos* (Four Years of Governing), Athens, 1940.
12. F.A. Voight, *The Greek Sedition*, London 1949, p.58. 'His regime was not a tyranny like Hitler's. There was no systematic brutality. The main object of his dictatorship was to create a modern and efficient state, for the Greeks had shown themselves incapable of effective administration under a democratic Constitution', C.M. Woodhouse, *Modern Greece, A Short History*, London, 1968, p.232.
13. Having returned from a quick tour of the Peloponnese, absorbed the Boy Scouts into EON, and inaugurated a new Dry Dock, Metaxas discovered on 26 June 1939 the disloyal letter by Tsouderos and, with the King's approval, fired him within the hour. See Daphnis, *op. cit.*, II, pp.460–5, and Metaxas, *Diary*, IV, p.376, for the text of his cable to the King. 1939 for Metaxas was on the whole a very busy and wearing year. As of the beginning of the year Metaxas suspected British-inspired conspiracies to create a rift between him and the King, and he suspected several Greeks, among them, Tsatsos, Tsouderos and others. Previously, at the end of December 1938, after the difficult episode of the election of the Archbishop of Greece, Metaxas was recording in his *Diary*, IV, pp.321–2 the fact he had to face a palace conspiracy, one that was being woven around the King. Cf. Demosthenes Koukounas, *O Archiepiskopos Damaskinos* (Archbishop Damaskinos), Athens, 1991, pp.42–3, where Metaxas is reported to have suspected Georgakopoulos, Spiridonos and Logothetis of constituting a conspiratorial front in the Royal Palace against him. It looked as if his closely controlled team would unravel. And on top of that came the Easter crisis over the Italian threat. A deterioriation in his health marked by dizzy spells was not surprising [*Diary*, IV, p.391].
14. See S. Maximos, *Koinovoulio I Diktatoria* (Parliament or Dictatorship), Thessaloniki, 1930.
15. See several articles on this in the journal, *Neon Kratos* (The New State), edited by Aristos Kambanis. The extant issues of this journal were in 1978 available at the Benaki Museum Library, Athens.
16. See Athenian, *Inside the Colonels' Greece*, translated by Richard Clogg, London, 1972, pp.25–6.

13

On the Eve of War

At least according to his *Diary*, Ioannis Metaxas was rather philosophical and introspective by the end of February 1939. In an entry in his 'Notebook of Thoughts' he considers the fate of man, and believes that no one can know that fate. Therefore life is not only action, but reaction too. The only permanent reality is that of activity and creativity. The only thing that can stop these is the loss of consciousness either from illness or with death. One must transcend the sentimental complaints and lamentations of the poets and artists if one is to prevail in one's confrontation with reality [*Diary*, III, p.357]. By 1 March, he was recording intensive work over state security to combat the activities of General Plastiras and the Venizelist Pepe (Pericles) Argyropoulos to recruit the support of foreign powers against him and his regime.[1] He also refers to the breakfast meeting with the outgoing Italian ambassador and rues that he had not been more forthcoming. The new Italian Ambassador was E. Grazzi. He also records meeting with Lord Lloyd, British Council Representative, and intensive work on security, when he is reassured by Governor General Sfakianakis that all rumours out of Crete are unfounded. The fact remains that Metaxas was at that time possessed by fear of being overthrown especially as he suspected the British of supporting his opponents. In his *Diary* [III, p.359], Metaxas describes the week of 13–19 March as 'Passion Week', when there was a public British announcement about Greece's debts as a prelude to demanding the overthrow of the Metaxas regime. Metaxas suspected the role of the banker E. Tsouderos.[2] But he believed the King steady in his support of him. Greece however was in no position to repay the debt. He dispatched an old trusted friend from Cephalonia, Lorandos, to London to look into and report on the question of the debt. Meanwhile, Metaxas worried

over the new understanding between Romania and Germany, and feared
that Mussolini would initiate an anti-Greece campaign. Generally, events
in Munich and elsewhere had their echo in Metaxas's anxieties about
the domestic security of his regime and the foreign threats to his country,
so that the entry in his *Diary* for 18 March simply records, 'My terrible
decision in the event of an Italian threat.' The month of April began
with the visit of Dr Goebbels, followed by increased Italian activity in
Albania, preparation of the state budget, control of the odd pro-Nazi
member of the Metaxas regime, viz., C. Kotzias, Mayor of Athens. The
Italians had landed troops in Albania; Metaxas became distracted with
worry, especially when the King called him to hand him a note by Sophoulis
of the Liberal Party, demanding a national coalition, or an All-Party
government. Displaying an extremely alert presence of mind, Metaxas
replied by telling the King that if he wished to try implementing this
proposal he could dismiss him from office and invite Sophoulis to form
a government. The King exclaimed, 'I haven't gone mad!' 'In that case',
retorted Metaxas, 'I will make no changes for there are no political parties;
the ones that exist are moribund. And I recommended to the King to
advise Angellopoulo, Chief of his political office, to stop encouraging the
parties.' With that Ioannis Metaxas returned to his Ministerial office and
called in his military chiefs of staff to consider and plan resistance strategy
against the Italians.[3]

What is interesting and perhaps in character is that Metaxas was not
content with the normal diplomatic, political and military efforts and
measures of his government. He persisted with the more covert measures
applied by his state security organization presided over by the clever and
wholly dedicated and loyal Maniadakis. Extensive telephone tapping
established the disloyal proclivities of Professor Constantine Tsatsos[4] in
collaboration with Sophoulis and implication of the Palace's Theodoros
Angellopoulos: Metaxas even suspected a conspiracy against him led by
the King. So he confronted the monarch demanding that he make
Angellopoulos apologize. At the same time, he spent the whole day with
members of his government – Mavroudis, Melas, Papadakis, General
Papagos, Admiral Sakellariou – alerting them to the situation, while
keeping a close eye on developments in Italy and reports that the Italian
occupation of Corfu was imminent. Metaxas now put the pressure on
the British by seeing Waterlow and Hopkinson of the British Embassy,
and by 9 April announced to them that he had decided to resist fiercely
till the end, and that consequently the war would spread throughout the
whole of Greece, and that he preferred the utter destruction of his

country to disgrace and dishonour. Typical of the man's behaviour throughout his career, he proceeded to galvanize his 'natural' constituency by visiting army camps (in any case a tradition of such visits at Easter), generating some loud enthusiasm for the regime. But in the evening the visit of the Italian Chargé Fornari, brought with it news of Mussolini's more aggressive policy in Albania, despite public protestations of friendly and peaceful intentions to the contrary. To be on the safe side and not prevent any misunderstandings of his recent decision regarding resistance to any external threat, the clever Cephalonian cabled the Greek ambassador in Rome telling him that even though Greece may allow the fleeing King Zog of Albania to seek asylum on her territory, she will not permit him to indulge in any political activity from her territory, and informed the Italian Chargé in Athens of this decision. By mid-April, the crisis seemed to have passed and things simmered down, especially after Italy offered Britain assurances that it would respect the territorial integrity and independence of Greece. Metaxas was now able to issue a public proclamation reassuring the Greeks of having ensured the independence and integrity of their country.[5]

With the weathering of this crisis, Metaxas turned his attention briefly to private matters when his older daughter underwent an appendectomy, and then proceeded to concern himself with domestic politics, starting with a tour of the Peloponnese to gauge his popularity and the strength of his Youth Organization, *EON*. But as he neared the third anniversary of his dictatorship Metaxas was no less paranoid about himself than before: 'Is all this enthusiasm (I encounter) real, or is it my fantasy, an extravagance?' [*Diary*, III, p.369]. He also continued to mistrust Bulgaria's irredentist intentions as described in his cable to the Greek Embassy in London, in which he also pointedly referred to British support for Bulgaria. It is interesting in this connection that Ath. Korozis in Volume 1 of his book, *The Wars 1940–41*, Athens, 1958, reported that in 1938 the British Military Attaché in Athens told the Chief of Greek Military Intelligence that Bulgaria constituted for Britain a major strategic interest, and that Greece should therefore cede Western Thrace to protect and promote this strategic interest [*Diary*, III, p.370, fn. 1].

Although 1938 and 1939 were years of intense, at times frantic, government activity in the 4th August Regime, one can hardly characterize the regime as a whole from its launching in August 1936 to its virtual end in April 1941 as exciting. Excitement came with the War, the Albania Epic. Before that the launching of *EON*, the National Youth Organization, could qualify as one of its other exciting features. From its early days it was clear Metaxas would emphasize agriculture and light industry in his public economic policy and programme, and that he would otherwise follow his predecessors, especially Venizelos, in attracting foreign capital and foreign companies for the further development of Greece's infrastructure – transport, irrigation and public works, and major utilities. In fact, his public economic policy – despite the spurt to reduce Greece's heavy dependence in its financial and economic affairs on Britain – which briefly suggested Metaxas was serious about seeking an ill-defined self-sufficiency or old-fashioned autarky – Metaxas favoured, among foreign, British capital investment: this was practically a traditional option since the War of Independence. The regime's public finance policy featured high indirect taxation which tended to affect if not punish the poorer strata of society; not a mark of radical, let alone progressive, reform. And in a way this was diametrically opposed to the regime's commitment to social reform legislation, the reinstatement of the eight hour Law of 1927, the creation of IKA (Foundation of Social Insurance) in November 1937, based on the first National Insurance legislation of the 1920s,[6] and the much vaunted fight against unemployment; the improvement of public health facilities and the fight against endemic disease; and the early earnest tackling of agricultural indebtedness when the regime tried to fix it by law. Thus the regime's social and economic policy, especially in its first two years was confused and contradictory and definitely less substantial than Metaxas managed to project to the public and to foreign governments. Its hopes and intentions to alleviate the burdens of the agricultural population were undermined and frustrated by its arrangements for loans, agricultural unions and cooperatives, and farming methods. There were hardly any improvement loans and credit to cooperatives. The Agricultural Bank preferred short-term interest-generating loans. Then legislation in 1938 transformed the Federation of Agricultural Cooperatives into a quasi-state compulsory organization, a state agency for other than agricultural aims. A year earlier the Union of Vineyard Owners, founded in 1926 to protect the interests of wine growers, was disbanded. Nor was there much improvement in the average income of the agricultural family which in 1936 was just over 20,000 drachmas per annum, partly because farming methods remained technically underdeveloped. The average daily wage in Greece remained at about 30 drachmas; the annual per capita income at about $60, about a sixth of that in France. Trade and labour union disputes were subjected to compulsory arbitration, thereby curbing and eventually abolishing the right to strike, until a form of corporatist syndicalism was evolved and consecrated. The regime tended to squeeze via taxation now one group then another. Its taxation policy on the whole made for greater inequality of national income. Even though the various social reform measures the 4th August Regime launched in its first two years were intended to benefit the agrarian and working classes, Metaxas appealed to the bourgeois class to make certain sacrifices for the less privileged classes. Moreover, the regime introduced extraordinary taxes based on the requirements of national defence and the social welfare programme. These were levied on agricultural production, on profits from shipping, especially freighter or cargo ships, which were up to 30 per cent in 1939, luxury taxes on tobacco consumption and games of chance. It is therefore fair criticism to point to the huge sums of money expended on *EON*'s activities and so-called special programmes. Surely much money was squandered in that direction to finance all the perks, including the rather silly one of free cinema tickets for *EON* members. But *EON* was the dictator's spoilt child, the preferred star of his 4th August Regime.

The social reform programme of the regime entailed not only complex economic–financial arrangements and provisions, but also promised sizeable propaganda mileage for the 4th August Regime and its chief Metaxas. In that sense it constituted another of the exciting features to the extent that the 4th August Regime could claim that it was founding something new and different from what went before. Regimentation and control was largely accomplished through *EON* and the so-called Worker Battalions, ostensibly to utilize the unemployed in the execution of public works, but actually a praetorian guard under the control of two of the stronger men in the 4th August Regime's administration, the ministers C. Kotzias and C. Maniadakis. Soon *EON* evolved its own elaborate bureaucracy, and hierarchy, and generated its own financial–political scandals, especially as it degenerated into a secondary state secret security service with its own army of informers. Inevitable too was the beginning of a leader cult around the person of the Chief of the 4th August Regime; a development that placed the King in an ever more difficult position, especially as the 4th August Regime was becoming more of a personal rule by Metaxas. And it was bound to impinge on politics, including the delicate matter of the role of the royal family in *EON*, and its relations with the Chief of the Regime, Metaxas. As *EON*'s activities spilled over into the schools and other existing youth organizations, the Minister of Education, K. Georgakopoulos, was opposed to this development.[7] But members of the royal family were brought into

EON. With *EON* now a state institution with its own Government Inspector, the industrialist Alexandros Kanellopoulos, Metaxas was able to disband the Boy Scouts, whose titular head had been the Crown Prince Pavlos. In a decree dated 21 June 1939, setting out the role of national youth, Metaxas declared the Boy Scouts absorbed into *EON*. A similar fate awaited the YMCA and YWCA soon thereafter. With this Metaxas could consider his original objective of a national state education and preparation of youth towards the goals of the New National State to have been achieved. And to proclaim, 'For me the success of *EON* is the success of all my political life or career.'

The decisive role of the King in the political drama of 1935–36 that marked the exit from the political impasse of partisan politics cannot be gainsaid or minimized. Reform was urgent in order to arrest economic and social disintegration. The country was unarmed and undefended. Its Army was inadequately armed and ill-equipped; it lacked combat capability. The Air Force was embryonic and without a future; the Navy needed modernization. And the purges following the Venizelist coups of March 1933 and March 1935 deprived the Army of large numbers of qualified officers.

These were some of the pressing reasons for the political factions to look to the Crown for a solution and an end to the National Schism. The King responded with massive intensive political effort against the forces of party politics and fragmentation in order to clear up the legacy of the past. But in doing this, he opened the way for radical political change during the last two months of 1935 which soon led to the Metaxas coup that established his autocracy in the 4th August Regime. The 4th August Regime was the inevitable, the only, exit from the domestic political impasse. It is to the credit of Metaxas's presence of political mind that it was brought about quickly and smoothly. Moreover, it was made to look as if both the King and all the political leaders of the day believed in it and were gasping for the relief it offered them, since it was a drastic, radical clean-up.[8] All the arguments for its justification were ready to hand: with war coming, it was imperative and vital for the Greeks to put an end to the National Schism, unite the Nation, equip, train and organize their Armed Forces. On this at least, the King and his new Prime Minister, the Chief of the 4th August Regime, were wholly agreed, and within a year they were also agreed on the Anglo–Greek alliance. It is therefore almost superfluous to note that on 4 August 1936 Metaxas decided to have done with partisan politics and disputes, to establish a strong government, and to build up a strong Army. There was no doubt, by the way, that when Metaxas became Prime Minister Greece badly needed a stronger Executive and Administration, and this soon meant or was translated into the personal autocratic rule of Metaxas.[9] The King too was anxious to clear up the political decks in order to prepare for the approaching war; and thus the views and interests of the two men converged at that time. Their agreement on this score is illustrated further by the King's assumption of a key role in the war of October 1940 to April 1941, and a greater political role after the death of Metaxas. In fact, by 1945 he had become the indispensable link between Greece and its major wartime allies, Britain and the USA.

II

One of the most difficult periods of the Metaxas regime were the two years 1937 to 1939, leading up to the outbreak of the Second World War, dominated by Metaxas's attempt to secure an agreement with Britain, preferably a treaty of alliance, that would secure much needed arms and equipment for the Greek Armed Forces. But this was a very difficult objective to attain, entailing an uphill struggle as he had to battle with a British bias against him personally and his 4th August Regime as fascist, totalitarian and oppressive: the British Establishment were reluctant to abandon their salon presumed liberal clients of ex-parliamentary politicians among the Greeks. Their most important client though was the restored King George II who seemed stubbornly content with his allegedly fascist dictator-premier, Metaxas. The closer he became identified with the 4th August Regime the deeper he embarrassed his British supporters. And as the regime became more populist – and popular – with an impressive National Youth Organization (*EON*), led by the 'eternal Great Leader-Governor', Metaxas, so did the latter's popularity soar at the expense of the King's and his Royal Family. These were all difficult, prickly matters for the British Foreign Office to grasp, handle and manipulate. But they equally constituted a great trial and testing time for the diplomatic–political talent and competence of the erstwhile Germanophile Metaxas.

Specifically, there were a series of critical outstanding issues, as for example that of the British bondholders of the Greek Debt, the renewal of the several franchises of such British monopoly enterprises as Cable and Wireless, Eastern Telegrams, Electric Traction and Transport – the so-called Power. A new contract with Cable and Wireless in April 1937 was followed in July of the same year by another with Power and Traction Company ('Power'). There were other problems with British insurance companies when Metaxas tried to nationalize all social insurance in the country, and lesser enterprises such as the aircraft industry Blackburn in Faleiro which Metaxas tried to control by monitoring via the Bodosaki–Athanassiadi local armaments enterprise.

These difficulties, although transient, soured relations between the Metaxas regime and Britain further. The latter was loath to push the dictator hard for fear of alienating him and undermining the position of their client, King George II. At the same time there were those among them who hoped to find a way of overthrowing him via a military coup god-fathered by the King and the old-world politicians especially when after January 1938 many of these issued anti-regime proclamations as the regime itself increased its repressive measures against them. But the King's options were limited: it was difficult to find a replacement for Metaxas, let alone the means of dismissing him or overthrowing his regime. Then the British found the Metaxas regime the most acceptable, because it was the most stable, in the circumstances. By the end of July the Chania uprising in Crete had failed for it was quickly suppressed by Metaxas and his agents. But the banker Emmanuel Tsouderos tried unsuccessfully to convince the British that the Chania abortive coup had wider significance, that the continued inability of the King to effect any political change in the country would lead to a revolution against the Metaxas regime. Metaxas, however, was quick to neutralize Tsouderos and his fellow-conspirators. The weakness of British intelligence about these events was that much of its information came from the so-called educated liberal classes. The poorer mass of the general public were indifferent if not even perversely satisfied with the regime's populism, and more importantly the regime had the support of the Armed Forces. So the British soon concluded that British interests were served best by a stable effective regime in Athens, even one headed by a 'fascist dictator'.

An equally major foreign trade problem was that of the sale of Greek tobacco, a lucrative cash export crop. Until the appearance of the highly competitive US Virginia, Britain was one of the major customers for Greek tobacco, and the crop was in danger of suffering a fate similar to the Greek currant/raisin after the development of the California wine industry. As with other Balkan countries in the interwar period Germany became the major client for the purchase of Greek tobacco in the 1930s. Eventually Britain agreed to purchase a limited amount of the Greek tobacco crop, representing a compromise arrangement, but not really a satisfactory solution to this particularly difficult problem of foreign Greek trade. So that by 1939 the particular crisis these outstanding problems constituted in Anglo–Greek relations was weathered by Metaxas and his regime even if not properly resolved. It was followed by two major preoccupations of Metaxas, to neutralize conspiracies at home against his regime, and to prepare the defence of the country in the War that was surely coming. At the end of 1938, the British government could not have any complaint about the stand of the Metaxas regime: the arrangements of 1937 secured important concessions for a variety of British interests in Greece, while the reassurances of Metaxas especially in October 1938 regarding Greek policy towards Britain were altogether satisfactory.[10] And yet perversely it would seem that at this point the British government decided to consider the possibility of interfering in Greek domestic affairs in order to modify the Metaxas regime into a less oppressive one. They worried about the denial of popular freedoms, the dissatisfaction of the politicians and the difficult position of the King. But the latter was notoriously indecisive. In fact the King told the British Ambassador, Waterlow, that he was not interested in replacing his Prime Minister as, contrary to widespread rumour, he was in complete agreement and harmony with him, and went on to add: 'The Greeks are orientals; they consider moderation in the exercise of power weakness. They are the most democratic people in the world, but once they take over power, they become automatically tyrannical. All know and accept this.'[11]

Metaxas had irritated and perhaps alienated members of the royal family when he absorbed the Scouting Movement in his own new Youth Organization, *EON*. Soon thereafter it was alleged there developed a clique around government which introduced widespread corruption in the Metaxas 4th August Regime. Naturally, the British were anxious to strengthen King George II by proving that he was really in charge in Athens; but they were hopelessly wrong about the political orientation of his Prime Minister, Metaxas, and eventually concluded that Metaxas in power served British interests far better than the old politicians of the ancient regime. But when Waterlow told the Turks that a military coup in Greece was imminent, Metaxas was furious: he decided to clear out all suspects of British-inspired conspiracies and have Waterlow replaced as Ambassador. By this time moreover, the Foreign Office had decided not to oppose Metaxas any longer, but on the contrary to strengthen him, for Metaxas in British eyes meant stability, and that was best for British interests.

In order to make its intentions quite clear and to put the seal of final approval on its new policy, the Foreign Office sent out on a special mission to Greece Lord Lloyd of the British Council who was also a personal friend of King George II. This marked the formal end of the crisis in Anglo–Greek relations for the period from December 1938 to February 1939. Since Metaxas too was keen to get rid of Waterlow he dispatched his friend Dr Lorandos on a special mission to England. In January 1939 Waterlow was replaced by Sir Michael Palairet. Meanwhile, the exile of political dissidents further weakened the pro-British elements in the country.

But then there was the special case of General Nicolas Plastiras in relation to the unsuccessful Tsouderos conspiracy and the attempt to lead an anti-Metaxas movement in Athens. Metaxas succeeded in clearing Tsouderos out by 30 June, placing him under house arrest. At the same time the press in Athens was actively involved in all these political trends. While the London *Times* referred to Balkan barbarism, and its fascist regimes, some of the Athens papers – *Bradyni, Estia* – made pro-Axis, anti-British noises. *Kathimerini* was prominently monarchist but neutral, and *Eleftbero Vima* remained staunchly though vaguely Liberal. Metaxas may have been unpopular but he was surrounded by incompetents: he was insecure, but the King was isolated and alone. People were in open despair against the regime which they considered as being controlled by a gang of crooks. And the Army was in a terrible state. In the meantime, the British managed to gain the collaboration of Maniadakis, head of state security, who also happened to consider Costas Kotzias, along with Tambacopoulos of Justice, as the most pro-Axis of Greek government ministers. Both were put under close surveillance. What is important is that all of these political trends and conspiracies were controlled and kept within certain limits so long as Metaxas was alive; the real problem would arise after his death: would there be a total collapse, especially as the regime could not accommodate itself with the old political parties.

By 1940 Greek foreign policy was typically and formally neutral, but essentially pro-British. In the face of the impending Axis invasion of Greece, the question of British military assistance to Greece occupied centre stage. Related to this was also the choice of a successor to Metaxas as Prime Minister, a vital matter that bothered both Greeks and British alike in view of the peculiar position of Metaxas in relation to the King. After the death of Metaxas, the latter wanted Koryzis of the National Bank of Greece, but Palairet thought the King should himself assume the premiership. Koryzis was seen as a mere stand-in for the King, and eventually he was opposed by Kotzias and Diakos of the original 4th August Regime.[12]

While these concerns became paramount, and the Greek Army was in desperate need of transport and other equipment, the new difficulties generated by the imminent German blitz through Macedonia and its effect on the Albanian front led to the first rumblings of a negotiated ceasefire with the Germans. This was particularly true among some of the military commanders, leading at some point to a widespread feeling of defeatism which in turn rendered Anglo–Greek relations, or at least those with the Greek Military High Command, difficult. In these circumstances one may note the failure of the King to put together a government of national cooperation and thus put an end to the dictatorship of Metaxas that was to create so much trouble for his cause and by extension that of the monarchy in the future.[13] But there may have been a major misconception in all of this, namely that Metaxas was wholly dependent on the King, which he was not.[14]

May to June, in fact the whole of that summer in 1939, was an equally unsettling and difficult period for Metaxas. It was marked by the frantic reporting of Skeferis, from the Greek embassy in Tirana, about heightened Italian activities in Albania, which Metaxas saw as ultimately hostile to Greece. Both he and his Army Chief of Staff General Papagos, fretted over the concentration of Italian forces on the Greek–Albanian border. At the same time Metaxas underwent a difficult spell of bad health marked by a recurrence of his stomach trouble, when he was desperately seeking renewed assurances from Britain and hoping to abolish the Boy Scout movement by having it merged with and taken over by his Youth Organization, *EON*; in this way he hoped to strengthen the base of his personal support and minimize further any challenge from organizations closer to potential opposition, including the Palace. And all the time he pursued E. Tsouderos whom he suspected of intriguing against him until he replaced him as Governor of the Bank of Greece with Drosopoulos. As he was recovering from the bout of ill health Metaxas succumbed to his old paranoia of suspicion and insecurity: he could not decide how firmly or securely he was in power and suspected everyone around him with the exception of Yannis Diakos and Costas Maniadakis, his major domo or factotum and confidant and the tough head of his state security, respectively. By July Metaxas felt good about his one important creation, *EON*, and was back to dealing with the petty jealousies and differences of his minions in government. He was also impressed by the celebrations of the third anniversary of his regime on 4 August 1939, but also concerned over his health [*Diary*, III, p.391]. While General Papagos was submitting a situation report to Metaxas, Maniadakis was tightening up control of public and state security immediately upon the outbreak of War. November and December 1939 was a disquieting period for Metaxas, with a new bout of illness, depression and insecurity: 'I feel weakness and fatigue; and a sense of disquiet with Anglo–French negotiations.' By New Year's Eve he was jotting down in his private notebook, 'Justice does not rule the world, but necessity' [*Diary*, III, p.411]. He saw the end of the year, fairly satisfied with the progress made by the country, but highly apprehensive about his own health.

In April 1940 Metaxas was unwell. There was a heatwave that summer which did not help his disposition: he was nervous, indecisive, and more suspicious than ever, so that even reduced applause he found suspect. A month later Merton attacked him in the *Telegraph*, encouraging his suspicion of a conspiracy originating in the Palace. He also suffered a bleeding ulcer. Earlier, in January of that year, he had sent a delegation to Britain to negotiate the economic relations between the two countries. Headed by Finance Minister A. Apostolidis and comprising Merchant Marine Minister Amv. Tzifos and the Deputy Governor of the Bank of Greece Varvaressos, it managed to agree on 43 per cent servicing of the debt for the duration of the war, increased Greek exports to Britain and France, and the chartering of sixty Greek cargo ships to Britain [*Diary*, IV, pp.446–8]. Metaxas hoped Britain would help Greece get out of German 'Clearing', and German domination of the Greek economy by buying more Greek products. Also earlier that year Metaxas sought from Britain aircraft and heavy transport vehicles with which to resupply troops on the Albania front so as to successfully complete that military campaign before the expected German blitz. But the British were unable to help.[15] Even the year before when in April 1939 Britain spontaneously guaranteed Greek territorial integrity and sovereign independence, it failed to impede the transport of Italian troops and equipment across the sea from Otranto. No wonder Metaxas's health suffered in November 1939 – 'I am a torpedoed ship' [*Diary*, IV, p.338]. The visit by Wavell and Longmore in November 1940 was unproductive; had unsatisfactory results. The Greeks declined British military assistance with ground troops unless it was in sufficient numbers.[16] Despite all these efforts at placing Greek–British economic relations on a wartime footing, Britain allowed bondholders of the Greek Debt to blackmail Greece into increased interest payments of 65 per cent; the Greek government and public had the feeling that the British Foreign

Office preferred Turkey and Bulgaria as wartime allies to Greece. In the circumstances it was perhaps inevitable that security became an obsession, especially with the discovery of two underground press publications *Eleftheria* and *Machi*. But no serious organization was found behind these publications; simply one or two people, Kolyvas and Kyrkos[17] [*Diary*, IV, p.319].

In volume A of his memoirs,[18] the young diplomat Angelos Vlachos, who had been with the diplomatic service for about a year and assigned to the Cryptographic Service, describes the months of July, August and September 1940 as one of the most trying periods for the sang froid, coolness of the Greek government, the Greek political leaders and Greek public opinion. Even as early as June Count Ciano would summon I. Politis, the Greek Ambassador in Rome, and harass him about Greek facilities for the Royal Navy in the Mediterranean, as well as other matters relating to Corfu, Greek agents in Albania, the murder of the wanted criminal Daoud Hotza, etc. The young diplomat and his equally young colleagues tended to crack jokes against Metaxas. The cheerful and without malice chief of Metaxas's office, Pindar Androulis, would admonish them, 'Keep your voices down lest Maniadakis hears you.' [i, pp.33, 34]. The collapse of the French Army highlighted the crisis of the imminent Italian menace for Greece, but 'Metaxas with a sober and calm look much younger than his 65 years exuded self-confidence, and the growing Italian challenges and threats focused his Cephalonian stubbornness, determination' [i, p.38]. He reprimanded the Italian Ambassador about his country's aggressive anti-Greek propaganda in the period July–September 1940. One can accuse Metaxas of many things, but one must recognize his sang froid in facing the Italian challenge. Thus the statement read by Nicoloudis after the torpedoing of the cruiser *Elli* consisted of twenty lines, was handwritten by Metaxas and concluded that until then it was impossible to ascertain beyond the shadow of a doubt the nationality of the attacking submarine. [i, pp.51, 52]. And while waiting all this time for the delivery of urgently needed war materiel from aircraft to explosives and other ordnance, Metaxas requested Berlin to intervene with a view to limiting Italian propaganda and aggression. The Italian press campaign against Greece on the contrary became more vociferous. In the meantime, Italy massed more troops on the Albania–Greek border, and Metaxas strengthened units in Epirus and East Macedonia, but via individual summons thereby avoiding a general or even partial mobilization. The exchange between him and General Pitsikas over this matter as reported by Vlachos is interesting [i, p.57].

III

There is a touching note written in longhand by Lela Metaxas, widow of Metaxas, about the days leading up to the Italian ultimatum on 28 October 1940, in which, among other things, she reports,

Eight days before 28 October 1940, I believe a Sunday, returning from the Ministry, Metaxas sat at table for lunch and in a cheerful mood said, 'Now they can come, we are ready. We will defeat them.' There were only the two of us at table, and what impressed me was his calmness and the satisfaction etched on his face. I was very impressed because after the torpedoing of the cruiser *Elli* which was a signal – and no one was to mention the episode – I had forgotten what he had said exactly then at the same place but vaguely something to the effect 'now we will keep quiet, we will ignore the torpedoist until the time is right, when we will be ready. We shall take our revenge, but we must get ready first.'

And so to 3 a.m. when we heard suddenly the telephone ring. Surprised we wondered who it could be at that hour. He put on his dressing gown and hurried to the phone. Travlos of Security was at the other end of the line who told Metaxas that the French Ambassador was asking to see him. Travlos had made a mistake: it was actually the Italian Ambassador, Grazzi, who was at the door. He returned to our room and said, 'What's up with Maugras(?); what indiscretion and how inconsiderate at this ungodly hour.' He straightened his hair quickly and went to meet him. He opened the main entrance door; they entered into the lounge with the desk in the middle of the room in front of the large green divan in which E. Grazzi sat to the right. Their conversation began calmly, but soon I heard an animated exchange, and an angry tone in my husband's voice followed by a loud bang of the palm of his hand on the top of the desk. It was the exact moment of the 'OXI' (NO), and there followed Grazzi's departure.

When he returned to our room Metaxas told me right away, 'We are at war; I must dress quickly.' He was ready in fifteen minutes and rang first the Ministry of Foreign Affairs where his office was located instructing it to inform the King and the border guard posts. Then he briefed Nicoloudis (Undersecretary for Press and Information), and Sir Michael Palairet of the British Embassy who was spending the summer nearby in Kifissia. All this happened within minutes as the Italian ultimatum expired at 6 a.m. We received Palairet and Nicoloudis in the main entrance, when Metaxas told them we are at war; help us for we are ready to fight for our country's honour. Then he returned to our room and told me, 'God is our help,' and that he may not be back home till late at night. But as it turned out he was back for lunch.

Vlachos gives us a vivid picture of the scene outside the Ministry of Foreign Affairs very early in the morning of 29 October 1940, only hours after Grazzi had handed the Duce's ultimatum to Metaxas, and the outbreak of war.

> All of Athens was out in the street … Thousands of people shouting and trampling over the Ministry's garden and orchard, having also surrounded Metaxas's parked car. Metaxas himself was by the outer gate surrounded by his two bodyguards, whom he ordered to step aside as the crowd got to him and swept him on its shoulders across to Army GHQ. I saw the dictator live the best moment of his life. [i, pp.64–66] … The open cable Metaxas sent to all Greek embassies abroad concluded that the Italian Ultimatum meant war and added that Greece will defend itself with all its forces against the Italian invasion. [i, p.67]

In the meantime he sought assistance with food and other essential provisions from Turkey. The capture of Koritsa a month later sent the cheering Athenians out in the streets again.

IV

The period before Christmas 1940 was exceptionally difficult and trying for Metaxas. He was particularly distressed when the King and most of the Royal Court stayed away from the annual 4th August Regime anniversary celebrations. Highly suspicious, as he was, Metaxas interpreted this massive absence of the Palace as directed against him personally, and as signalling a withdrawal of royal support for him and his regime. While he reiterated his faith in *EON*, Metaxas feared Palace-led conspiracies against him.[19] Although satisfied with the first batch of regime graduates from the Military Academy, *Scholé Evelphidhon*, he remained uncomfortable over possible intrigues by a certain Mavromichalis and Prince Peter of the Royal Family.[20] Thus the pathologically suspicious and insecure Yannakis even suspected his own man Kotzias, of his inner cabinet, of intriguing or conspiring with the royals against him. All the same, on 12 August 1940, Metaxas informed the Cabinet that Greece would resist either or both of the Axis aggressors to the end, but noticed the hesitation of some ministers and General Papagos.[21] Metaxas now suffered personal attacks in the Italian press as part of the mounting wider Italian campaign against Greece, culminating in the torpedoing on 15 August 1940 (*Ferragosto*) of the Greek light cruiser *Elli* during the traditional annual Greek celebration 'The Panagias' on the island of Tenos. Within a fortnight Metaxas told his foreign affairs Undersecretary Mavroudis, as well as Melas and Kyrou, that he will not bow before the Italians.[22] He also briefed Palairet of the British Embassy about this, while trying to get to the bottom of the suspected conspiracy in his midst. Thus he arrested and exiled or banished Tourkovassilis, one of the co-founders of his *Eleftherophrones* party nearly twenty years before. He was still plagued by the General Platys affair whom he had dismissed in September 1940 as pro-German, and was still troubled by Kotzias, Rangavis and Kyrou for their defeatism.[23]

As the Italian troops massed along the Epirus Albanian–Greek frontier, Metaxas wisely mobilized the independent 8th Division, commanded by the gifted and charismatic General Katsimitros, whose memory seems to have been erased from Greece: nobody seems to have heard of him since. He also mobilized the 9th Division, proclaiming not too quietly, 'I am ready for every sacrifice for the honour of Greece.' But he was not wholly free of misgivings over the loyalty of some of his ministers and senior Army officers, who he suspected intrigued with the Palace, if not the King himself directly, against him. Thus in his *Diary* Metaxas mentions captiously and in passing Elias Krimbas, his Minister for Social Services, Ath. Filonos, a staunch monarchist, even Mavroudis. Throughout this turmoil and crisis, Metaxas and his family completed their move into their villa home in Kifissia. Pressure of work and the accompanying stress was taking its toll. Less than two months into the Greek–Italian armed conflict, the old stomach ailment returned to plague Metaxas; he sought relief in the palliative traditional remedy of orange blossom water (*anthonero*), but reiterated for good measure his old-fashioned Greek dependence on God (*prosfigé mou o theos: my refuge is God*).[24] What really worried Metaxas were his suspicions regarding General Papagos who by mid-December was promoting the reinstatement of the 1935 coup rebel officers who were probably needed for the war. An episode involving Nicoloudis and Koryzis, together with advice from Rangavis to seek Hitler's mediation for a ceasefire – which incidentally Metaxas considered a dishonourable surrender, describing Rangavis as mischievous and bonkers – pushed Metaxas to the state of paranoia, believing that all around him were conspiring against him. There were troubles with some of the royal princes over *EON*, but the King himself remained steady. At a tea party Metaxas was miserable. 'I do not know English', he complained, 'I am short and nobody takes notice of me.'[25] The re-supply of the country was now critical. By early December 1940, the thirty-third day of hostilities, there was a shortage of ammunition and other essential supplies. His confidant, I. Diakos, expressed his own unease about the loyalty of some Army officers, and wondered if the Greeks should cease fire. Metaxas however rejected the idea of a separate peace. On 7 December he was unwell, marking the collapse of his health leading to his demise a month later.[26]

NOTES

1. See Pericles Argyropoulos, *Apomnemonevmata* (Memoirs), 2 vols, Athens, 1970–71.
2. Governor of the Bank of Greece, Tsouderos succeeded A. Koryzis as Prime Minister in May 1941. See his *Diplomatika Paraskenia, 1941–44*, Athens, 1950.
3. See *Diary*, IV, pp.338–46.
4. First President of the Greek Republic after the restoration of constitutional parliamentary government in 1974.
5. See *Diary*, IV, pp.364–7.
6. P. Kavellopoulos claims that back in 1926–27, together with his friends Andreas Zakkas and Christo Angelopoulo, director of the Tobacco Workers Provident Fund, he wanted to found a comprehensive National Insurance scheme on the basis of an old piece of legislation passed by the Chamber in 1922 with the support of his uncle, D. Gounaris. The later 1932 law of Venizelos was inconsequential because the Plastiras-led coup of 1932 intervened. *I Zoe mou* (My Life), Athens 1985, pp.35–38.
7. Actually, he was sacked in December 1938 over the episode of the election of the Archbishop of Greece, when he did not support Metaxas's preferred candidate, Chrysanthos. See *Diary*, IV, pp.320–2.
8. See P. Pipinelis, *George II*, Athens, 1951, Sir Reginald Leeper, *op. cit.*, and Sydney Waterlow, *op. cit.*
9. See Apostolos Alexandris, *Politikai Anamniseis* (Political Reminisences), Patras 1947, pp.130–5, who refers to the fact that when Metaxas first succeeded to power, or to the office of Prime Minister, he planned to hold elections very quickly, because of his lingering adherence and loyalty to the old representative political system, but he also realized the urgent need of a strong Executive and Administration.
10. Yannis Koliopoulos, *I Diktatoria tou Metaxa kai o Polemneostor Sarauda '40*, Thessaloniki, 1994, p.130.
11. *Ibid.*, pp.131–2.
12. See Sir Alexander Cadogan, *Diaries, 1938–45*, London, 1971.
13. I.S.O. Playfair, *The Mediterranean and the Middle East*, 2 vols, London, 1956.
14. The best narrative of the crisis of 1937–39 is that by Yannis Koliopoulos, *H Diktatoria tou Metaxas kai o Polemeos tor '40*, Thessaloniki, 1994, which is almost wholly based on British Public Record Office Papers.
15. The rift between Metaxas and his Army Chief of Staff General Papagos was now

rather wide. Metaxas was irate when he discovered that Papagos was reinstating and promoting officers who had taken part in the 1935 Venizelist coup. At the same time, he complained of insomnia, worrying over lack of transport (esp. heavy vehicles), shortage of ordnance and ammunition, and all the other difficulties of resupplying the troops on the front line in November to December 1940. See *Diary*, IV, pp.546–7.

16. See Churchill, *The Second World War*, New York, 1951, vol. iii, pp.73–7.
17. Among the many rumoured conspiracies, a member of his government, Elias Krimbas, reported to Metaxas that Crown Prince Paul did not think it right for the monarchy to be associated with the 4th August Regime, suggesting a wider web of intrigue in the Palace. See *Diary*, IV, pp.456–7.
18. Angelos Vlachos, *Mia fora ke ena keyo Enos diplomatis* (Once upon a Time a Diplomat) Vol. A, Athens 1984, pp.46–7.
19. His *Diary* for the period from May to December is replete with references to his suspicions, and the measures he took against suspected conspirators. He was particularly irked by those he called pro-Axis and defeatists, prominent among them General Platys, Deputy Chief of Staff whom he dismissed – actually suspended from active duty. See *Diary*, IV, p.465ff.
20. *Diary*, IV, p.491.
21. *Diary*, IV, p.429. There were also disagreements between Metaxas and General Papagos and his staff over mobilization. Considering the uncertainty over German policy towards the anticipated Italian aggression against Greece, Metaxas hesitated, until in September–October he fatefully, as if guided by instinctive premonition, activated the independent 8th and 9th Divisions in the Florina–Yanina region. As it turned out the 8th Division commanded by General Katsimitros stopped the Italian invasion in October–November dead in its tracks and followed it up with a brilliant counterattack that threw the Italian forces back into Albanian territory. See also Ath, Korozis, *Oi Polemoi tou 1940–1941* (The Wars of 1940–1941), 2 vols, Athens, 1958. See also A. Papagos, *O Polemous tou 1940–41* (The War of 1940–41), and D. Kokkinos, *Oi Dio Polemoi, 1940–41* (The Two Wars, 1940–41), 2 vols, Athens, 1945, 1946 for details of operations and related matters. See also *Diary*, IV, p.507ff.
22. *Diary*, IV, p.502.
23. *Ibid.*, pp.502–4.
24. *Ibid.*, pp.504, 550, 551.
25. *Ibid.*, p.540.
26. *Ibid.*, pp.542–60.

PART IV

Radical Reformer and Wartime Leader, Architect of Military Victory

14

The Nature of
the 4th August Regime

Metaxas saw the need for the adoption of extraordinary powers: the country needed discipline, political parties and partisan politics had to be banned. There would be no more elections for the foreseeable future, marking the end of parliamentary government in Greece. Metaxas however went beyond this; he wanted to create a new *weltanschauung* if not quite an ideology (even though he used the term *kosmotheoria*) for his 4th August Regime, and looked for its basis in the political and social institutions of ancient Sparta. The Metaxas regime was to be based on total state discipline, a freedom of the individual strictly limited by the needs of the state. This would constitute the starting point of a new Hellenic civilization, consisting of an improved synthesis or amalgam of the ancient Greek Byzantine civilization. The signal for the need to create a new – the Third – Greek civilization, was given by Metaxas in his address to the *EON*, the National Youth Organization, on 13 June 1937. In earlier speeches Metaxas had spoken of the bankruptcy of the prevailing civilization and the need to tap the sources of ancient civilization for the ideals needed by the contemporary Greek in trying to fill the spiritual vacuum and confusion of the interwar period.[1] From the first days of his 4th August Regime, it was clear Metaxas would proceed to fulfil his commitments. Drastic measures to suppress opposition and sedition against his regime were introduced and decreed almost immediately. Thus on 5 August 1936, a decree provided for the guidance and direction of the press as per its prototype in the totalitarian states.[2] More dramatic and exciting of course was his major attempt to secure a wider popular base when he founded the *Ethniki Organosis Neoleas* (*EON*), the National Youth Organization, by decree dated 7 October 1936.

The immense expansion of state jurisdiction, of its activities and its writ, as well as the radical transformation of governmental functions were perhaps terrifying even if they did not amount to a totalitarian Behemoth. This ominous underlying tone is reflected in a leader article in the London *Times* of 5 August 1940, entitled 'Authoritarian Greece', which was uncertain from the Metaxas reforms whether the Greek dictator was aiming eventually at a constitutional monarchy for the country.[3] As an intelligent man, Metaxas realized that finding a successor as committed to the same goals of a new authoritarian National State as himself would be difficult if not impossible, and that his highly personal 4th August Regime would not survive his own demise. Is that why perhaps he left behind a Last Political Will and Testament in the form of an outline of a fairly strong monarchic or presidential state.[4]

The intensity with which Metaxas tried to convey and inculcate his vision and the principles of his new National State during the 4th August Regime is reflected in practically all his speeches in which he sounded as if he were badgering, not simply haranguing, his audiences. His emphasis on youth, the family and other traditional institutions of Greek society very early on in his regime is interesting, for it enabled him to project a paternalistic, albeit didactic, image which to some degree assuaged any portrayal of him as a ruthless dictator. In a radio broadcast on 10 August 1936, barely a week after his assumption of dictatorial powers, Metaxas made a special appeal to the youth of the country to rise to the 'only reality (which) is the Greek Nation', and to resist foreign ideas. After an interesting press interview with the *Echo de Paris* on 18 September 1936[5] the interviewer noted, 'Metaxas does not look like an organizer of coups, a man of brute force, but a soldier similar to Lyautey; a ruler and soldier inclined to study and thought, who dislikes being referred to as a dictator, or that his politics follow foreign models. He insists on personal responsibility for his work.' Perhaps Metaxas would have accepted being compared to Salazar.[6]

In a speech to parents and teachers on 19 October 1939, Metaxas tried an interesting new approach by discussing the importance of the institution of the family.

> It is important to us here in Greece, and we are not particularly interested what other societies and foreign countries think of it. Here it is simply linked to the very existence and survival of Greek society. For many centuries, having suffered so many catastrophes and enslavements, the Greek national identity was not really encompassed in a territorial state, so that all the cultural heritage of the Greek Nation was concentrated in and transmitted from generation to generation by the family. Then, we

Greeks are mainly Orthodox in religion, so that of 8 million Greeks in the modern State, barely 250,000 belong to other religions, rites or sects. And the Church emphasizes the two sacraments of marriage and baptism! The family therefore is the cell of Greek society. And the Nation for Greece is the same as society. So the family must participate in the education of the children; the major forces of the society other than the Nation are the Polity or the State and the Church. In the West there is a total separation between Church and State, and the Church is denied a role in education. Here in Greece, Church and Nation constitute one whole. The Greek Nation and the Greek Church share the same history since the rise of Christianity. Thus the State in Greece never dared seek anti-religious aims: even the parliament of 1927, when and where there was such an inclination, did not dare undermine the special position of the Orthodox Church. So that one of the conditions that gave rise to the 4th August Regime was the period of irreligion preceding it. But now Family, Nation and Church are the new pillars of the Greek society, nation and the state. State and Church work each in its own way towards the same national goals. In these circumstances, the State has the right to interfere in the education of children for national purposes. School, parents, *EON* and the State are involved in this important national endeavour. It is the duty and role of the State and the new national structures (institutions, such as *EON*) to ensure that no teacher or professor promotes ideas for the overthrow of our society, our state, and our nationalism: no intellectual has the right to do that, and *EON* in particular has a special role of vigilance against such threat.

Metaxas, incidentally, highlighted the two features of *EON* as being, first, that membership was voluntary, and second, that it practised autonomy in the management of its affairs and training programmes. In October 1939 it had 750,000 members. As an army of the Youth of Greece which turned its members mentally and physically into (patriotic) Greeks, it could also be seen as a future combat army. It is only fair though to point to the massive evidence, including the regime's appointment of the Director of *EON*, its close control of the Organization's finances, as well as the funding and organization of its summer camps, the control of the syllabus, the agenda of its Information and Education programmes, all of which contradict the claim by Metaxas of *EON*'s autonomy. On the contrary, there was great social and political pressure as well as several attractive perks for Greek youth to join the *EON*. Like most other similar youth organizations elsewhere, *EON* too became the cause of family divisions, and the alienation of children from their parents and vice versa. Furthermore, Metaxas himself kept a keen and close personal control over *EON*: it was, he thought, his greatest accomplishment, '*kamari mou*', his pride and joy, and referred to its members as his children people [*Diary*, IV, pp.769–851].

There are those who assert that Metaxas represented Fascism in Greece, and impute to his 4th August Regime a Fascist ideology. Such is the case argued by the author on the Left, S. Linardatos. The same is true of Yannis Andrikopoulos.[7] A careful examination of the bases of these charges suggests they are tenuous, even unfounded, and over-simplified. There was no elaborate background preparation for a Fascist regime; there were hardly any Fascists in Greece before 1936, or at least in any meaningful numbers. Equally, there were hardly any significant, active Fascist organizations. Andrikopoulos himself manages to list only five: The *National Union of Greece* (*Ethniki Enosis Ellados*) in Thessaloniki which was patriotic and anti-Semitic; *The Greek National Socialist Party* of George Mercouris, founded in 1933 as a poor, unsuccessful imitation of the Hitler movement by the son of the ultra-royalist Mayor of Athens, S. Mercouris, a close collaborator of King Constantine during the Great War; *Iron Peace*, a national defence organization led by Colonel Niklambis, an old cohort of the dictator General Pangalos, whose members were mainly cashiered officers of the Pangalos regime; *National–Socialist Party of Macedonia–Thrace*, very insignificant; and *University Students Club*, a national union to counter the strong Communist student organizations in the University of Athens. There was also a small local group of the *Italian fascio*.[8] There is no evidence however that Metaxas himself was associated with them. Being influenced by Fascism and Fascist ideas is not in itself tantamount to being Fascist. To concede or recognize the failure of parliamentary government to provide political stability in Greece after the Great War, or in the interwar period, and to seek as a remedy to impose a regime with a stronger executive and a more regimented polity free of unfettered partisan politics for that purpose, or to opt to do so via a more regimented and disciplined society, including a National Youth Organization at a time of international crisis, economic difficulty and an impending European war; in short, to choose a strong – even powerful and unopposed – central government and forcefully extend its writ to cover most social and political activity and institutions, is not necessarily synonymous with Fascism. It was autocratic: Fascism is also one variant of autocracy.

Nor did Fascism in Greece have a prominent or even a disguised theoretician or ideologue. The published articles about the 'new state' or 'new order' in Europe, of strong government and the National State, which appeared in the publications of Aristos Cambanis and others do not allow such an assertion.[9] To be sure, the local manager of Lufthansa, Nicolopoulos, was found to be a Nazi agent, and several senior Army officers on active duty were pro-German. It was inevitable that, as in other European countries of that time, there would be those in Greece, both in private and public life, who were attracted by the idea of the strong national state and that of the powerful charismatic leader. It was also a period when many Greeks sought and received their university and other higher education in Germany; to that extent Germany enjoyed a strong, if not dominant, and widespread cultural–educational influence in Greece. But there were hardly any Greeks prepared to subscribe to the biological racist theories and programmes of Fascism. Nor did Metaxas himself. It is difficult if not impossible for someone to be simultaneously a humanist and a racist, or a racist and a Freemason! Those who accuse Metaxas and his regime of Fascism cannot have it both ways; for they also accuse him of being a creature of the King, and that his regime was no more than the King's bidding. The King they viewed as an anti-Fascist agent of the British, actually a guarantor of Greece's alliance with Britain against the Fascist aggressors in Europe.

It is difficult, or at least risky to assign Metaxas and his regime to facile categories of the extreme Right, Fascism and the like. Even the exemplary liberal democrat Panagiotis Kanellopoulos among Greek politicians and the last Prime Minister before the April 1967 Army coup d'état is circumspect and hesitates to state unequivocally that Metaxas belonged to the extreme and typical traditional Right. But, he does assert that the Metaxas regime did sow mistrust between the Army and the politicians, the Army and Parliamentary democracy, the Army and the civilian population; for he encouraged their belief that the public was unable to deal with political issues, and made Army officers feel superior to the average citizen like some *deus ex machina* protecting the Nation, the moral fabric of its social order, and its interests. Kanellopoulos thus further justifies his two long memoranda to Metaxas in June 1939 and August 1940 by his claim that the 4th August Regime had made Greece belong ideologically to the Fascist political systems of the Axis countries, and he therefore feared Greece would not resist Axis aggression. He also claims the 4th August Regime had made no contingency preparation for the fate of the people under enemy occupation, so that everything would unravel in a matter of a few hours or days, and that the end of Metaxas's dictatorship would leave a huge vacuum behind it.[10]

The Metaxas regime may have taken on some of the then fashionable political features associated with the Fascist trend and the fear of the Communist threat in Europe championed by the Axis states, but without any ideological commitments to the eternal verities of Fascism. It may be argued that Metaxas and his regime perversely committed suicide by rejecting the Duce's Ultimatum on 28 October 1940 and going to war against him. More perverse is the fact that the Metaxas regime, its successors and remnants, did not determine the rule of the so-called Right from 1950 to 1967 and beyond, especially when so many elements from the liberal wing of the so-called Conservative political world joined the Right after 1942, and especially after 1950. If Kanellopoulos is to be believed the Axis Occupation and the Civil War (1941–44, 1946–49) generated a new National Schism (*Ethnikos Dichasmos*) between the Left and an expanded – practically transformed – Right, led first by Field Marshal Papagos of wartime fame and by Karamanlis after him. The Metaxas regime did not quite represent the political Right – perhaps only a faction of it; what it did do was to encourage the expansion of the old or Traditional Right by its incorporation of diverse elements from the wider Conservative forces and strata of the country.

Any facile description of the Metaxas regime as Fascist is perforce confusing and misleading. To be sure at the heart of the conflict between Greek resistance organizations during the Axis Occupation, say, between Left (Communist) and Right (Nationalist/democratic/monarchist) was King George II's endorsement of the 4th August Regime in 1936, which many people perceived as being Fascist-oriented. What they did not expect however was its resistance to the Axis Ultimatum of October 1940 and subsequent German invasion of Spring 1941, the rearguard resistance to further Axis aggression in the flight from the mainland to Crete and from Crete to the Middle East, the Western Desert and, on the way back, Italy. In fact the King led a pro-Allied anti-Axis Greek government throughout the War. It threw off all British calculations based on their pre-War assessment and conclusion that the presumably Fascist 4th August Regime would reach some accommodation with the Axis and collaborate with the Occupation. It came as a great shock to all the clever Foreign Office and British Intelligence analysts when the successors or remnants of the Metaxas regime, now led by the King as a government in exile, continued their resistance to the Axis and its occupation of their country. What this suggests is that not all National

Social rhetoric surrounding a Greek dictatorship constitutes Fascism or a commitment to a Fascist regime.

It should have come as a great shock to the average British liberal, leftwing, even socialist/communist Oxbridge type in the Foreign Office, or serving with the British forces in the Middle East and Eastern Mediterranean, especially those among their Intelligence Services who were detailed to do underground work in occupied Greece, that the Fascist dictator Metaxas and his royal mentor and accomplice behaved completely out of character: instead of welcoming and embracing the Axis invader they resisted him until the end of the War. In fact there was the typical – and costly – confusion that accompanies blinkered ideological predilection. Incidentally, much of this anti-4th August Regime prejudice derived from the initial hostility of the British Embassy's S. Waterlow to the Metaxas Regime in August 1936.[11]

An interesting gloss on the censorship policy of the Metaxas Regime accompanies an exchange of letters between him and the widow of Venizelos in February 1938. In a letter from 22 rue Beaujour, Paris VIII, dated 7 February 1938, Mme Venizelos objected to a book by Prince Christopher of Greece in which the Prince alluded to dark circumstances surrounding the birth of Venizelos, and asked Metaxas to force the Prince to delete the passage, especially, she added, since Metaxas was in the process of 'purifying classical texts and old books'. In his reply dated 14 February 1938, Metaxas informed Mme Venizelos that firstly, no such purification of classical texts had been ordered or would be ordered by him; that classical texts were sold as they were; and secondly, that he or his government were not in a position to exercise or impose censorship on books published outside Greece, and especially in countries where complete freedom of the press prevails. On the contrary, 'in our country where there is fortunately today control over all publications, I can assure you however that as of 4 August 1936, since I govern the country, nothing has been allowed to be published that impugns the memory of your late husband'. Another concerns the British Ambassador Sir Sydney Waterlow who protested against the censorship of Embassy mail and newspapers in the spring of 1937, but six months later in November he wrote to Metaxas proposing a programme of English-language classes for Greek Army officers.[12]

Under Metaxas Greek foreign policy came temporarily under German influence, not because of Metaxas's background and military education, or any affinity between the two regimes, but because of the economic grip Germany had secured through 'Clearing' over the country. At a cabinet meeting on 28 October 1940, Metaxas said:

Gentlemen, I've been accused of two things: one, the first, that I am a Germanophile, and two, the second, that I lack the sensitivity and imagination of Venizelos. It is true I was educated in Germany and had many ties with that country. But as one who comes to hate a friend who betrayed the friendship, that is how I hate Germany now. I am of course a Cephalonian and weigh things carefully. But there are times when after all this one lets the heart dictate the final decision. And my heart tells me I cannot betray a 3000-year history. He who disagrees with me can resign.[13]

During the Italian press and diplomatic campaign against Greece, Theo Nicoloudis asked Metaxas if he should approach Bulgaria with a view to ceding to it a corridor to the Aegean. Metaxas snapped back at him, 'So long as I am Prime Minister I do not give away an inch of Greek territory.'[14] One notes in much of this a kind of sentimentalism in Metaxas's patriotism echoing the idiom of the humblest of Greeks.

There are letters and other documents relating to the odd protest of politicians against the Metaxas regime, in particular what they considered to be his secretive conduct of foreign policy in 1937. These came mainly from established party leaders such as George Papandreou of the Radical Socialist Party, Tsaldaris of the Popular Party, Sophoulis of the Liberal Party, Mylonas and Kafandaris of other groups in the Liberal camp. Quietly Metaxas appointed his own men in key state positions, ranging from provincial governors to ministers. Thus a month after the proclamation of his 4th August Regime he appointed Skylakakis, an ex-officer with suspected fascist leanings as Minister of the Interior; the avuncular and massive Maniadakis in charge of State Security, 'the faithful dog of Metaxas',[15] and the one who led all government policy regarding internal order and domestic security; and Papadakis as Minister of Army Affairs. Next, Metaxas embarked upon a measure of 'economic nationalism'. In addition to being a response to those who claimed that Greece was a 'protectorate of foreign banks' the new policy had the added advantage of promoting greater state control over foreign enterprises in the country, especially in telecommunications, urban transport and insurance. Yet less than two years into his regime and despite its repression of the old political parties, politicians resurfaced to launch manifestos attacking it.[16]

Metaxas was bothered by the question of succession and to this extent his so-called Last Political Will and Testament, *To Politevma tou Ioannou Metaxa* (The Political Regime of Ioannis Metaxas), setting out the general outline of a future constitution for the new Greek State to be submitted to the King for promulgation at the end of the War, to replace in a more permanent way the old parliamentary system is important as reflecting his political intentions and objectives had he survived till after the end of the War, and representing his own political ideas and vision. The document itself was published in Athens in 1945, and added by his daughter Loukia to his archive is an edited version (1941) by his son-in-law, the lawyer George Mantzoufas, of an original document dictated by Metaxas to Nicolaos D. Koumaros at the Grande Bretagne Hotel on 19 December 1940. Koumaros took the dictation down in shorthand. According to this document all powers would be vested in the government. The King would appoint the Prime Minister, and in consultation with him the rest of the government ministers; that is, an Executive appointed by the Sovereign. Instead of a Parliament there would be three representative councils, an eighty-strong Legislative Council, and Executive and Judicial Councils consisting of forty councillors each. This substitute parliament, however, would be strictly advisory. In case of irreconcilable differences between the appointed government and these advisory councils there would be a plebiscite to decide the matter. Only the government would have the right to propose and initiate legislation; no political parties would be allowed; and individual rights would be subordinated to those of society, of the state. Members of the Councils would receive no salary; they would be reimbursed for expenses only incurred in the discharge of their duties. Everyone must work. Those unemployed and living off unearned income would lose their political rights. The state would have control over the 'social benefits' implications of private property. The press would constitute a state service. The Prime Minister would be elected directly by the people and must poll two-thirds of the vote. But the King could appoint someone without the required vote. In order to qualify for elected office, men must have done their military service; women must be over thirty. The Executive Council could only question government acts, but its deliberations had no official status or validity, and this would limit discussion. As for the Legislative Council it had no legislative initiative; it would merely take decisions on the basis of government proposals. The three Advisory Councils together constituted a 'Review Assembly'. But there could be no discussion of the review of the permanent structures and fundamental elements of the political system and in particular: (1) the prevailing religion; (2) the person of the reigning monarch; (3) the separation of powers, the existing representative institutions and the concentration of powers in the monarch and the Government; (4) ownership of property and work. Moreover, no court could declare a law or decree unconstitutional without the prior consultation of the government. Local government was to be curtailed.

The 'cultural' nationalism of the Metaxas regime was manifested in his dealings with the YMCA. Metaxas had no objection in principle to such a foreign social–cultural international youth organization with Protestant missionary overtones, but he insisted it had to be a Greek corporate entity subject to Greek law,[17] and comply with Law 1789 of June 1939 concerning the education of youth which in the Metaxas regime was directed and controlled by the Ministry of Education and *EON*. There was in this approach no emulation of other existing political systems in Europe. Rather Metaxas preferred to invoke the position of ancient Greek philosophers, Plato and Aristotle, in this connection.

Metaxas claimed he was a Platonist and an Aristotelian, in the sense that in politics the basic Platonic premise was that the interests of the state, the polity, take precedence over those of the individual, and the obstacles to the attainment of the common good must be set aside, even by force if necessary. He followed Plato in his belief that politics or political conduct at least is a teachable art, and that authority is not accessible to all and sundry, but only to an elite. To this end the education of youth is a task for the state, and legislation must direct the youth towards an orthodoxy of ideals.[18]

NOTES

1. See *Epilogue* to his published debates with E. Venizelos, *Istoria tou Ethnikou Dichasmou, op. cit.*, Thessaloniki, 1994, 'The New Generation can restore the Ideals that were shattered by the calamity of Venizelos', dated 23 January 1935, pp.523–9, and in *Kathimerini* Edition of 1935, pp.379–84.
2. See Daphnis, *op. cit.*, ii, p.469.
3. Referred to and cited in *Diary*, IV, pp.737–8. See also Fivos Gregoriadis, *4 Avgoustou – Albania, 1935–1941* (4 August – Albania, 1936–1941), Athens, 1972. See *Diary*, IV, pp.737–8.
4. See printed pamphlet *To Politevma tou Metaxa* (The Political System of Metaxas), published from the Metaxas Private Papers in Athens in 1945, with a preface by his daughter Loukia, dated November 1944.
5. Reproduced in *Diary*, IV, pp.645–55.
6. See *Diary*, IV, pp.654–55. Salazar, who became the strong man of Portugal in July 1932, produced in 1933 a Constitution of the *Estado Novo* (The New State), an authoritarian state based on principles of social justice. He also rehabilitated Portugal's finances and freed his government of all effective opposition.
7. See S. Linardatos, *I Tetarti Avgoustou* (The Fourth of August), Athens, 1966, and

Y. Andrikopoulos, *I Rizes tou Ellinikou Fasismou* (The Roots of Greek Fascism), Athens, 1977.

8. Andrikopoulos, *ibid.*, pp.56–7.
9. See my 'Metaxas – the Man', in *The Metaxas Dictatorship*, edited by Robin Higham and Thanos Veremis, Athens, 1993, pp.179–92.
10. See *Istorika Dokimia* (Historical Essays), Athens, 1975, p.209 and typewritten memos in the Metaxas Private Papers.
11. See realist dispatches supra; see also P. Kavellopoulos, *Ta Chronika tou Megalon Polemou 1939–1944* (The Years of the Great War, 1939–1944), Athens, 1964; C.M. Woodhouse, *The Story of Greece*, London 1968 and 1977; Hugh Seton-Watson, 'From Fascism Right and Left', Walter Laqueur and George Morse, editors, *International Fascism, 1900–1945*, New York, 1970.
12. The Metaxas Private Papers also contain the correspondence with British Ambassador Sir Michael Palairet about Churchill's offer of aid to Greece in the event of war with Italy (26 August 1940), letters from Greek embassies in Rome and Paris containing particular warnings about the impending war, as well as many documents dealing with problems of domestic security. See *Diary*, IV, p.501ff.
13. See G. Seferis, *Diary A, 1935–1944*, Athens, 1979, 1981, pp.32–3. In connection with his flight to Italy in 1923 – his second exile – there is in the Metaxas Private Papers an interesting scrapbook of press cuttings; documents relating to the efforts of General Plastiras to arrest him, and accusations against the ambassadors of Italy and Norway, as well as the officers of the Patras port authority of assisting Metaxas to flee the country.
14. *Ibid.*
15. *Ibid.*, p.95. Maniadakis also headed the very ambitious, highly suspect pro-German Skylakakis. See Fivos Gregoriadis, *op. cit.*, pp.265ff.
16. See S. Waterlow, *Political Quarterly*, *op. cit.*
17. See the correspondence with Lonsdale regarding compliance with Law 1789 of June 1939 about the education of the Youth, mentioned in the typed French text of the statement by Metaxas about his dealings with Lonsdale over the YMCA in Greece in the Metaxas Private Papers. December 1938 was, it seems, the month for dealing with cultural, educational and ideological matters. See *Diary*, IV, pp.312–22.
18. See the A. Tzifos *Diary* document referred to earlier, above, as well as that by Rammos; and see also D. Svolopoulos, *op. cit.*, and File 45, Metaxas Private Papers Archive.

15

How Others Saw Metaxas
and His Regime

I

It is interesting to consider the early British reaction to Metaxas's dictatorship as this is reflected mainly in the dispatches of Sydney Waterlow, the British Ambassador in Athens, in 1936–37. The ambassador was reporting mainly on what he referred to as the 'Metaxas reform', or the Social–Economic 'New Deal' under Metaxas. One notes here the apparent initial success of Metaxas in impressing foreign diplomats in Greece with the reformist thrust of his regime, as this could be detected in his new legislation. Thus Waterlow reports about new laws in the New Year (January 1937), barely six months after Metaxas's assumption of dictatorial powers, to burden the state budget with an annual charge of 500 million drachmas for poor relief over and above funds already reported 'as having been allocated to social assistance'; the money to be raised by supplements to postal and telegraph charges, to stamp duties, tobacco duty, playing cards and lotteries. The government argued that the structure of the taxation system was not being changed; the new law simply credited the budget of the Ministry of Public Assistance (of which the Department of Health was an Undersecretariat) with the proceeds of these supplementary charges up to a total of 500 million drachmas. Thus Metaxas's promise, Waterlow concludes, 'to finance his New Deal without fresh taxation has not been broken'.[1] There were those, however, who argued that the new charges were a form of indirect tax, but the retort of Metaxas to these critics was that it was a levy on human weakness, viz., smoking and gambling, and announced a Budget surplus for fiscal 1935–36 despite a bad harvest. Waterlow did report the fierce opposition of the Bank of Greece to these measures, 'which taken in conjunction with the rearmament programme and the country's inevitably heavy commitments for the importation of cereals from abroad, must impose a severe strain on the stability of the currency,' suggesting that Metaxas's New Deal was incompatible with sound finance. He also observed that contrary to the recommendation of the Financial Commission of the League of Nations, Metaxas was raising public expenditure instead of reducing his State Budget, leading to unease among foreign creditors and disagreement among his government ministers as to the best way of raising money for the New Deal.[2] Those who believed it ought to be extracted from the rich endangered Metaxas's political position, further aspirations and objectives. On this point Waterlow remarks that Metaxas was 'not … actuated merely by demagogic motives'. Developing an overweening confidence in his powers as an administrator, 'he sincerely believed (without, in my opinion, much justification) that he can reform and inspire the public services to such a degree that they will be able to spend large sums to the enduring benefit of those whom, in conversation with me, he now calls "my people" – or the poor – his new constituency? And it must be admitted that much has been done to help the poorer classes.'

Were these the first indications of Metaxas's popular autocracy, unaccountable to an elected parliament, and unlimited (by a written constitution). He projected his rule as one of radical social reform, opposed to unfettered capitalism and a wholly free market economy. Waterlow further reports that Metaxas considered the state of public health and public welfare generally in Greece as a disgrace to civilization, and to remedy this was a basic aim of his policy of national regeneration. But also in order to avoid social unrest, Metaxas put forward national regeneration as a premise for the legitimacy of his rule and regime, so that as soon as he assumed power he considered the promotion of the country's social welfare as a fundamental part of his programme. But the implementation of such a programme was 'dependent not only on the availability of abundant financial resources, but also on inspired leadership'. The role of the Minister of Public Assistance, A. Koryzis, was crucial in this situation.[3] Metaxas called on the generosity of private individual philanthropy, and created a new Free School of Social Welfare to train social workers.

It would appear then that Metaxas was very serious about social welfare as a prerequisite of his policy of national regeneration, apart from the fact that if successful it provided greater legitimacy for his power and rule.[4] Clearly though his immediate difficulty was one of money: how all this was to be financed. He may have felt strongly about social welfare being a sacred trust of government, but so was an accelerated rearmament programme a national necessity and a state priority, as well as a massive financial outlay. Metaxas had moreover announced an ambitious ten-year public works plan of agricultural development, land reclamation, road and railways construction, totalling some 7.5 million drachmas.

Now as chief of his own regime Metaxas was anxious to avoid piece-meal policies in favour of a better planned national programme, informed by his ambitious programme of reorganizing the country along national lines. But as Waterlow observed, 'the Greek mind, as usual (had), taken little account either of technical difficulties or of inexorable economic costs'. He considered all these schemes as 'almost entirely unsound'; beyond the capacity of the Greeks, and not a realistic economic propo-sition.[5] 'It therefore looks,' Waterlow confidently opined, 'as if the present regime were embarking on an ambitious career of largely wasteful expenditure. This is the inevitable result of patriotic ambition combined with excessive self-confidence.' But Waterlow was giving vent to his anti-Metaxas bias, and betraying a massive lack of insight: he was opposed to Metaxas and his regime, because he believed it was a Fascist regime that would not oppose the Axis. But Metaxas did not share the average Greek's haphazard view of such national ventures or undertakings. He was highly rational and calculating. In fact with his policy of national regeneration, he was introducing planning as a new departure, perhaps a new experience for the Greeks. Even Waterlow had to concede that the unusual nature of Metaxas's New Deal was enough to make it a success for a while. However one looks at it, Metaxas did, through his plan of national regeneration, reduce the import requirement of wheat by several thousand tons a year; he did improve public health, and helped the growth of home industry to a level of satisfying three-quarters of home demand for industrial products.[6]

II

A very interesting sketch of Ioannis Metaxas as Chief of the 4th August Regime, leader and ruler of the Greek State was left by Ambrosios Tzifos, Minister of Merchant Shipping in 1938–40, in his *Diary*. The material in this typewritten document, found in the Metaxas archive, in File 45 of his private papers, is in two parts: one covers the premiership of Metaxas, 1936–41; the other consists of comments about his ideas and policies, concluding with an Epilogue. What is interesting is the Diarist's declared objective or intention: 'To forestall myths about one of the most glorious periods of contemporary Greek history.'

Tzifos had a background in banking in Switzerland and the UK. When Metaxas interviewed him he was an official of the National Bank of Greece. He noticed that Metaxas's questions were general and searching on a broad front, and he became convinced Metaxas was more interested in how Tzifos's mind worked. When he offered him a ministry in the Government, Tzifos hesitated and protested that he had no university degree when he was hired by Rallis Brothers in banking. Metaxas, according to Tzifos, was apparently delighted with this information and told his Finance Minister Apostolidis, 'This man is quite a find: diplomas, university degrees, multilingual proficiency, a dearth of practical minds with common sense destroyed Greece,' and added to Tzifos, 'I demand hard work, honesty and a practical spirit.' Tzifos interpreted all of this as an indication of Metaxas's approach to government, having found parliamentarism cumbersome, especially as Metaxas was fond of saying, 'During periods of extreme parliamentarism and party politics we forget we are Hellenes and become Greeks.'

After commenting on his experiences and setting out his observations on Greek politics in the period 1926–34, Tzifos hazards one or two conclusions and generalizations. Thus Venizelos, Tzifos believed, was the 'only politician who had the required standing to exercise essentially dictatorial powers albeit in parliamentary guise' (p.8), and 'was the first Greek politician to strengthen the Executive, in a democracy led by a strong man'. Tzifos did not believe in dictatorship as the ideal form of government, but in a polity with a strong Executive, a period led by a strong man in order to introduce reform and even radical change (viz., *à la* Caesar, Oliver Cromwell, Napoleon?). Whenever Executive power has been in the hands of strong leaders, Tzifos avers, Greece has known periods of political change and reform – Char. Tricoupis, E. Venizelos, I. Metaxas. (should one here add C. Karamanlis in the 1950s?) He further essays the pros and cons of Metaxas as Prime Minister or Chief of the regime: in his favour were hard work, positive dynamism, a strong will, determination, broad education and culture, and high military reputation and standing: as a staff officer Metaxas learned planning and acquired discipline. He was not a lawyer – lawyers made Greece suffer so much politically. Metaxas on the contrary inspired self-confidence and led a productive government despite any mistakes in 1936–38. As for the proverbial pressure on politicians for patronage and nepotism, instead of 300 parliamentary deputies, there were under Metaxas only thirty government ministers. Moreover, Metaxas eroded Greek atomism, and sought to relieve the pressure of the bureaucracy.

The discussion of the international situation in 1938–40 by Tzifos is interesting insofar as it tells us what Metaxas was about during that critical period on the eve of the Second World War, and the kind of Premier he was too – at least one version of that story. Given the global plans of the Axis for the control of the world, Metaxas in 1938 did not believe that Italy would seek to take Corfu or northern Epirus. Neither would the German Reich allow a Bulgarian war in the Balkans until that could serve its wider strategic war aims, in the East in general, and in Egypt and Russia in particular; and so Metaxas came to believe that if the Axis won the war, Greece would lose. Conversely, if Greece was on the winning side as one of Britain's allies, it would recover the Dodecanese Islands and possibly Cyprus. According to this reasoning, Metaxas considered the belief that Greece could escape getting embroiled in the War as utopian, 'and only a 100 per cent pro-British Greek policy without bargaining is possible'. He also felt that any concessions to the Axis Powers would be futile and to no avail, 'because the Germans – I flatter myself I know their character well – will benefit from every one of our weaknesses, and will respect only a serious steady stand (on our part). We must therefore remain honourable to the core towards the British and the French, who offered a guarantee (of our security), and who do not covet our territory like the Italians and the Bulgarians.'

Despite certain positive results of a dynamic radical reforming regime unencumbered by parliamentary or party political delay, many claimed the Metaxas regime was an unbearable tyranny. This was partly the reflection of the pathological devotion of the Greeks to abstract notions of freedom, unfettered and undisciplined, even when this was against the vital interests of the nation. They complained there was no control over government, that it was unaccountable, that there was suppression of popular freedoms, the exile of politicians and opponents of the regime. The fact is, Tzifos asserts, that the Communists exiled to the islands were fewer than under previous governments, especially since the Venizelos Government introduced the so-called *idionymo* legislation to combat the spread of radical and seditious groups. The political exile of leading opponents was already a well-established convention in Greece; it was not an innovation of the Metaxas regime. Without an elected Chamber, and with the suspension of the bill of rights articles in the Constitution, the accountability of government was of course a problem; although some have argued that it was checked by the monarch. Be that as it may, Metaxas was a patriarchal dictator of the classical variety, approaching an Alcibiadic figure as per the Plutarch cameo, an enlightened despot who achieved national unity by introducing into Greek society and the Greek polity, among other things, an element of discipline.

NOTES

1. The Metaxas government turned out to be most efficient in collecting taxes.
2. Thus the Minister of the Interior, Skylakakis, resigned over this issue in December 1936. See text of Metaxas letter dismissing the Minister, dated 26 December 1936, *Diary*, IV, p.660.
3. Alexandros Koryzis was appointed Prime Minister upon the death of Metaxas in January 1941, but he committed suicide soon thereafter.
4. See Waterlow to Eden, despatches of 6 and 9 April 1937, FO371/21143, and FO371/20387, 20 August 1936. See also Th. N. Anastasopoulos, *op. cit.*
5. The same view prevailed incidentally of the Egyptians after Nasser nationalized the Suez Canal in 1956. It is perhaps incorrigible imperialist arrogance and its racist derogation of the 'Wogs' that makes such misjudgments inevitable.
6. See Waterlow to Eden, *op. cit.*

16

Assessments and Conclusion

The feelings of Metaxas in November 1940 are reflected in his lament: 'They accused me, exiled me, sentenced me to death (in absentia, incidentally), but finally even for me there came in my seventieth year the moment of recognition.'

Metaxas believed that if the Greek forces could clear the fleeing Italians from Albania by Spring 1941, they would be able to face the German onslaught in Macedonia. He counted of course on British naval supremacy in the Mediterranean and RAF assistance. He discounted reports that Hitler was sympathetic to Greece; he believed if it became a necessary part of his Eastern (Russian) and Aegean strategy Hitler would attack Greece – as he did. German neutrality in the Albanian War was, Metaxas believed, strictly a formality; thus he rejected Berlin's proposal of a separate peace with Italy. By 5 January 1941 German military activity in Romania and Bulgaria prompted Metaxas to cable Simopoulos, the Greek Ambassador in London, to warn Eden that Greece was determined to resist a German invasion, especially when Metaxas was convinced that the Italian attack was with German acquiescence, if not connivance.

On his Nameday on 7 January 1941, Metaxas was praised by enemies, political opponents, followers and supporters alike, and he responded:

> All this is not my doing, but that of the Greek people, who always stood up true to their tradition, so long as they were united and disciplined, rather than slavish blind political followers. Under these conditions the divisions of the past – the factionalism – these virtues and attributes disappeared, so that all my efforts from the start – when I assumed power – were directed at recovering these virtues, so that the nation would be psychologically ready for the 28th of October.[1]

Tzifos reports briefly the difficulty the King had in appointing a successor Premier immediately after the death of Metaxas on 29 January 1941. His choice of banker Alexander Koryzis was opposed by the press Minister Nicoloudis who insisted on an appointment from the Army, or failing that, the Athens Archbishop. Poignant though is the comment by Tzifos on the funeral of Metaxas, and the fear and apprehension that possessed the Greek public.

> At that moment Metaxas was the symbol and inspiration of our great national struggle at its most critical moment. The same fear possessed both friend and foe … So much talent, determination and glory were gone for ever. In my eyes Metaxas does not represent a mere ordinary mortal, but an idea, and it was impossible for me to accept that he was gone forever, never to return.

Theologos Nicoloudis, Undersecretary of Press and Tourism, wrote Metaxas on 13 August 1939 proposing a separate Ministry of Culture (which presumably he would head). In his reply[2] the following day, Metaxas told him bluntly that

> culture is the work of a whole period of a whole people led by an inspirer (*empsychoti*) in whom it believes and who acts upon and influences all the agencies of state and society; he inspires and guides them directly and personally. Thus an independent ministry of culture cannot exist. Popular enlightenment, the education of the people, is conducted by many, if not all, the departments of the state; it is not the function of a particular or special minister. The coordination and direction of all these departmental efforts is the responsibility of one individual among them who has the authority by virtue of his position and personality, and that person is the Chief or Head of the Government, the Leader, *O Archegós*. And this is how it is done now, and fortunately quite successfully. The work and activities of the several government departments are coordinated, and guided by the directions and spirit of the Chief (*Kybernytes: Governor*).

One cannot ignore the peculiarity of some of Metaxas's perceptions about such matters as the function of government ministers, cultural and educational state policy, and his hegemonist tendencies.

The political testament of Metaxas as formulated in his *Politevma* suggests that his political inclinations were more often than not anti-democratic and anti-parliamentarian [see also *Diary*, I, p.500]. When in power he presented us with a paradox: while still clinging to the notion of freedom, or liberty, deriving from the Enlightenment, the French Revolution, classical Greece, and nineteenth-century European idealism and nationalism, Metaxas had come to believe also in the need for enlightened despotism; his reaction to the Axis threat to his country, in 1937–40, illustrated this paradox: he considered himself an enlightened despot and a patriot who defended his country's independence and honour.

In the same letter however, he refrains from commenting on Nicoloudis's judgements on various individuals (i.e., his gossip), and in a way reprimands his correspondent, claiming that he listens to many views, but always forms his own independent judgement about people and events.

In philosophy Metaxas believed, like Plato, in the superiority of ethical values over material interest, and in the immortality of the soul. Was this an aspect of Metaxas's romanticism? But he also subscribed, like Plato, to Pythagorean geometry (to numbers, which fits in nicely with his Freemasonry?). Intellectually Metaxas was a rationalist, considering what is feasible, possible or even probable. Thus during his exile in Corsica, Sardinia and mainland Italy, Metaxas read much Platonist and Pythagorean literature (under the influence of Freemasonry, he may have also read Neo-Pythagorean materials, especially dealing with the mysticism of numbers, and Neo-Platonism). In European literature, Metaxas read the tragedians of classical Greek drama, as well as Goethe, Schiller, Shakespeare; the historians Montesquieu, Burke, Pascal. St Augustine's *Confessions*, and the Gospel of St John.

When he came to power, Metaxas held radical social views, or at least radical views about Greece's social problems.[3] He felt there was a decadent rotten streak in the Victorian influences of the bourgeois system. He was unhappy about the country's parasitic mercantile class and the glaringly unfair distribution of wealth. Overprofessionalism and urban inflation Metaxas considered two very serious problems, and he believed social change was inevitable and social reform imperative. But he wanted it to be rational and properly channelled, that is, controlled by the state from above by reviving Greek patriotism, loyalty to church and family; in other words a redistribution of wealth without destroying the basic traditional values of Greek society. He aimed at a social transformation while maintaining a basically civil bourgeois regime or political order. Wealth, according to Metaxas, should not be a simple right of the individual; it must have a social role, especially in his new State.

Like many others, the position of Metaxas regarding religion shifted. Personally, he had passed through an agnostic – even atheist – phase. Tortured by doubts however he became a believer, or acquired a faith of sorts. He also believed post-war society would be wholly different; hence the central role of the state in the education of youth, avoiding the old Greek anarchic atomism, and inculcating a state-directed spirit of national cohesiveness and solidarity; the rule of freedom with order, defined by limits to personal freedom set by the needs of the state and society. This he hoped to achieve through the *EON* organization.

Metaxas was no gifted orator; nor was he a demagogue, charismatic or otherwise. He came across as unbending and inflexible. Whereas Venizelos, who was all these things, combined what was essentially a dictatorship and at the same time satisfied the Greeks' love of partisan politics.

There is an ironic complementarity between the two great rivals, Venizelos and Metaxas, in terms of the effect of their respective political leadership and control, as well as their policies, on Greece. Both men's reforms were prompted by pragmatic necessity. One, Venizelos, submerged the landowning class forever; the other, Metaxas, suppressed factionalism and abolished partisan politics as the principal impediments to internal recovery and security long enough to implement his preparations for war.[4] So that Venizelos–Metaxas constituted a political continuum, not a break in recent Greek political history.

II

How valid or fair would it be to argue that if it were not for the Italian Ultimatum on the dawn of 28 October 1940, so dramatically presented by the Italian Ambassador Emmanuelle Grazzi and equally dramatically rejected by the Greek Prime Minister Ioannis Metaxas in his pyjamas and dressing gown, and the subsequent Albanian epic of the Greeks defending their country against the enormous odds presented by the Italian invaders, Ioannis Metaxas would have been relegated to historical oblivion.[5] How true is the contention by some that the Italian Ultimatum of 28 October 1940 was not a surprise; that there is evidence of advance notice from Berlin, where the Führer Adolf Hitler was advising Athens not to do anything to provoke Mussolini against Greece. Hence, Metaxas's reluctance to mobilize early despite pressure from his military chiefs, General Papagos and others, and his awful dilemma, consisting

of his need of British assistance and his wider search for arms procurement, especially aircraft on the one hand, and his wish on the other to
avoid greater Italian and Axis hostility in the Aegean. How justified are
the accusations that he and the King were not willing to re-arm, leaving
the Greek armed forces hopelessly unprepared to cope with a war contingency; that Metaxas and his government were reconciled to the
prospect of defeat, and that the successful defence of the country's
frontier in Pindos and subsequent victories in Northern Epirus and
Southern Albania before Christmas 1940 were all a lucky and pleasant
surprise.[6] Thus it was widely reported that in 1939 Metaxas instructed
all Greek consular representatives in Albania to discourage the Greek-
speaking communities or population from demonstrating against Italy.
There are even more extreme accusations to the effect that as a dictator
Metaxas was psychologically attached to dictatorial and fascist regimes,
that he was not simply an admirer of Germany, but also pathologically
a worshipper of that country and all things German; and that he planned
to make Greece a province of Nazi Germany, declining British military
assistance until it was too late (in April 1941), despite a public pledge by
the British Prime Minister Neville Chamberlain to defend Greece and
Yugoslavia against any Axis attack.[7]

It is not easy to resolve these controversial matters on the basis of the
available evidence. There are documents which suggest that Metaxas
was desperate to procure arms, especially aircraft, from Great Britain,[8]
that he managed all the same to secure supplies and equipment for the
mobilization of a maximum of 750,000 men. Moreover, serious extensive
manoeuvres were held in the spring and summer of 1940, and the
exceptional quality of Greek field and mountain artillery was maintained. What was not anticipated was the heightened, frantic and fierce
duplicitous game of Mussolini in 1939–40; part of it, one suspects, a
consequence of his military failure in the Western Desert, and the
accompanying humiliation by his Axis ally and senior partner in the
War, Adolf Hitler.[9] Nor is there any hard evidence to suggest that Metaxas
had meaningful Italian connections. And his contacts in Germany were
mostly via the Royal Court in Athens, and especially the Queen Mother.[10]

What probably was a real surprise was the manner in which the Italian
Ultimatum was delivered on 28 October 1940. In his *Diary*, Metaxas
indicates clearly that he feared Italian aggressive moves against Greece.[11]
He was also emerging from a long period during which a series of conspiracies against his regime represented the culmination of the reaction
of the Greek political world to the 4th August change.[12] By this time the

friction and confrontation between a powerful dictatorship and the monarchy was being sorted out in a growing national consensus to defend the country against any aggression emanating from the Axis Powers. By mid-May 1940 when the German blitzkrieg through Holland and Belgium was materializing, Ioannis Metaxas already wondered how long Germany could maintain such military momentum, and how far the aggressive noises emanating from Italy were serious [*Diary*, IV, p.468]. He was also under immense pressure from his military and diplomatic chiefs to mobilize. 'In order to salve my conscience,' Metaxas states bluntly in his *Diary* [IV, p.469], 'I called one age group to the colours.' Several though disparate problems of state and private life crowded the Metaxas calendar for 1940, so that by the end of May when France was rapidly succumbing to the relentless German occupation, Metaxas reported the purchase of the new family home at 10 Danglis Road in Kifissia, his satisfaction with *EON*, the National Youth Organization – 'my only consolation', as Metaxas exclaimed [*Diary*, IV, p.471] – along with his bitter complaint, 'The English and the French have left us unarmed and almost unprotected.' Although less insecure about his regime on the eve of the Italian aggression, Metaxas was still disturbed about his relationship to the monarch, and concerned about any moves by the politicians. On 6 January 1940, Metaxas made a Last Will and Testament. Within a matter of days British and French ambassadors asked to see him together. Italy was about to declare war against the Allies, and although under pressure to react, Metaxas managed to prolong Greece's neutral stand for another few days, and instructed the Greek Embassy in Rome, as well as informed the Italian Ambassador E. Grazzi in Athens, accordingly [*Diary*, IV, p.475]. He desperately sought to deny that the British fleet was using any Greek naval base or port facilities, especially in Crete, and to keep Greece out of the War for as long as possible.[13]

If opposition to the Metaxas regime consisted of political intrigue and conspiracies, there was a great deal of both, the most serious being the Chania uprising in Crete two years before the war. By then however Metaxas's Chief of State Security C. Maniadakis had a near perfect security system in place; the Army Officer Corps had been purged of potential rebels; and the leadership of the old political parties had been decimated and neutralized by dispersal via removal from Athens to various islands and isolated locations in the countryside. As for the uncertain relations between dictator and monarch, Metaxas had by then acquired greater confidence especially in the new pillars of his regime which he had put in place and nurtured, such as the *EON* Youth Organization and Workers Battalions ('*i froura mou* [my guard]') as he referred to them.

This view is supported by the early reaction of the Venizelist political leadership, and the wider, but now defunct, parliamentary establishment. A sharp correspondence, consisting of long letters by Pepe (Pericles) Argyropoulos to General Nicholas Plastiras in August and November 1936 regarding the political situation immediately after the proclamation of the new Metaxas regime of 4 August 1936, and the relationship between the monarch and this regime and its leader is important and revealing. For it suggests that there was little the political establishment could do; opposition to the regime was weak, sporadic and ineffective; it was no match for the regime's State Security apparatus, headed by a good police department and efficient censorship. Nor was the King, it seems, keen on restoring parliamentary government. But neither were the politicians so inclined. The Metaxas regime would have been succeeded by another dictatorship. Argyropoulos was certain of this, and comments extensively on the relations between Metaxas and the King. Most enlightening is his discussion of the early tactics of Metaxas, especially in neutralizing all possible opposition, and emphasizes the measures reported against senior military officers, Generals Reppas and Platys, and Admiral Demesticha. Thus Metaxas pestered the King until he got him to sign the order dismissing these officers. Argyropoulos reveals that Metaxas planned a four-year transition period, but that it is difficult to outline the regime's administrative and economic plans, if any. In fact, he wonders what form Metaxas intends to give to his regime, but finds that the latter has made no statements in connection with this, if indeed he has a programme for the regime in mind. Argyropoulos further remarks that only one member of the Metaxas government, namely Constantine Zavitsianos has made any public statements and these not of a serious nature. In the meantime the political parties disintegrated – no great loss, incidentally – since they had been reduced to mere obstacles to the proper governing of the country, to national reconciliation and constitutional reform. Thus even after the fall of Metaxas we will not see the return of parliamentary government. The present dictator will be succeeded by another. According to gossip among the insiders and palace watchers, the King, who does not want a parliament, is nevertheless unwilling to tie his own political fate to that of Metaxas, so that if the present Metaxas government fails, he will look for another: the 'Condition Metaxas', i.e.

the Metaxas regime, will be succeeded by another. Alongside the party political disintegration, the communist mass will remain intact and compact, without however impressing or attracting the sympathy of the mass of the nation. As for our own (i.e., Liberal Party and Venizelist) stand the transition of a dictatorship is necessary; the dictator will be judged by his use of power, while the abolition of parliamentarianism is inevitable. In the final analysis though the head of government must have his mandate from the people. And in the perception of many, you (Plastiras) are seen as the successor to Metaxas. They are in fact pleased with the turn of events, and see no reason why they should systematically oppose him, since such opposition would be interpreted as disagreement with the abolition of parliamentarianism, whereas you yourself agree with Metaxas on its abolition. Today Metaxas faces no significant opposition, especially since the Communists are terrorized and deflated. As for the party leaders who cannot accept the fact they have been neutralized, look to a situation which seeks to rearrange internal or domestic issues, and plan to judge Metaxas on his works and how he will use his position to deal with these. A flexible stand which could be transformed: abstention without actual support of the regime. Metaxas therefore remains so to speak basically in limbo (*xekremastos*), his only strength being that he is in power and depends on the King. He lacks of course a wider popular base. The letter dated 18 August 1936 concludes with the following interesting recommendations: Metaxas's lack of a popular base is exactly the condition we can exploit, together with any organized opposition to the regime, as well as the use of political allies in the army in order to contribute to the abolition of the anti-Venizelist state. Metaxas would have to take punitive counter-measures which, because of his political nudity, would put him in an awkward difficult position. In this connection, many believe – and I agree with them – that we should initiate contacts with Metaxas, especially as it would be the height of delusion and destructiveness for the nation to allow power to revert to the control of political party leaders without having resolved the military problem, and when this would be the basis of any understanding (with Metaxas).

In his second letter, dated 28 September 1936, Argyropoulos lists the pros of the Metaxas regime, especially social reform measures pertaining to the working classes, and its efforts at administrative decentralization. He refers to the regime's handling of the currency and its stabilization, measures that would affect Greek bondholders in Egypt, as well as Greek merchant shipping. He focuses on the heightened rivalry between Metaxas and the King over the control of the regime, and singles out

the attempted purge by Metaxas of senior military officers considered
to be close to the King, such as Reppas, Papagos and Platys, as well as
an undisclosed number of other senior officers whom he would replace
with 'apotaktous' of his choice. While such moves freed Metaxas of
troublesome elements in his regime, the King's position was becoming
more difficult, especially with British and French criticism of the
economy, and the broadly pro-German policy of Metaxas. Reference
elsewhere to the role of Theodore Angellopoulos,[14] Chief of the King's
Political Office, becomes relevant when Argyropoulos writes about his
links with him. As for the cons of the regime, Argyropoulos cites the
harsh police, which terrorizes people, or its victims, with castor oil, while
the officers dismissed after the abortive Leonardopoulos coup (1922–23)
now run things with a tendency to establish a German or Nazi-type
tyranny. The position of Metaxas is not wholly secure; his only support
is the King, and the major support of the King is the Army Officer Corps
which is largely Popular–Monarchist, but not pro-Metaxas. Hence the
latter's scheme to rid himself of leading monarchist senior Army officers.
At the same time he turns to the masses, organizing mass rallies to show
the King that he enjoys popular support. Thus not all of Metaxas's
collaborators, including government ministers, are in agreement, and
many of the army officers are opposed to the appointment of Nicoloudis
who happens to be the ablest member of the government. Whatever the
difficulties and whatever the nature of the opposition, the King's support
remains crucial to the security of Metaxas in office. He pours cold water
on any notions of the restoration of constitutional government, especially
when none of the party leaders has a proper programme, and when
Kafandaris aspires to the leadership of the Liberal opposition front. Yet
the Popular Party–Monarchist army is the key to the whole situation. If
it expresses strong disapproval of the Metaxas regime, it could undermine the King's confidence in Metaxas. The attempt by Theotokis to
represent the parties' unhappiness with the Metaxas regime was doomed
to failure when Kafandaris was willing to accept a short-lived collaboration with Metaxas if this would restore parliamentary government.[15]

If the charge against Metaxas of conducting a secret foreign policy is
unjustified, his handling of the country's defence policy was even more
intensely personal, as this is illustrated by his desperate efforts to secure
aircraft for the Greek Air Force from Britain and other European
countries. He paid great attention to all the reports, confidential or otherwise, of Army GHQ from 1935 to 1939 regarding the strategic, logistical
and other requirements of the defence of Greece in the event of war, the

strength of the armed forces, the procurement of weapons for them, etc. Interesting is the report by General Papagos, Chief of Army Staff, submitted to Metaxas in mid-July 1940 about the involvement of his own Deputy, General Platys, with the Germans to obstruct and frustrate his cooperation with Anglo–French military institutions and commands. Metaxas immediately ordered the Undersecretary of War, Nicolas Papadimas, to conduct a full inquiry. Otherwise involved was the Under-secretary of State Security, C. Maniadakis. His department's surveillance reports on the activities of professors, lawyers, doctors and others, especially Liberal and Popular Party politicians, increased. The regime's immediate influence began to impinge upon and be directly felt in the appointment of professors, judges, and directors of galleries and museums, especially as in the case of Costis Batsias and the National Art Gallery. There are interesting handwritten raw reports on several people involved in the 'Organization of National Renaissance', most of them in their late twenties, which would affect their employment and profes-sional prospects. In fact, Metaxas demanded the CVs of such people early in 1940 with this aim in mind. Clearly, the 4th August Regime of Metaxas was one of very close surveillance, supervision and control. But there were also on the other hand reams of personal letters directly addressed to the Chief of the 4th August Regime, pleading admiration, undying devotion and enthusiasm for his new State. One of these dated 11 December 1939, called Metaxas 'the maker of a new Greece'. Another dated 31 December 1939, waxed lyrical when it told the Chief, 'May you govern us for a hundred years, and may your spirit do so for a thousand years.' Diaspora Greeks in the USA and Africa showered Metaxas with messages of support during the War. Subsequently in Greece 'the plain folk' *(o kosmakis)* held on to the epic of Metaxas. Old ladies would hold up his photograph and say, 'If our Yannakis were alive we would not have suffered all these trials and tribulations.'[16]

The wartime British Ambassador to the Greek Government in exile, wrote soon after the end of the war about the Metaxas 4th August Regime:

> Greece has had several dictatorships before Metaxas assumed power and dispensed with Parliament, and it would be a mistake to imagine that the Metaxas regime aroused anything like the fierce hostility throughout the country that Greek politicians would have you think. Metaxas had no patience with Greek politicians and exiled most of the more prominent ones to islands in the Aegean, where their most serious hardship was to

be removed from the game of politics, the king of sports in Greece.[17] The Fourth of August, the birthday of the Metaxas dictatorship, was always mentioned to me as something one could hardly speak about, some terrible stain on the fair record of Greek history ... And yet, let it be remembered that it was Metaxas who said 'No' to Mussolini, who not only brought the Greeks into the War but had already built up the army into a force that outmatched the Italians, and who was the brilliant military brain that directed the strategy of the campaign. When I followed the uneasy course of Greek politics for three years I was not altogether surprised that King George had allowed Metaxas a free hand in 1939.[18]

In his book, *Greece's Anatolian Adventure*, A.A. Pallis described Metaxas as 'clearheaded, practical, even unsentimental with all the old logic of a German trained staff officer. Metaxas had the courage to state what was bound to be ...', and commenting on the Memorandum by Metaxas as Acting Chief of Staff to Venizelos regarding Greek military operations in Asia Minor, Pallis opines, 'His words were almost prophetic. The principle of the expedition as originally planned and launched by Venizelos in 1919 was, as Metaxas had rightly anticipated, intrinsically unsound and contained within itself the germs of ultimate failure.'[19]

The end result of Venizelos's *Megali Idea* policy of 1919–20, had it succeeded, would have been a neo-Byzantine empire with a hybrid population of Greeks, Turks, Slavs, Albanians, Armenians and sundry other Levantines. Its failure left a homogeneous Greek state within internationally recognized territorial boundaries. The All-Party Government in 1926–27 in which Metaxas was Minister of Communications, patched up the state finances and raised new foreign loans, sponsored by the League of Nations for refugee resettlement, currency stabilization and road construction. The 'nearest thing to a national government Greece had ever known'[20] was succeeded by one led by Venizelos after his triumph in the elections of August 1928. But his four-year administration (1928–32) was a failure, plagued by ministerial scandals and maladministration, and buffeted by the World Depression. By the end of 1932 the Republic was dead, and monarchism, dormant since 1926 was revived. As Pallis wrote, 'the institution of the Republic ... had been the result not so much of any deeply rooted republican feeling among the people, as of the hostility felt by certain military and political circles towards the Dynasty ... The Republic through all those years from 1924 to 1932 had been acquiesced in, but neither loved nor respected.'[21] The Republic had failed because it had been monopolized by one party. 'Its fall was the work of its friends rather than its foes.'

The last year of his life was crowded with regime celebrations, suspected conspiracies, frantic preparations for war, the battle against the Italians in Albania and illness. As of April 1940 Metaxas was dogged by recurring illness. He was really dying throughout those nine months. Having made his position clear to senior officials of the Ministry of Foreign Affairs – Mavroudi, Melas and Kyrou – as well as to Sir Michael Palairet, namely, that he will not bow to the Italians, Metaxas felt free to enjoy more time with *EON*, with his family, as well as to nurse his bouts of illness. But he was more nervous and irritable than ever, especially over General Platys and the defeatism of Rangavis and Kyrou. He managed to order a partial mobilization amidst moving house completely to Kifissia. Among the spate of suspected conspiracies, Krimbas reported to Metaxas that Crown Prince Pavlos did not think it right for the monarchy to be associated with the 4th August Regime, suggesting a wider intrigue in the Palace [*Diary*, IV, pp.456–7]. On top of all this Metaxas introduced additional taxes in his new Budget for that year and wondered if the public could withstand them [*Diary*, IV, p.459]; it was actually a risky thing to do when his regime harboured a pro-German cabal (Kotzias–Platys).[22] In the Spring of 1940 Metaxas was depressed and unwell, only to feel worse throughout the heatwave of that summer, making him nervous and indecisive, as well as so maudlin as to wonder on National Day, 25 March, if anything will remain after his death [*Diary*, IV, p.459], and to sigh fatalistically that whoever wins the War Greece will be its client [*Diary*, IV, p.484]. He was in such a state, that even reduced applause Metaxas found suspect. To make matters worse and to feed his paranoia, Merton attacked him in the *Telegraph*, encouraging further his suspicion of the Palace. This was doubly unfortunate as it came when Metaxas was seeking aircraft and heavy transport vehicles to resupply the troops in the Albanian theatre so as to successfully complete that military campaign before the now certain German blitz. The British, alas, were unable to help. Even the year before when Britain spontaneously guaranteed Greek territorial integrity and independence it failed to slow down, let alone prevent, the transport of Italian troops and equipment to Albania across the sea from Otranto. Then shortly before the German blitz through Greece, there was a visit of Eden and senior British military commanders in the Mediterranean and the Middle East, Wavell and Dill, to confer with the Greek King and his government in January 1941. This, just as with an earlier visit of Wavell and Longmore in November

1940, had unsatisfactory results when the Greeks declined British military assistance of ground troops unless it was in sufficient numbers.[23]

III

According to his younger daughter, Mrs Nana Foka, Metaxas died at the family home, the modest villa on Danglis Street, Kifissia, at 5.30 a.m. (the official bulletin of the attending physicians put the time of death at 6.00 a.m.) on the morning of Tuesday, 29 January 1941. Cause of death, as reported in the official death certificate and the official medical bulletin, was septicaemia after a streptococcus infection. Typically, his death was shrouded in mystery, including a myth of his assassination. Metaxas's older daughter, Loukia (Loulou), however, in an undated handwritten statement states that her father suffered an intestinal or internal haemorrhage in the spring of 1940, at least a good six months before his death, possibly due to arteriosclerosis. Actually, Metaxas in his *Diary* reported periodic internal haemorrhages over a period of years, and when these occurred when he was in power he worried about his ability to govern.[24] Loukia reported further that by 26 January 1941 her father was gravely ill, having suffered a serious throat abscess. His personal physician Yeroulanos attended him when Dr N. Georgopoulos, an otorhenolaryngologist (ear, nose and throat specialist), lanced the abscess. But Metaxas suffered an intestinal haemorrhage the following day and was given a blood transfusion. By then urea had set in and Metaxas was given yet another blood transfusion. One suspects kidney failure at this point and the imminent risk of heart failure, especially as he was put on an oxygen mask.[25] Mrs Nana Foka told me in November 1996 that a soldier of the British Armed Forces from a nearby British Army depot arrived with an oxygen cylinder on Tuesday, 29 January. Metaxas was already dying when he was connected to the oxygen cylinder, and the British mechanic went to sleep on the adjoining bed. After Metaxas was pronounced dead, the British soldier took the oxygen cylinder and left. One suspects that it is this particular action of the British which gave rise to the rumours about the killing of Metaxas by poisoning or other means. But it is all speculation.

IV

The 4th August Regime presents an extraordinary picture. Metaxas sought not only to lead the country into a new type of state, a united nation physically and mentally prepared to face the impending war in Europe, but also to handle the day-to-day details of governing it. Needless to say both tasks were enormous, requiring great stamina, will power and determination; and Metaxas, despite his recurring bouts of ill-health, seemed to find vast resources within himself to call upon until he was struck down terminally. However one assesses his public as well as his private conduct, his was nonetheless a great achievement in very difficult circumstances. Can one really confine comment about Metaxas to the banal, 'he was a dreadful dictator'? On the contrary, the man was not only an extraordinary Greek political figure in the first half of the twentieth century; he was also an imaginative – albeit conceited and pompous – original, because he was a rational, disciplined and deter-mined, leader of the modern Greek state and polity. Beyond standing up to gigantic aggressors, the Metaxas regime of 4th August may have been on balance a failure, especially since its very embodiment and per-sonification, Metaxas himself, died. Yet he himself was at the end of the day a success, especially since the 4th August Regime and the Albania Epic were in great measure his personal achievements – and triumphs.

After all, the fundamental cultural–political problems that exercised Metaxas and his regime, especially that of a secular state and political identity, the conservative primordial insistence upon a Hellenic national identity deep in the recesses of the country's past history and separate from its modern independent territorial national state structure, the relation of the citizen to the state, the question of an elite and a civic culture have yet to be resolved by the contemporary Greeks, and parti-cularly leaders of their successive regimes since the end of the Second World War. Until very recently, the Greeks found it difficult to reconcile themselves between East and West: recently, some have even proposed identity cards which implied that Greek identity was synonymous with the Greek Orthodox rite or faith. In a way therefore, Metaxas was ahead of his time when he set an agenda of social, economic and political reform. Until it became a full member of the West European Community, Greek political leaders had failed to neutralize the political intervention potential of the military, to reform national education in such a way as to bring its standards nearer to the most advanced in Europe, and to elevate the country's cultural norms. In fact, in at least two instances hegemonist leaders of political parties competed with the head of state (in both cases a monarch) for the leadership of the country, and did not rest until they abolished the relatively short-lived institution of the monarchy in favour of a curiously elected republican presidency, so far held by unimpressive political figures, far less cultured or erudite than Metaxas, thus lowering with their occupancy of the top office of state the whole cultural standard and tone of the country itself.

In characterizing the Greek political experience since Independence, I ventured some twenty years ago the following remarks about the Metaxas episode:

> The mutual interdependence of army officers and politicians introduced a new factor into Greek politics in this century, reminiscent of civil–military relations in the Middle East. It contributed to the further erosion of parliamentary government, which in any event was a delicate implantation in difficult soil. The prolonged dictatorship of General Metaxas (1936–1940) meant atrophy of civilian institutions. At best one could argue that it was headed by an educated general who from the turn of the century had been versed in the ways of Greek politics.
>
> A combination of fascist-inspired national socialism and religious fanaticism served as the basis of the Metaxas regime and the background to his 'August 4th' New Era. Typically, forced social reform for the improvement of the conditions of the urban and rural lower classes was accompanied by a police state system, so that Greeks of all classes and occupations were made even more dependent on the state. Paramilitary youth organizations and other corporatist structures of a dictatorial government forced an alliance between the petite bourgeoisie, traditionalist and individualist small landowning farmers, the army, and the Church. The army was purged clean of all republican officers. The power and authority of the old landowning upper classes had been eroded by the liberal experiment of Venizelos after 1910. Now the liberal, middle class followers of Venizelos were decimated by the *Megalos Kybernitis* – the Great Leader, Metaxas.
>
> The most pernicious legacy of the Metaxas dictatorship was that of political atrophy and its by-product, political irresponsibility: a recourse by Greek politicians to extralegal and extrainstitutional means for the attainment of both their political and their most selfish personal ends. Whereas Venizelos toward the end of his career cheapened the meaning of parliamentary democracy by dispensing extensive patronage among army officers and by personalizing party political strife, Metaxas undermined the system further by suspending it for five years.[26]

Needless to say, the whole experience of this episode undermined legality and eroded the legitimacy as well as credibility of both the Crown and the older political elite. Yet given the concatenation of events after the National Schism of February 1915, the 4th August Regime was perhaps inevitable. That it was on balance harmful to the normal political evolution of the country is arguable, even true. But so were subsequent episodes, viz., the Communist challenge to state power in 1944–49, the so-called Colonels Regime in 1967–74, and the PASOK pretentious yet quite anachronistic and unsophisticated Socialist 'crusade for change' led by the charismatic but mercurial, unpredictable and ineffectual Andreas Papandreou in 1981–95.[27] There have been too many saviours of Greece since its independence, and one wonders where this soteriological pretension, and salvationist–apocalyptic zeal of its politicians comes from.

NOTES

1. See text in *Diary*, IV, pp.859–60.
2. See text of Metaxas's reply in Metaxas Private Papers, and *Diary*, IV, pp.715–17.
3. See Speeches, 2 vols, and D.K. Svolopoulos, *Ai ideai tou Ioanni Metaxa dia tin Ellada kai ton Ellinismo* (The Ideas of Ioannis Metaxas about Greece and Hellenism), Athens, 1952.
4. See F. Voight, *The Greek Sedition*, London, 1949. General Mazarakis in his *Memoirs*, Athens 1948, pp.611–14, accused Metaxas of having neglected the defence needs of the country; that instead he spent his billions on *EON*, ignored and scorned the services of able army officers for political reasons, and failed to construct proper fortifications for the Thessaloniki area.
5. See Emmanuele Grazzi, *I Arché tou Telous: I Epicheirisi Kata tis Ellados* (The Beginning of the End) Greek translation from the Italian of Grazzi's *Memoirs*, Athens, 1980. See also *Diary*, IV, pp.440ff.
6. But very much the brilliant and brave improvisation of General Katsimitros, CO the 8th Independent Division.
7. See I.A. Peponis, *Nikolaos Plastiras sta Gegonota, 1890–1945* (The Political Activities of Nikolaos Plastiras 1890–1945) 2nd edition, Athens, 1948.
8. See his correspondence with Charalambos John Simopoulous (1874–1942), Greek Ambassador in London 1935–42, Metaxas Private Papers, Files 35–81, and *Diary*, IV, passim.
9. Along the Alex–Marsa Matrouh Road in the Western Desert, retreating Italian forces set up a marker on which they wrote, '*Non manquo il coraggio, manqua la fortuna*'.
10. So much so that several times in the period from 1913 to 1923, the Queen is reported to have uttered to her immediate entourage the oft-quoted, '*Wir haben unsere man in Athene, das ist Yannaki*'. See Philip Dragoumis, *Diary*, and other sources. P. Kanellopoulos concludes that although he was a dictator, and oriented more or less to Fascist ideology, including *EON*, when the moment came on 28 October 1941 to say 'yes', he said 'no' to Mussolini's Ultimatum, *op. cit.*, p.44.
11. *Diary*, IV, pp.413–15.
12. The most serious at Chania, Crete, was quickly suppressed. See *supra*.
13. *Diary*, IV, pp.428–30. Cf. Papagos, *The War of Greece*, Ath. Korozis, *The Wars, 1940–*

1941, and P. Pipineli, *History of Foreign Relations*, pp.330–1.

14. There was frequent, albeit random, mention to his 'Memoirs' in Greek sources, but a published version of these does not seem to exist anywhere, despite repeated searches. Angelopoulos died fairly recently, at a very advanced age.

15. Pericles Argyropoulos, 1881–1966, a lawyer, one of the leaders of the National Defence (*Ethniki amyna*) and Thessaloniki rebel government of 1916. He was also involved in pro-Venizelos moves in Istanbul in 1921–22, and was a supporter of the Democratic Defence in the 1935 Venizelist coup. See File 15, Correspondence of Plastiras, Benaki Museum Archives.

16. G. Seferis, *Diary A, 1935–1944*, and see also Metaxas Private Papers, esp. Files 43, 44 and 80.

17. See Sir Reginald Leeper who succeeded Sir Michael Palairet in the Greek post in 1943. See his *When Greek Meets Greek*, London, 1950, p.10.

18. *Ibid.*, p.10.

19. A.A. Pallis, *Greece's Anatolian Adventure*, London, 1937, p.126.

20. *Ibid.*, p.160.

21. *Ibid.*, p.164.

22. Ath. Korozis, 2 vols, *op. cit.*

23. See W. Churchill, *The Second World War*, Boston, 1948, III, pp.73–7.

24. Bouts of recurring illness are recorded by Metaxas in his *Diary*.

25. The Loukia (Loulou) document about the death of her father is in the Metaxas Papers Archives.

26. *Greece: A Political Essay*, pp.30–1, in *The Washington Papers* series of the Georgetown University Center for Strategic and International Studies, Sage Publications, California and London, 1974.

27. See my 'Greece: The Triumph of Socialism', *Survey*, Vol. 26, No. 2 (Spring 1982), pp.50–65, the published version of my Montague Burton Chair in International Relations Lecture delivered at the University of Edinburgh on 2 November 1981.

Index

Bibliothèque Université d'Ottawa Échéance	Library University of Ottawa Date Due